Land Records
of
SUSSEX COUNTY DELAWARE

1782–1789

Deed Book N No. 13

Elaine Hastings Mason
& F. Edward Wright

HERITAGE BOOKS
2011

HERITAGE BOOKS

AN IMPRINT OF HERITAGE BOOKS, INC.

Books, CDs, and more—Worldwide

For our listing of thousands of titles see our website
at
www.HeritageBooks.com

Published 2011 by
HERITAGE BOOKS, INC.
Publishing Division
100 Railroad Ave. #104
Westminster, Maryland 21157

International Standard Book Numbers
Paperbound: 978-1-58549-167-4
Clothbound: 978-0-7884-8972-3

INTRODUCTION

Sussex County researchers should be aware that the southernmost portions of Sussex County were once part of Somerset and Worcester Counties, Maryland, and that other lands as far north as the Nanticoke and Indian Rivers, plus most of Northwest Fork 100, were claimed by both the Calverts and Penns for several generations. It is important, therefore, for Lower Sussex researchers to be familiar with the historical data presented below.

Somerset County, Maryland, was created in 1666 with the Atlantic Ocean and Chesapeake Bay its eastern and western boundaries, and its northern boundary ......which today lies well inside Sussex County, Delaware......the Nanticoke River.

Dispute over the location of Delaware's southern boundary began in 1680 when William Penn received his charter. It continued until 1732 when both parties signed an agreement that the line would lie at 39°43'19" and be surveyed to continue to the midpoint of the peninsula, then turn north to a point 15 miles south of Philadelphia. Unfortunately for Lord Baltimore, his decision to agree to this compromise was based on an inaccurate map which showed 39°43'19" as lying at Cape Henlopen. In fact, Cape Henlopen lay 25 miles further north, and Baltimore had inadvertently signed away present-day Little Creek 100 and parts of Broad Creek, Dagsborough and Baltimore Hundreds that had never been claimed by Penn.

Realizing his mistake too late, Baltimore fought the agreeement in the courts for the next 20 years. When Worcester County was formed in 1742 from the eastern and southern sections of Somerset, he set the northern boundary of Worcester at "Broad Creek Bridge"....at the site of present-day Laurel, Delaware.

In 1750 Baltimore was forced to capitulate. The survey was begun in 1751, but the death of Charles, fifth Lord Baltimore, and subsequent litigation of his estate, delayed further progress til 1763. From 1763 through 1768 Charles Mason and Jeremiah Dixon conducted the final survey of the so-called *Mason-Dixon Line*, and finally, in January 1769, the new line was officially accepted.

Prior to 1769, therefore, all records of the residents of lands south of the Nanticoke and Indian Rivers should be sought in Maryland record books. For persons who resided in the disputed territory near the two rivers, or in Northwest Fork Hundred, both Delaware and Maryland records should be consulted prior to 1769.

Though the two proprietors had finally agreed, there was no mad rush to transfer records from Maryland to Delaware. Most southern Sussex residents continued to think of themselves as Marylanders, and passively resisted the change. Typical of their feelings is the story passed down in one family of the Little Creek 100 ancestor whose farm was split in two by the new boundary (as many others also were), with his home left just north of it in Delaware. Absolutely clear in his loyalties, he dismantled his house log by log and rebuilt it on the Maryland side.

Adding to the resentment of the transplanted Marylanders, the Sussex County seat of Lewes was northerly and remote from them, constituting a two day ride by horseback for those living in the Little Creek region. Many new Sussex inhabitants simply stopped recording their legal papers. A few isolated deeds from Lower Sussex are found in Lewes Town record books during this period, but not many.

During the chaos of the Revolution, few records were filed by anyone. After the war, beginning about 1782, there was a period of 'catch-up' when people took time to record the land sales, wills and other events of the war period along with the records of contemporary events. It is at this time a steady trickle of Lower Sussex records appears in Lewes.

In 1791, in response to numerous petitions and relentless pressure, a new, centrally-located county seat was erected at Georgetown, and southern Sussex residents finally began filing their legal papers in Delaware courts on a consistent basis.

From 1769 to 1782, therefore, researchers of Delaware lands south of the Nanticoke and Indian Rivers will find discouragingly few records in either Delaware or Maryland. The situation improves from 1782 to 1790, and normalizes in 1791 with central-ization of the county seat in George-town, when all Sussex County records that survive can finally be found in Sussex County.

Elaine Hastings Mason
May 27, 1990

Somerset County MD
in 1724, based on a
map from *The National
Genealogical Society
Quarterly*.

DORCHESTER CO

SUSSEX CO

Nanticoke R

Indian R

NANTICOKE 100

BALTIMORE 100

S O M E R S E T   C O

WICOMICO 100

MONIE 100

POCOMOKE 100

BOGETENORTEN 100

MANOKIN 100

ANNEMESSEX 100

MATTAPANY 100

ACCOMACK CO

IN 1742, WORCESTER COUNTY, MD, WAS CREATED FROM SOMERSET COUNTY. In setting the northern boundary at 'Broad Creek Bridge', site of present day Laurel, Lord Baltimore reaffirmed his claim to Sussex County lands even though, in 1732, he had signed an agreement in which he ceded them to Wm Penn. *A word of caution: information derived from the above map should be interpreted very broadly, based as it is on vague descriptions of Lord Baltimore's boundaries which often conflict with maps from the period. Surviving maps, in fact, often conflict with one another, and even bear obvious inaccuracies like the transposition of Somerset and Worcester Counties.*

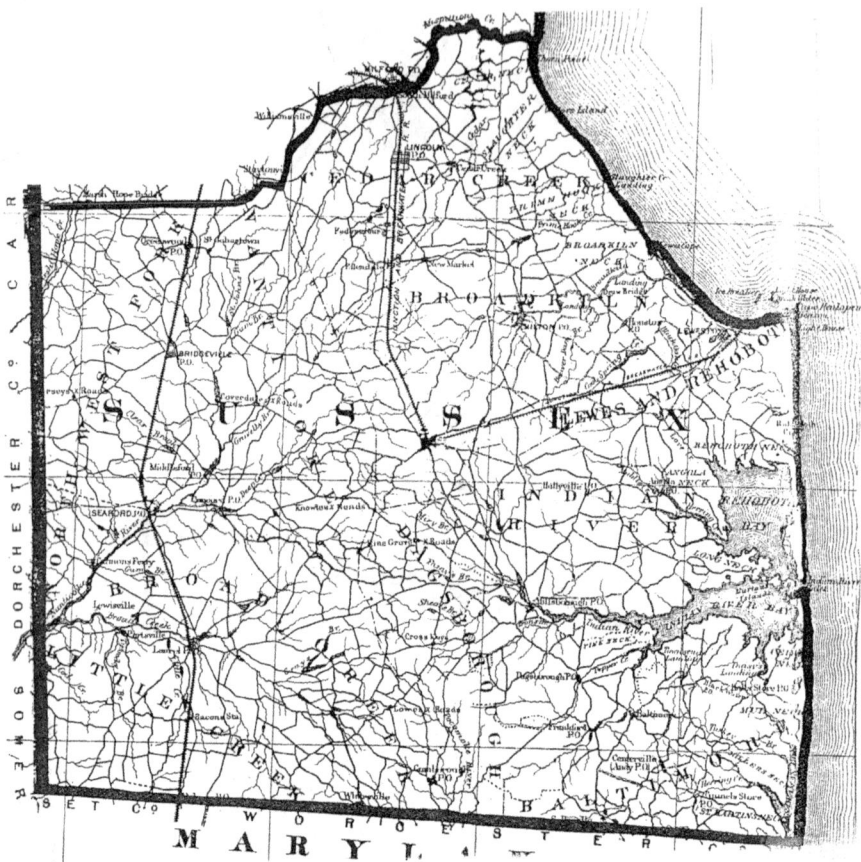

SUSSEX COUNTY, DELAWARE, FROM AN 1868 PROPERTY MAP. The
various hundreds are located approximately as they were in 1780-86.

ABBREVIATIONS USED

ac - acres
adj - adjoining
ackn - acknowledged
adminr - adminstrator or
   administratrix
afsd - aforesaid
amt/o - amount of
atty - attorneys
Co - County
cr - creek
dau(s) - daughter(s)
decd - deceased
DEL - Delaware
e - east
examr - examiner
Hund - Hundred

mar - married
mi - miles
MD - Maryland
n - north
PA - Pennsylvania
pt/o - part of
purch - purchased
rd - road
s - south
Suss - Sussex
tr - tract
uxor - wife (latin)
wit - witness
w - west
w/o - wife of

1 Power of Atty from WOOLSEY HATHAWAY, mariner of Sussex Co, to his bro JAMES HATHAWAY of same place, 12 Feb 1784. Wit: JOHN BURTON, ISAIAH BURTON. Ackn: 27 May 1784.

1 Depositions of JOHN BRADEY & EZEKIEL WEST, 9 May 1783, before JOHN WILTBANK Esq & Assoc, JPs: JOHN BRADEY, yeoman of Sussex Co age 23 or thereabouts, saith about 4-5 yrs ago he was at EBINEZER CAREY's house & looking at CAREY's papers & saw a bond of conveyance for parcel of land situate in Indian River Hund from JOHN HILL, late of Suss decd, to CAREY, & one of the witnesses was JOHN LACEY now decd. EZEKIEL WEST, yeoman of Suss age 52 thereabouts, saith he heard JOHN HILL say he had sold his land to EBENEZAR CAREY & he believes it to be that land he owned in Indian River Hund adj land of JOHN REGUA; & he heard HILL say he must go git plank from CAREY for he owed him money. Ackn: 9 May 1783.

2 Deposition of EBENEZAR CAREY, 5 May 1784, before JOHN WILTBANK Esq JP. EBENEZAR CAREY, yeoman of Suss age 50 thereabouts, saith he purch in 1768 a parcel of land, 100 ac, in Indian River Hund from JOHN HILL, yeoman of Suss now decd; & that he posted bond for payment of 25£ & after paying bond made several payments to HILL in plank & shingles in amt/o 8£ 18 shillings sixpence, the cancelled bond now in hands of EZEKIEL WEST, HILL's Adminr. CAREY further saith he afterwards sold a tr to GEORGE WALKER whom HILL accepted as paymaster for residue of 25£ + interest, & that he took bond from HILL for conveyance of land, & he thinks one of his sons tore off & destroyed pt/o said bond; & that he afterwards sold land to SMITH FRAME.

2 Petition of EZEKIEL WEST, Adminr of JNO HILL decd, to sell lands, 5 May 1784: sheweth that JNO HILL owned tr, 100 ac, being 1 moiety or pt/o larger tr in Indian River Hund in forks of Swan Creek, 208 ac originally granted to JOHN WALKER & after sold to EBENEZAR CAREY; bond to CAREY is now torn & destroyed; CAREY afterward sold the land to SMITH FRAME 2 Jun 1775; SMITH FRAME sold the land to DAVID STREET 19 Feb 1777; DAVID STREET sold it to WOOLSEY HATHAWAY 21 Apr 1783; that JOHN HILL died intestate & admin of estate was granted to petitioner EZEKIEL WEST, & he believes CAREY's debt for the land was paid in full; therefore WEST prays the Court's permission to give HATHAWAY a good & sufficient deed.

4 Deed, 5 May 1784, from EZEKIEL WEST adminr of JOHN HILL to WOOLSEY HATHAWAY: 100 ac in forks of Swan Creek in Indian River Hund being 1 moiety or pt/o larger tr estimated at 208 ac, originally granted to JOHN WALKER 16 Dec 1714 by warrant, & surveyed by ROBERT SHANKLAND Dep Surveyor 9 Apr 1716. Afsd JOHN WALKER afterward died intestate leaving 1 dau SARAH to whom the land descended; & SARAH after married JOHN PARSONS, & they sold the land to GEORGE DAY 6 Feb 1738, who in his will of 27 Feb 1744 devized the land to his 2 cozens GEORGE HILL & abovenamed JOHN HILL to be equally divided between them (will reg at Lewes, Bk A, fol 392). Land adjoins lands late of WM STEVENS decd (lands described). Bond from EZEKIEL CAREY dated 26 Sep 1768 found in HILL's possessions recently. Wit: ROBT HOUSTON, SOF. RUSSELL. Ackn 27 May 1784.

7 Deed, 4 May 1784, ISAAC HORSEY of Little Creek Hund from CALEB BALDING, miller of Little Creek Hundred, et uxor: 149 acres, part of a tract called STRAWBERRY

PLATT laid off for use of the Indians by Deed of Bargain & sale by BARKLEY
TOWNSEND for him, 186 ac pt/o the afsd tr on Little Creek in Little Creek Hund
of Sussex Co, being the now dwelling plantation of CALEB BALDING ; & whereas
BALDING now owns 2 tr situate as afsd called BATCHELOR'S DELIGHT, 250 ac, &
BATCHELOR'S INVENTION, 250 ac, surveyed for Col WM STEVENS, granted to JAMES
WITH & MARMADUKE MISTER who sold same to JAMES McMURRAY late of Summerset Co
MD, decd, who after having it many years died intestate so the 2 tr descended
to his eldest son, and so to ANN w/o PRICE RUSSELL & REBECCA w/o ARTHUR DENWOOD
of Summerset Co MD, by whom the same has been sold to JOHN MITCHEL of Sussex Co,
from whom CALEB BALDING obtained bond of conveyance for same 2 tr/o land.
BALDING also owns tr WELLBROOK situate as afsd; and in 1776 obtained warrant
to resurvey the pt/o afsd tr STRAWBERRY PLATT & to include any vacant land
contiguous thereto, & hath surveyed or included 78½ ac. BALDING now sells
STRAWBERRY PLATT, 149 ac, 58ac pt/o tr BATCHELOR'S INVENTION, & 6¼ ac pt/o tr
WELLBROOK, plus all the afsd 78 ac resurveyed to STRAWBERRY PLATT (Land described: near mills, near ditch emptying into Little Creek, adj COX'S DISCOVERY)
totaling 284¼ ac with dwelling house, etc, to ISAAC HORSEY for 600£. BALDING
represented by friends JOHN RODNEY, PHILLIPS KOLLOCK & ISAAC HENRY ESQ. Wit:
ELIJAH DAVIS, CHAS MOORE. Release of dower by SARAH, w/o CALEB BALDING. Wit:
JNO WILTBANK, ELIJAH DAVIS. (SARAH BALDING of full age.) May 6 1784 proved by
ELIJAH DAVIS; ackn by PHILLIPS KOLLOCK atty; J HALL Prothny.

10 Bond to CALEB BALDING/BALDWIN from JOHN MITCHEL, merchant of Sussex Co,
30,000£, 11 Nov 1780, for BATCHELOR'S INVENTION, 250 a, and BATCHELOR'S DELIGHT,
250 ac, in Little Creek 100. Wit: JAMES BRATTAN, JOHN MITCHELL JUNR. Ackn 27
May 1784 by J HALL, Proth'y.

10 Bond to JOB INGRAM from RICHBELL ENLESS/INLOSS of Kent Co DEL, blacksmith,
100£ , 1 Nov 1781, for 100 ac on the east side of Sheley's Branch in Sussex Co
near JAMES THOMPSON. Wit: BENJAMIN PHILLIPS, WM BURTON.
Afsd bond assigned by JOB INGRAM to MINIS MESSICK 6 Jan 1784. (Also called
Shealoe's Branch.) Proved 5 May 1784.

11 Deed to JOB INGRAM from MINIS MESSICK, yeomen of Sussex Co, 5 May 1784: land
in Broadkill Hund granted by warrant to THOS PARKER; PARKER sold it to JACOB
INGRAM 1 Feb 1737; JACOB INGRAM devised it to afsd JOB INGRAM in his will: 150
ac, bounded by Gravelly Branch proceeding out of Nanticoke River (s side of said
Gravelly Branch, also referred to as Bever dam) and other fork of said branch,
called PARKER INHERITANCE. MINORS MESSICK, his mark; wit: JACOB KOLLOCK, ELIJAH
CANNON, JOS MORRISON. Ackn 27 May 1784, D HALL, Prothn'y.

12 Bond to SUSANNAH HOPKINS from JNO DAGWORTHY, both of Worcester Co MD, 600£,
7 Aug 1774. Wit: EDWD DINGLE, GINNETHON HARNEY. Proved 5 May 1784, D HALL Prothn'y.

12 Deed to JOHN LAWS ESQ from WM OWENS, s/o ROBERT, planter, both of Sussex Co,
28 Oct 1783. Warrant of 11 May 1745 for survey by WM SHANKLAND, Dep Surveyor,
for JONATHAN FOWLER, 100 ac more or less in forest of Cedar Creek Hund; JNO
FOWLER sold 110 ac of afsd land to WM OWENS 18 day instant; WM OWENS now sells to
JOHN LAWS 50 ac of tr for 40£, being pt/o tr HORSE POUND adj JOHN LAWS ESQ .
Wit: NATHANIEL MORRIS, JOHN HEMMONS. WM OWENS appoints JOHN RODNEY or RHOADS
SHANKLAND, gentlemen of Lewes, his atty. Proved 5 May 1784, D HALL, Prothn'y.

14 4 May 1784, deed from MEIRS CLARK, yeoman of Broadkiln Hund, to STEPHEN TOWNSEND
yeoman of Cedar Creek Hund: tr in Slaughter Neck in Cedar Creek Hund, bounded by
other ½ of whole tr now owned by ALEXANDER DRAPER, by survey of WM POLK of 15 Apr
last 81 ac + more or less; being same land owned by NEHEMIAH CLARK at his death,
& which his adminr JOSHUA CLARK sold by decision of Orphan's Court for payment of
debts of intestate; buyer was JOHN CLARK late of Sussex, 5 Mar 1760?; JOHN CLARK

2.

later died intestate leaving a wid & 2 children, being the afsd MEIRS CLARK &
JOHN CLARK, to whom the land descended: to wit 2/3 to eldest son MEIRS CLARK &
to JOHN CLARK 1/3, subject to right of 1/3 dower of wid MARY, now w/o ANDREW
COLLINS. Tr sold to STEPHEN TOWNSEND for 115£ 10 shillings gold & silver coin,
all the undivided 2/3 pt/o above described land -- swears to protect against
any claim by afsd MARY COLLINS, or by heirs of JAMES WHITE & MARY WHITE. Wit:
DAVID TRAIN, JACOB KOLLOCK. MEIRS CLARK appoints PHILLIPS KOLLOCK ESQ & CORD
HAZZARD ESQ of Lewes his attys. Proved 5 May 1784, D HALL Prothn'y.

15 Deed, 27 Dec 1783, from BARTHOLOMEW TWIFORD, planter of Sussex, & NANCY his
wife, to SOLOMON TWIFORD, planter of Sussex, 200£, tr TWIFORDS MEADOWS and the
resurvey made on same called ADDN TO TWIFORDS MEADOWS in Northwest Fork Hund
bounded by CLARKSONS INDUSTRY & another tr owned by SOLOMON TWIFORD & BANINGS
CHANCE. BARTHOLOMEW & NANCY TWIFORD appoint PHILLIPS KOLLOCK & ALEXANDER LAWS
their attys. Wit: DANIEL POLK, FRANCIS WRIGHT. Proved 5 May 1784, D HALL.

17 Deed, 5 May 1784, from LEVIN DERICKSON ESQ, Commissioner For Sale of Forfeited
Property, to JOHN CLOWES of Sussex: pursuant to Act Of Free Pardon & Oblivion of
26 Jun 1778, DERICKSON sold at public auction to afsd JOHN CLOWES, on 23 Sep 1778,
113 ac, pt/o forfeited estate of BOAZ MANLOVE, for 135£; said land lying on n
side of Broadkill Creek a little below Ozburns Landing, bounded by ELIJAH MELLSON's
lands, JONES' land, ISAAC DRAPER's field & the Creek beginning at the Cripple;
cont 127 ac being sold to ISAAC DRAPER off the sw corner of whole tr -- defend
against any claim of afsd BOAZ MANLOVE. Wit: WM POLK, WM HARRISON. Proved 5 May
1784, D HALL, Prothn'y.

18 Deed, 13 Jan 1784, from WHEETLEY HATFIELD of Sussex to JONATHAN HATFIELD,
blacksmith of Sussex. By patent granted to JAMES HAILES of Dorchester Co, 50
ac HAILES CHANCE, 22 Mar 1742; said JAMES HAILES died leaving 2 sons WAITMAN &
EZEKIEL HAILES who inherited land according to his will; then they sold land to
WM HATFIELD who later died without issue so the land fell to COTTENHAM HATFIELD,
heir at law, who also died without issue, so the land fell to WILLIAM HATFIELD,
father of the two deceased, and he gave up admin to his son WHEETLEY HATFIELD.
HAILES CHANCE, 44 ac, 40£, lying on s side OF Bridge Branch issuing out of ne
fork of Nanticoke R, whole tr 93 ac. Wit: JOHN CLOWES, JOHN LAWS, signed
WHITLAY HATFIELD. Proved 5 May 1784.

19 Deed, 4 May 1784, from FRANCES CAHOON, spinstress of Sussex Co, to SAMUEL
THOMPSON, pilot of Sussex Co, 85£ , tr situate in Lewes Town between 2nd & 3rd
Sts, adj on nw lot now owned by DANIEL MURPHEY & formerly by COMFORT JENKINS, &
adj on se lot lately owned by NEHEMIAH FIELD but formerly by DIANA MARSHAL, 60'
front on 2nd St & 200' back on 3rd St. This lot formerly owned by Capt BAILY,
decd, who sold it to FRANCES CAHOON on 4 Aug 1742. Wit: JAMES SYKES, JNO RODNEY.
Proved 5 May 1784.

20 Deed, 30 ___ 1783, from JOSHUA HITCH of Somerset Co MD to JOHN ROBINS of
Sussex Co DEL: tr granted by patent on 10 Jun 1734 to JAMES JONES called JONES
VENTURE, 50 ac situate then in Somerset Co, & tr granted by patent to ISAAC JONES
on Jun 20 1749 called JONES CHOICE, 50 ac then situate in Somerset Co & nearly
adj afsd tr, which by sundry legal conveyances duly became the estate of ALEXANDER
RECORDS of Somerset Co, who on 5 Jan 1775 sold both tr to afsd JOSHUA HITCH for
200£; afsd land now in Little Creek Hund, Sussex Co DEL, whereon JOHN ROBINS now
dwells. JOSHUA HITCH appoints JACOB MOORE, JOHN WILTBANK & JOHN LAWS Esqs his
attys. Wit: WM RELPH, CHAS MOORE. Ackn by MARY, w/o JOSHUA HITCH; wit: ROBT
HOUSTON & CHAS MOORE. Proved 5 May 1784.

3.

21 Deed, 17 Oct 1783, from JACOB LOCKERMAN, planter of Dorchester Co MD, to
SOLOMON VINSON of Sussex Co DEL: whereas CONSTANTINE HODSON 50 yrs ago owned 7
tr then in Dorchester Co (2 of which hereinafter described) & voyaged to England
where he after settled, married & died leaving his lands undisposed of, & his
family hasn't been heard of for 26 years so it is presumed they are extinguished
& dead, & he left in Dorchester 3 sisters who after his death & presumption of
family extinction became his heirs at law, & who themselves are now all dead
leaving lawful issue; & whereas VIENNA HODSON, eldest sister, married THOMAS
LOCKERMAN & by him had several children including the afsd JACOB LOCKERMAN, their
eldest son, who is entitled to 1/3 of the lands, JACOB LOCKERMAN now sells 2 tr:
CONSTANTINOPLE & WOODEN MINE for 54£, now lying in Sussex Co due to a division
line lately established separating DEL from ES MD. If heirs of CONSTANTINE
HODSON come forth & claim land, then LOCKERMAN swears to return the purchase
price to SOLOMON VINSON, & appoints JACOB MOORE & RICHARD BASSETT ESQs his attys.
Wit: JNO HAMMOND, R STEVENS. Proved 5 May 1784.

23 Deed, 6 May 1784, from JAMES ROWLAND, pilot of Lewes Rehoboth Hund, & wife
DEBORAH, to NATHANIEL HICKMAN, yeoman of Broadkiln Hund; land devised by SAMUEL
ROWLAND, pilot late of sussex, decd, to all his children equally by will dated
15 Dec 1765 (to children after death of wife); widow now decd & partition sub-
mitted to PARKER ROBINSON, HAP HAZZARD & WM PERRY, gentlemen, who laid off lands
on 9 Mar 1783 to the children: the afsd JAMES, SAMUEL & COMFORT who married
STEPHEN WARRINGTON; to JAMES went tr of marsh on w side of Coolspring Creek, 45
ac, which he now sells for 67£ 10 shillings. Wit: WOOLSEY BURTON, DAVID TRAIN.
Ackn by wife DEBORAH ROWLAND, to JNO WILTBANK. Proved 6 May 1784.

24 Deed, 6 May 1784, from JNO ABBOTT WARRINGTON, yeoman of Sussex, to WOODMAN
STOCKLEY, yeoman of Sussex, land in Angola Neck in Indian River Hund where JOHN
ABBOTT WARRINGTON lately dwelt, pt/o larger tr called WEBLEY originally patented
to ROBERT BRACY, 800 ac, who deeded to his son ROBERT BRACEY JUNR 600 ac; & on 25
day of 1st month, 1697, ROBT BRACEY JUNR sold it to WM CLARK; who on 10 Apr 1702
sold 400 ac to JAMES WALKER; & he, with JAMES SHIRLEY, mortgaged land to Genl
Loan Office who sold it at auction when he defaulted (RYVES HOLT ESQ then High
Sheriff of Co) to THOMAS WARRING on 12 Aug 1730; & he sold sold 179 ac on 7 Feb
1732 to HANNAH DAVIDSON, now decd; & her heirs LEWES DAVIDSON, MARY DAVIDSON,
JOHN ANDERLY & SARAH his wife, late SARAH DAVIDSON on 6 Aug 1752 sold same to
JACOB WARRINGTON, father of afsd JOHN ABBOTT WARRINGTON. And one other tr adj
afsd 179 ac which is also pt/o larger tr WEBLEY granted as afsd to ROBERT BRACEY
who sold it to WM CLARK whose executor sold it to JOHN CAREY who sold it to THOS
GRAY, who mortgaged it to Loan Office so that CORNELIUS WILTBANK, then High
Sheriff sold it on 28 Feb 1739 to ROBERT SMITH who sold it to THOMAS WARRINGTON,
who devised it in his will to his son JOHN WARRINGTON, who on 4 May 1763 sold it
to afsd JACOB WARRINGTON, f/o afsd JOHN ABBOTT WARRINGTON, being 225 ac. And
afsd JACOB WARRINGTON died intestate leaving several children, so that afsd JOHN
ABBOTT WARRINGTON brought petition to Orphans Court on 24 Feb 1774 (being eldest
s/o JACOB) saying JACOB had died leaving a widow & 8 children & that widow was
now decd, & prayed the Court to divide the land among the children, & the court
appointees reported the land could not be fairly divided without spoiling it, so
JOHN ABBOTT WARRINGTON requested valuation for sale of land on 29 Oct 1774 & it
was valued at 26 shillings per ac; & on 8 Feb 1776 J A WARRINGTON sold 198 ac to
afsd WOODMAN STOCKLEY (pt/o 225 ac tr); & now sells the 179 ac tr to same: tr
standing on head of small branch running into Middle Creek, adj land formerly
owned by WM REED, & adj w side of Gum Branch which runs into Braceys Branch, adj
land late owned by JOSHUA STOCKLEY decd. Also now sells remainder of 225 ac tr.
Wit: DAVID TRAIN, RICHARD BURTON. Proved 6 May 1784.

27 Petition of SMITH FRAME, adminr to ROBERT FRAME decd, 5 May 1784, to sell land of latter on w side of Pocomoke Cypress Swamp at its head called FORREST, 50 ac, granted by patent on 24 Oct 1754 to afsd ROBERT FRAME, who on 23 Nov 1754 gave bond to EDMAN TAYLOR of Worcester Co MD, planter, (FRAME also planter, of Sussex Co); afsd TAYLOR assigned bond on 13 Feb 1759 to MOSES TIMMONS, who on 22 Jan 1769 assigned it to EZEKIEL TIMMONS, who on 19 Nov 1768 assigned it to THOS PARRAMORE, who in turn on 9 Dec 1770 assigned it to JOHN WINGATE. Afsd ROBERT FRAME died intestate before executing any deed to EDMOND TAYLOR or any of assignees, and that part of ROBERT FRAME's estate remaining unadministered by the surviving adminr NATHAN FRAME were committed to SMITH FRAME adminr, who prays the court to make a good & sufficient deed to JOHN WINGATE for the land. Approved 5 May 1784.

29 Deed, 5 May 1784, from SMITH FRAME, adminr DBN of ROBERT FRAME, yeoman decd, who died intestate, to JOHN WINGATE: tr FORREST in Broad Creek Hund (descr above). Adminrs for ROBERT FRAME were ISABELLA & NATHAN FRAME, now both decd; JOHN WINGATE yeoman of Sussex Co. Wit: JOHN WILTBANK, D HALL. Proved 5 May 1784.

31 Bond, 4 May 1784, from ROBERT HODSON, blacksmith of Sussex Co, to NOTTINGHAM JACOBS, yeoman of Sussex, for land in Slaughter Neck, Sussex Co, 50 ac. Wit JAS WHITE, AARON WILLIAMS. Proved 6 May 1784.

31 Deposition of LUKE WATTSON & THOMAS GROVES, 6 May 1784, verifying signature of JAMES WHITE.

31 Petition of SARAH CLARK, adminr of ROBT HODSON, 6 May 1784. SARAH CLARK, late _____, adminrx of ROBERT HODSON, blacksmith of Sussex Co, who owned tr in Slaughter Neck of Cedar Creek Hund, 50 ac called BOWMANS FARMS, same tr JOSEPH HICKMAN sold to him 6 Aug 1747. Afsd HODSON gave bond 4 May 1754 to NOTTINGHAM JACOBS in amt 100£, & died intestate without making deed to afsd JACOBS; & afsd NOTTINGHAM JACOBS also died leaving a wid MARIANNE & issue, only one son JEHU JACOBS to whom the lands descended; & the said MARIANNE later married JAMES KENDRICK late of Sussex by whom she had issue, only one son WM KENDRICK, & afterwards died, & JEHUU JACOBS her son also died w/o lawful issue leaving his bro-in-law WM KENDRICK his next of kin, to whom the land descended. SARAH CLARK therefore prays the court to make a good & sufficient deed to WM KENDRICK. Wit: D TRAIN. Proved 5 May 1784.

33 Deed, 6 May 1784, from SARAH CLARK, adminrx of ROBERT HODSON (she late SARAH HODSON), tr BOWMANS FARMS, 50 ac, adj JOSEPH HICKMAN's lands & JAMES WHITE's lands & near WM HICKMAN's fence "where his father lived", being part of land left to afsd JOSEPH HICKMAN by his father who purch same from HENRY BOWMAN decd. SARAH CLARK wid/o ROBERT HODSON. Wit: DAVID TRAIN, MARY TRAIN. Ackn 6 May 1784.

35 Commission of the Peace directed to DANIEL POLK, EDWARD DINGLE & LEVIN DERRICKSON, appointing them Justices of the Peace of Sussex co. Wit: His Excellency NICHOLAS VAN DYKE ESQ our Pres etc, 26 Apr 1784.

35 Deed, 4 Jun 1784, from MARGARET HARRIS, wid/o Philadelphia, one of daus & heiress of CHARLES PERRY late of Lewes Town, clothier decd, & late wid/o THOMAS KALE late of Lewes Town, carpenter decd, to JOSEPH GREENWAY, cooper of Philadelphia & HANNAH his wife. MARGARET HARRIS owns valuable real estate in Lewes including her father's plantation in Lewes Town & tr, 500 ac, at Nanticoke in MD, & farm house & land about ½ mi from Courthouse at Lewes, adj land of JOHN RUSSELL & MARGARET SIMONTON; last named land, 3 lots, granted by RUSSELL to JOHN TYRE who sold them to THOMAS KALE decd. MARGARET conveys to JOSEPH GREENWAY & her dau the afsd HANNAH his wife for love & 5 shillings all the lands & goods of her decd father CHARLES PERRY & of her sister CATHARINE KOLLOCK decd, incl all abovenamed est. Wit: SAML THOMPSON, LYDIA TOWN, R WHITEHEAD. Proved 10 Jul 1784.

5.

36 Letter of Atty, 24 Jun 1784, JOSEPH GREENWAY from MARGARET HARRIS wid/o
Philadelphia, one of daus/o CHARLES PERRY, clothier late of Lewes, decd; & late
wid/o THOS KALE carpenter of Lewes decd. CHAS PERRY left 3 daus: MARGARET, WIN-
IFRED & CATHARINE to whom his estate descended; CATHARINE mar SIMON COLLICK, & died
without issue. MARGARET finished building the house on 3 lotts ¼ mi from Courthouse & rented same to ROBERT JACKSON & empowered W PURNAL JOHNSON to collect rent;
she has not these many yrs received any part or benefit from rent or estates;
now appoints her son-in-law JOSEPH GREENWAY her atty to sue for debts & arrears of
rent, etc, & sell property if he so advise. Wit: SAML THOMPSON, LYDIA TOWN, R
WHITEHEAD. Ackn 20 Jul 1784.

37 Deed, 30 Jun 1783, THOS RODNEY mercht of Phila & ELIZABETH his wife, to THOS
FISHER, SAMUEL FISHER & JABEZ MAUD FISHER of Phila, merchants. JABEZ MAUD FISHER
late of Suss, decd, owned large tr FISHERS ISLAND incl great qty marsh PLUMB
POINT MARSH, & in his will of 30 Sep 1742 bequeathed to 3 daus MARGARET, SARAH &
ELIZABETH, latter now w/o afsd THOS RODNEY, 400 ac PLUMB POINT MARSH. MARGARET
& SARAH now decd; ELIZABETH survivor sells 400 ac for 400£. Wit: JOHN ASHMEAD,
NICHOLAS LITTLE. Testimony of ELIZABETH FISHER to JOHN GIBSON, Mayor of Phila.

38 Award on division of lands, 31 May 1783, between MARY BEVINS & JOSEPH MARVEL:
Dispute between BEVINS & MARVEL over land of which they are each part owners;
JOHN BEAVANS, late of Suss decd, owned 49 ac in Indian River Hund & his son JOHN
BEAVANS inherited it & it was sold at sheriff's auction by RHOADS SHANKLAND during
his ownership, to JOSEPH MARVEL; but ELIZABETH BEAVANS, wid/o JOHN decd has 1/3
dower right to land. Divided by arbitrators ABRAHAM ADDAMS, JOSHUA COSTON, ROBT
WATSON Mc CALLEY of Suss: 17 ac of westernmost end, benefit of 1/3 apple orchard
during her life to MARY BEAVANS + pymt of cost of MARVEL laying her 1/3 land.
Wit: ELI McCALLEY, BETSY MACALLY.

39 Deed, 9 Nov 1781, JOHN COLLINS of Broad Crek Hund to LEVIN VAUGHAN planter of
same place: MARGARET, w/o GEORGE BACON of Suss decd, died intestate owning 136
ac pt/o tr ADDITION & 80 ac pt/o tr CYPRESS SWAMP. ADDITION originally granted to
DAY GIVANE & CYPRESS SWAMP to ROBERT GIVANE, both of Somerset Co MD, & both were
adjudged to JOHN COLLINS by Orphans Court as eldest heir of afsd MARGARET. ROBT
GIVANE bequeathed his 80 ac CYPRESS SWAMP with other lands to his son THOS GIVANE
who died intestate, so land fell to ROBT GIVANE eldest bro/o THOS, & he sold to
GEO GIVANE of Worcester Co MD, 24 Jul 1747, CYPRESS SWAMP + 281 ac INCLOSED, bond
proven before DAY SCOTT Esq 30 Aug 1749 in Worcester Co, thence by various deeds
to afsd JOHN COLLINS. And JOHN COLLINS had surveyed & laid out for him in 1776
tr RUNNING MEADE in Broad Creek Hund, Sussex. LEVIN VAUGHAN paid COLLINS 405£
in 1779 for RUNNING MEADE, 85 ac +, pt/o CYPRESS SWAMP, 47 ac +, & ADITION, 69 ac
+, totalling 202½ ac, adj LEVIN VAUGHAN's shop & NEHEMIAH MESSICK's land, & adj
tr COXES PERFORMANCE. Wit: D HALL, ISAAC HENRY. Ackn 24 Aug 1784.

40 Deed, 30 Jul 1784, from JOSEPH CORD yeoman of Suss & JANE his wife, to ANDERSON
PARKER gentleman of same place: pt/o 4 ac lott in Lewes Town on n side southermost
street adj Block House Pond, originally granted 12th month of 1688/9 to CHARLES
HAINS who on 3 Mar 1690 sold it to LANCELOTT BECK?, who sold it thru his atty
THOS PEMBERTON to RICHARD WILLIAMS 7 Mar 1691, who sold it on 4th day 12th month
1692/3 to MARY HASLUM who after married JOHN MEIRS the Elder by whom she had 4
children: JOHN, JAMES, SARAH & MARY MEIRS; & having survived her husband afsd
MARY wid/o JOHN the Elder, by her will of 27 Aug 1727 devized 1 ac to her 4 sons:
JOHN MEIRS, JAMES MEIRS, DANIEL PALMER & JONATHAN OZBURN (afsd PALMER & OZBURN
having married abovenamed MARY & SARAH her daus), to be used as a burying ground;
and she devized remainder of 4 ac lott to her son JOHN MEIRS. JOHN MEIRS by his
will of 31st day 11th month 1749/50 devized land to his dau JANE CORD ("& if JANE
CORD have no issue, then to SAMUEL ROWLAND s/o THOS & SARAH ROWLAND, & to JOSEPH

6.

PALMER s/o DANIEL & MARY PALMER"), & at Court Of Lewes of May last, JANE CORD according to law caused a perfect common recovery, docking, cutting & barring all remaining estates. Now JOSEPH & JANE CORD sell for 35£ lott on nw side South Street adj land/o late EDWARD STRETCHER now owned by WM BRERETON, adj Market St, 3½ ac land & pond --- defend against SAMUEL ROWLAND, JOSEPH PALMER, JOHN MEIRS, MARY MEIRS, RICHARD WILLIAMS, LANCELOTT BECK & heirs, etc. Wit: CORD HAAZZARD, JOHN WOOLF. Ackn 30 Jul 1784.

42 Deed, 12 Jun 1784, from JOHN WOOLF cordwainer of Lewes Rehoboth Hund, to ANDERSON PARKER yeoman of same place: marsh in pasture of WRIXAM WHITE in afsd hund, adj line of patent of GREENFIELD & WHITE's marsh (pur/o WM PRETTYMAN late of Sussex, decd) & adj GRAY's & GREENFIELD's patents, 4½ ac land & marsh, pt/o tr GREENFIELD. Land was owned by WM PRETTYMAN afsd who died intestate; his admnx COMFORT PRETTYMAN died before admin complete & her admnr was PERRY PRETTYMAN who sold land   to WM DAVIS to settle debts of WM PRETTYMAN on 7 Nov 1772; & WM DAVIS sold it back to PERRY PRETTYMAN, who on 31 Aug 1776 sold it to ANDERSON PARKER. WOOLF purch for £21 5 sh from PARKER. Wit: J MAXWELL, JABEZ FISHER. Ackn 24 Aug.

43 Deed, 10 Jul 1784, JAMES BRATTON from JAMES TRUSHAM both of Suss: £100 pd to TRUSHAM for 1 moiety of tr TRUSHAMS CHOICE, 12 ac. Wit: JOHN MITCHELL, JOSEPH VAUGHAN. Ackn 24 Aug.

44 Deed, RICHARD HOWARD pilot of Lewes, from JOSEPH CORD yeoman of Suss & JANE his wife: lott in Lewes originally granted to JEREMIAH SCOTT who, by his attys COMFORT SCOTT & WM EMMOTT, conveyed it to THOS OLDMAN on 16 Dec 1692; & OLDMAN sold it on 8 Mar 1693/4 to JOHN MEIRS who on 26 Mar 1721 willed it to his son JOHN MEIRS; & that JOHN MEIRS willed it on 31 day 11th month 1749/50 to his dau & only child JANE CORD, saying "if she have no heirs, then to SAMUEL ROWLAND, s/o THOS & SARAH ROWLAND, to JOSEPH PALMER s/o DANIEL & MARY PALMER". JOSEPH & JANE CORD barred further claims at court of last May; & now sell to HOWARD for £72 lott fronting Lewes Creek & adj land/o heirs/o WRIXAM LEWIS ESQ decd & adj lott owned by NEHEMIAH DAVIS JR; 60'x200'; protect against claims/o SAML ROWLAND, JOS PALMER, JOSHUA FISHER, JOHN MEIRS younger, JOHN MEIRS elder, THOS OLDMAN etc. Wit: JOHN CLOWES, ___ RUSSELL. 1 Jul 1784. Ackn 31 Jul 1784.

45 Deed, 4 Aug 1784, LEVIN LANK yeoman of Sussex from MARY RUSSELL spinstress of Suss: tr in Broadkiln Hund which RICHARD STARR late of Suss decd bequeathed to his 3 sons: NATHANIEL, JONATHAN & JAMES STARR. SARAH STARR admnx of afsd JONATHAN & gdn/o his only dau & heiress BETHIAH STARR, through her atty ANDERSON PARKER, obtained bond of NATHL & JAMES STARR to accept division of WM STEPHENSON, HUGH KING & RHOADS SHANKLAND (appointed by court) according to true intent of will; so 146 ac was awarded to SARAH STARR wid & BETHIAH STARR d/o JONATHAN; platt made & recorded in Rolls Office Liber L No 11 Fol 216. Since JNO STARR's personal estate didn't cover his debts, 46 ac ordered sold at auction & purchased by THOS STATON on 8 Aug 1772; THOS STATON then died intestate & tr again sold by his admnr ANDERSON PARKER for his debts, & were purch by ANDERSON PARKER himself; & on 29 Apr 1776 he sold tr to afsd MARY RUSSELL. Adj NATHL STARR & Mill Creek; MARY RUSSELL sells to LEVIN LANK for £150. Wit JOHN BURTON, JOHN FUTCHER. Ackn 24 Aug 1784.

47 Deed, 21 May 1784, JOHN HART yeoman of Suss, from EDWARD CRAIGE yeoman of Lewes Rehoboth Hund & SARAH his wife: CRAIGE sells for £10 1 ac, pt/o tr south of Lewes 23 3/4 ac, being the same moiety JOHN SIMONTON the Elder devised to his 3 daus: JENNET, SARAH (w/o EDWD CRAIGE afsd) & MARY, the other moiety having been deeded to JOHN SIMONTON the Younger by JOHN MEIRS. JOHN SIMONTON Younger died intestate & without issue so land descended to 4 sisters: JENNET, SARAH, MARY & ELIZABETH. ELIZABETH m NOBLE LEWIS & released rights to other sisters who had it divided & SARAH recd afsd 1 ac: adj southernmost street of Lewes. Wit JNO WILTBANK, JNO RUSSELL. Ackn 4 Aug 1784.

7.

48   Bond of JULIUS AUGUSTUS JACKSON of Suss to JEREMIAH RUST JACKSON of Suss
for £500, 5 Nov 1783; conditioned upon J A JACKSON making over his several tr on sw
of Tuskel Creek Branch, including resurvey joining to LONG LOTT. Wit: CHAS MOORE,
PETER RUST. Proved 4 Aug 1784.

48   Deed, 20 July 1784, JOHN METCALF yeoman of Suss from BENJAMIN WYNKOOP gentle-
man of Phila: WYNKOOP sells for £100 small tr or island of marsh in Cedar Creek
Hund on w side Delaware Bay & se side of Cedar Creek; granted to ABRAHAM WYNKOOP
ESQ by warrant of 26 Oct 1742, & by his will of 15 Nov 1753 he devised it to afsd
BENJ WYNKOOP; adj Cedar Creek & Comfort's Gut, 90½ ac marsh. WYNKOOP appoints
JOHN RODNEY &/or JOHN WILTBANK Esq. Wit: DANIEL ROGERS, DAVID WILLIAMS. Proved
4 Aug 1784.

49   Deed, 24 Jul 1784, JOHN THOROGOOD yeoman of Suss from SHADRACH SHORT of Suss:
tr on n side of Shealos Branch at head of Indian River called SHORTS ADDITION,
granted by MD to EDWARD SHORT 17 Nov 1748 & bequeathed by him to afsd SHADRACH
SHORT; 100 ac. SHORT sells for £100. Wit: JOHN GIBBENS JNR, JOHN WINGATE.

50   Deed, 4 Aug 1784, ROBERT HOUSTON ESQ of Suss from LEONARD HOUSTON farmer of
Suss: 200 ac, pt/o tr ROUND POND INLARGED in Broad Creek Hund, 860 ac; devised
to LEONARD HOUSTON by his grfather JOHN HOUSTON; £129 paid to LEONARD by ROBT;
n end of tr, adj road from Broad Creek Bridge to Pine Grove Furniss. Wit: WM
VAUGHAN, JOHN GODDARD. Ackn 4 Aug 1784.

51   Petition of SYDENHAM THORN & BETTY his wife to convey lands to JOSEPH GRIFFITH:
THORN being exec of MANUEL MANLOVE of Suss decd. MANUEL MANLOVE gave bond to
JOSEPH GRIFFITH on 13 Oct 1772 for £300 or conveyance of 2 tr land; bond proved 3
Nov 1774 by oath of SARAH MERRICK, wit; prays court to permit execution of 2 separate
deeds to GRIFFITH for the parcels. 4 Aug 1784.

52   Deed, 4 Aug 1784, JOSEPH GRIFFETH yeoman of Suss, from MANUEL MANLOVE's execrs,
SYDENHAM THORN of Suss & BETTY his wife (late BETTY MANLOVE, execx): 2 tr in
forest of Cedar Creek, 350 ac, in Hindses Neck, 100 ac of which in MD patent &
other 250 ac by PA warrant to afsd JOSEPH GRIFFITH. Bond in Rolls Office Liber
L No 11 fol 448. When MANUEL MANLOVE died he apptd his then wife (afsd BETTY
MANLOVE) his execx. Deed for tr JENCOE granted by MD to DANIEL WELCH of Suss 14
Apr 1736, surveyed 10 Apr 1740, assigned by WELCH to JOHN MAY, assigned by MAY's
heirs to afsd MANUEL MANLOVE; adj OWENS FIELD, 255¼ ac. Wit: JNO WILTBANK, WM
POLK. Ackn 4 aug 1784.

53   Deed, 4 Aug 1784, JOSEPH GRIFFETH yeoman of Suss, from MANUEL MANLOVE's execrs,
SYDENHAM THORN of Suss & BETTY his wife (late BETTY MANLOVE, execx): 2 tr in
forest of Cedar Creek, 350 ac, etc (see above). Deed for tr JONATHANS LOTT
granted to MANUEL MANLOVE 14 Nov 1730?, MD Land Office Lib EJ No2 fol 785; adj
an Indian Oldfield, 100 ac. Wit as above. Ackn as above.

54   Deed, 4 Aug 1784, SHADRACH SHORT farmer from JOHN WINGATE farmer, both of Suss:
WINGATE sells for £50 tr DOWNSES CHANCE in Suss, nw side of Pocomoke River about
3 mi from w Province line; first granted to JOHN DOLBY; signed over to JACOB
DOWNS; conveyed from DOWNS to afsd JOHN WINGATE: on Bushy Ridge on nw side of
Whick Whack Swamp, 50 ac. Wit: ISAAC WITHERS, WM DRISKELL. Ackn same date

55   Deed, 3 Aug 1784, SHADRACH SHORT from THOS PAREMORE both of Suss: PARAMORE
sells to SHORT for £100 tr FRIENDSHIP in Suss, nw side of Pocomoke River about 3
mi from w Province line, first taken up by ANDREW COLLINS: w side of a cypress
swamp called CANNONS SWAMP about ¼ mi from said swamp, 28 ac. Wit: JOHN WINGGATE,
JOHN THOROUGHGOOD. Ackn 4 Aug 1784.

56 Deed, 21 Jun 1784, JOSEPH MELSON of Suss from JOHN JOHNSON eldest s/o HENRY JOHNSON of Worcester Co decd, who was eldest s/o WITTINGTON JOHNSON of Worc decd who d intestate owning tr MILL CHANCE & JONES NECK, 96 ac: both in county afsd, MILL CHANCE 9 ac, descended to said HENRY BLAIR JOHNSON & CHRISTIAN JOHNSON, wid/o WITTINGTON JOHNSON: after death of WITTINGTON, HENRY BLAIR JOHNSON obtained JONES NECK from THOS JONES of afsd county, dwelling plantation & sawmill of his father, then he & CHRISTIAN sold the 2 tr to JOHN MITCHEL 2 Jun 1772, which then became property of JOSEPH MELSON 27 Feb 1782: now JOHN JOHNSON & CHRISTIAN JOHNSON for 1 shilling & matters related sell same: originally granted by MD to EBENEZAR JONES 2 Nov 1730; MILL CHANCE being granted to WITTINGTON JOHNSON 26 Aug 1762: totally 105 ac in Broad Creek Hund; the JOHNSONS appt JOHN LAWS, JOHN CLOWES & JACOB MOORE ESQ their attys. Wit: JOHN LAWS, WM POLK. Ackn 4 Aug 1784.

57 Deed, 4 Aug 1784, JOHN BETTS yeoman of Suss from JOHN TIMMONS yeoman of Suss: TIMMONS sells for £45 tr in Broad Creek Hund, pt/o tr LONG TRUSTED granted by MD to afsd JOHN TIMMONS, 50 ac, originally granted by MD 7 Dec 1772. Wit: JOB INGRAM, D TRAIN. Ackn same date.

58 Deed, 4 Aug 1784, GEORGE HOWARD AYDELOTT planter of Worc Co from JOSEPH ROBERTS, exec of est of JESPER AYDELOTT of Suss decd: JESPER AYDELOTT owned tr in Baltimore Hund, pt/o tr JOINT MEADOW, & by will of 23 Jan 1783 dircted pt/o JOINT MEADOWS be sold for debts; so his exec sells for £147+, 53 ac of afsd tr: adj tr mentioned in deed from JOHN AYDELOTT SR to his son JOHN AYDELOTT. Wit: MARY TRAIN, DAVID TRAIN. Ackn same date.

59 Deed, 4 Oct 1783, THOMAS ALLCOCK FOWLER farmer of Caroline Co from WM ADAMS farmer of Kent Co DEL & NANCY his wife: ADAMS sells for 10 silver dollars 93 ac in Suss, pt/o tr ADAMS VENTURE & all that part not heretofore sold by WM ADAMS SR f/o said WM ADAMS, to JACOB NUNER then of Dorch Co on Jul 31 1766 --- refers to "said THOMAS ALLCOCK". Wit: JOHN LAWS, WM CAUSEY JR. Ackn same date.

60 Deed, 5 Aug 1784, LEMUEL WILLIAMS of Slaughter Neck & Cedar Crk Hund from JOHN SMITH of same place & SOPHIA his wife: SMITHs sell for £134+ plantation & tr at head of Slaughter Neck on both sides of county road, 1 mi below Cedar Crk, adj MITCHELL BLACK decd & ALEXANDER DRAPER's land; adj NATHL STOCKLEY; 83 ac pt/o tr PAGES PATENT & pt/o land willed by DAVID SMITH ESQ on 26 Apr 1753 to his 2 gr-sons JOHN & DAVID SMITH, who at age 21 divided lands. SMITH to protect against claims of heirs/o MITCHELL BLACK decd & of LITTLETON TOWNSEND & JOSEPH DRAPER & their heirs. LEMUEL WILLIAMS cordwainer. Wit: THOS GRAY, BENJN MCELVAIN. Ackn 5 Aug 1784.

61 Deed, 25 Sep 1784, JULIUS AUGUSTUS FLOWER of Suss from EDWARD WRIGHT & ANN his wife of Caroline Co: WRIGHTs sell for £25 10½ ac pt/o tr WRIGHTS MEADOW in Suss, adj ST DAVIDS formerly owned by SOLOMON TURPIN decd, e of MD state line. WRIGHTs appt JOHN RODNEY ESQ & ANDERSON PARKER ESQ attys. Wit: WM POLK, HENRY FLOWER. Ackn 30 Sep 1784.

62 Deed, 25 Sep 1784, JOSEPH TURPIN of Suss from JULIUS AUGUSTUS FLOWER of Suss & ELIZABETH his wife: FLOWERs sell for £200 tr BAR MEADOWS? & ST DAVIDS on e side of MD state line & TURPINS CONCLUSION. JOHN RODNEY & ANDERSON PARKER attys. Wit: WM POLK, HENRY FLOWER. Ackn 30 Sep 1784.

64 Deed, 25 Sep 1784, RICHARD TULL of Suss from THOS ANGE & REBECKAH his wife of Suss: ANGEs sell for £80 tr CURTECY given to THOS ANGE by his father JOHN ANGE decd, in Suss sw of branch where said TULL & ANGE & heirs of ANGE's bro JOHN ANGE have a sawmill & gristmill in partnership; & tr drowned by mills & their pt/o tr TULLS ADDN surveyed for RICHARD TULL, adj CURTECY. JOHN RODNEY & ANDERSON PARKER

attys. Wit: WM POLK, HENRY FLOWER. Ackn 30 Sep 1784.

65 Bond, 20 Mar 1775, WM RILEY EVANS of Worc Co from JOSHUA HILL of same, for conveyance of land: HILL bound to EVANS for £650,for tr HILL bought of DANIEL GODWIN called TOWER HILL, land w of Seder Neck Rd bot/o JONES RICKARDS called FRIENDSHIPS ADDN & all right to vacant land on n side Tuske Branch & w of afsd road, & watermill. Wit: NOAH COLLINS, WM WILKINS.

65 Deed, 3 Nov 1784, SAMUEL BETTS yeoman of Suss buys from JOHN COLLINGS gentleman of Suss, execr of ANDREW COLLINGS the Elder late of MD decd: tr formerly in Dorchester Co but now in Suss originally granted by MD to JOHN BROWN 22 Jul 1748, 50 ac, JOHNS FORREST, on s side cart road from Broad Creek to CANNONS SYPRESS SWAMP, e of swamp near BURTONS SEVANAH. JOHN BROWN devised land to bro JAMES BROWN 22 Oct 1766, who sold it on 4 Sep 1769 to afsd ANDREW COLLINGS who sold it to SAMUEL BETTS but died before conveyance made, but apptd said JOHN COLLINGS & ANDREW COLLINGS (his sons) his execrs, JOHN surviving. Now conveyed for £27 previously pd. Wit: DANIEL ROGERS, JNO RUSSELL. Ackn same date.

66 Deed, 3 Nov 1784, JOHN BURTON s/o ROBERT of Angola & Indian River Hund, yeoman, buys from MOSES ALLEN pilot of Lewes & ELIZABETH his wife: 217 ac in Angola & Indian River Hund pt/o 1200 ac tr ARCADIA originally surveyed by CORNELIOUS VERHOOF 30 Dec 1681 & patented by RICHARD BUNDOCK 1 Mar 1684, who on 19th of 1st month 1683 sold 500 ac to NORTON CLAYPOOLE who d intestate leaving 4 children: GEORGE, JOSEPH, MARY & JEREMIAH who inherited it, & they on 9 Mar 1722/3 sold to afsd JEREMIAH CLAYPOOLE, who on 3 Aug 1726 sold it to JOHN ALLEN. (JACOB KOLLOCK atty for 4 CLAYPOOLE children.) ALLEN bettered title by buying right of RICHARD BUNDOCK, s/o RICHARD afsd on 25 Jan 1722, also from BUNDOCK's wife SUSANNAH. Then ALLEN sold 100 ac to JOHN THOMPSON 7 May 1728, & by his will of 1 Feb 1767 devised 200 ac to his gr-son WM ALLEN (on LONG LOVE & BUNDICKS BRANCH), & devised residue to his gr-son MOSES ALLEN, & they had land divided between them. Now sell to BURTON for £650; adj JOSIAH MARTIN & country road from Lewes to St Georges Chapel. Wit: RHOADS SHANKLAND, JNO RUSSELL. Ackn same date.

68 Deed, 1 Jun 1780, AARON MCKEMMMY/MCKIMMEY of Suss, yeoman, sells to WM ROBINS shipwright of Suss: tr in Broadkill Forrest at head of Gravelly Branch, 200 ac, patented to RICHARD DOBSON 4th day of 8th month 1718, & he bequeathed to his 2 daus JANE & RACHEL who divided it; JANE later mar WALTER MCKIMMEY & had children: afsd AARON & 2 daus ELIZABETH & JANE who inherited, & the daus sold their part to AARON 6 May 1777. Now selling 7 ac. JOHN RODNEY, JOHN CLOWES attys. Wit: WM REDDEN, STEPHEN REDDEN. Ackn 3 Nov 1784.

69 Deed, 13 Jun 1784, JOSHUA WRIGHT & SARAH his wife of Somerset Co sell to JOHN TENNENT of Suss for £25: pt/o tr in Suss called GRAPEVINE THICKET, 25 ac. JOHN RODNEY atty. Wit: JESSE GRIFFETH, JOHN TURPIN, JEREMIAH CANNON, WM POLK. Ackn 3 Nov 1784.

70 Deed, 24 Jun 1784, CURTIS BROWN of Suss & RACHEL his wife sell to THOMAS LAWS yeoman of Suss for £457: tr GLADSTOWER in NW Fork Hund, 100 ac, plus tr CLEARANCE in NW Fork Hund, adj a swamp from a bridge branch from Nanticoke R, 94 ac. Wit: WM POLK, EDWARD MINNER. Attys JOHN WILTBANK ESQ, WM POLK ESQ. Ackn 3 Nov 1784.

71 Deed, 7 Nov 1783, HUGH PORTER planter of Somerset Co & JOHN his son sell to ANDERTON BROWN of Suss for £78+: parcel in Suss called WALLACES DELAY, 192 ac, patented by THOS WALLACE 2 Jul 1755, 96 ac being sold. JOHN RODNEY, JACOB MOORE ESQS attys. Wit: THOS LAWS, ROBT LAWS, GEO WALLACE. Ackn 3 Nov 1784.

73 Deed, 11 Oct 1784, CORNELIOUS BEVINS yeoman of Suss sells to PHILIP MARVEL yeoman of Suss, for £160, (reference to CORNELIOUS "BIBBINS"): pt/o tr granted &

10.

& surveyed for JOSHUA INGLISH formerly of Suss in forrest of Broadkiln Hund, which INGLISH sold to JAMES RICHARDSON, & then was sold by sheriff to WM STEEL of Suss; & STEEL on 24 Feb 1776 sold it to CORNELIOUS BEVINS, 100 ac. (Ref to CORNELIOUS BEVEANS.) Attys SIMON KOLLOCK, WM BUTCHER. Wit: SIMON KOLLOCK, WM BUTCHER, THOS MARVEL. Ackn 3 Nov 1784.

73 Power of atty, 11 Sep 1784, JOHN HANCE yeoman of Shrewsberry Twp, Monmouth Co NJ, to PETER WAPLES of Dagsburry Hund Suss, yeoman, to sell 150 ac of Cypress Swamp. Wit: JOHN WALKER, JACOB BURTON. Proved 3 Nov 1784.

74 Deed, 27 Sep 1784, PETER WAPLES farmer of Suss sells to WM DINGLE housecarpenter of Suss for JOHN HANCE: tr CYPRESS SWAMP owned by JOHN AYDELOTT granted by MD 9 Nov 1730, which AYDELOTT on 20 Nov 1735 sold to GEORGE HOWARD, 75 ac, who devised it by his will to his sons NEHEMIAH & GEORGE HOWARD, who on 11 Sep 1754 sold it to JOHN HANCE, & AYDELOTT also sold his part to HANCE, mariner of Monmouth Co East NJ; & JOHN HANCE bequeathed it to his son the afsd JOHN HANCE. Now sold for £150. Wit: PAUL WAPLES, THOS WAPLES. Ackn 3 Nov 1784.

74 Deed, 3 Nov 1784, WILLIAM JOSEPH yeoman of Monongahela Co VA sells to NATHAN JOSEPH of Suss: lands owned by JEREMIAH JOSEPH late of Suss decd in Indian River Hund. JEREMIAH JOSEPH died intestate leaving 8 children & 2 gr-children who were issue of 2 of his decd daus; so NATHAN JOSEPH obtained order of Orphans Court for survey & division of lands (WM PERRY ESQ, CLARK NOTTINGHAM, ABEL NOTTINGHAM, JOHN DUTTON & EDMOND DICKERSON apptd to divide who did so 4 Sep 1783): 65 ac laid off to WM JOSEPH which he now sells for £20. Wit: PETER F? WRIGHT, WM HARRISON. Ackn 3 Nov 1784.

75 Deed, 16 Sep 1784, JENNET BAILY widow of Lewes Rehoboth Hund sells for £4 10 pd annually for her life to her son JOHN ORR ship joyner of same place: tr 3½ ac near Lewes left to her by her father JOHN SIMONTON decd by will of 29 May 1751, to be divided between her & her sisters SARAH & MARY. Wit: JNO RUSSELL, ELIZABETH RUSSELL. Ackn 3 Nov 1784.

76 Deed, 5 Feb 1780, JOHN CLOWES mariner of Suss sells to STEPHEN REDDEN carpenter of Suss: tr in Broadkiln forrest granted to THOS WHARTON by PA 2 Jul 1757, which sold it on 15 Oct 1765 to afsd JOHN CLOWES; pt/o afsd tr now conveyed: adj FOSTER DULAVAN & ARON KEMMEY's lands, adj JACOB CARPENTER's land, adj ANDREW COLLINGS' land, adj FRANCIS CORNWALL's land, 101 ac; now sold for £320. Wit: ISAAC DRAPER, NICHOLAS ABBOTT. Ackn 3 Nov 1784.

77 Deed, 30 Mar 1779, BENJAMIN MIFFLIN of Kent Co Del sells to JAMES REED of Suss: tr in forrest of Suss adj lands of EDWARD STEVENSON, JAMES REED & FORSTER DONOVAN granted to THOS DUTTON by PA 14 Jun 1759, 84 ac, which DUTTON sold 6 Feb 1765 (Lib K No 10 fol 115). Now sold for £330. Wit: JOHN CLOWES, GEO ADAMS. Atty JOHN RODNEY. Ackn 3 Nov 1784.

78 Deed, 14 Feb 1784, DANIEL HOSEY/HOSEA champman & painter of Suss sells to ESTHER WOODS widow of Suss: ESTHER WOODS having on 7 Aug 1783 granted all her possessions including debts & lands to HOSEY, & having received no remuneration, HOSEY at her request now returns same. Attys CORD HAZZARD, JOHN RUSSELL, JOHN WILSON DEAN. Wit: JOHN INGRAM, WM PAREMORE. Ackn 3 Nov 1784.

79 Deed, 3 Nov 1784, WM STUART & SAMUEL LINGO of Indian River Hund sell to RICHARD BLOXOM of Suss, all husbandmen for £50: tr in forrest of Broadkiln Hund adj lands of WM BLOXOM decd & NICHOLAS ABBOTT & SOLOMON BACON?, whole tr 300 ac, 200 ac of which was sold to HUGH BACON?; originally patented to THOS BAILY 5 Mar 1740: STUARTS FOLLY, 100 ac. Protect aganst claims of heirs of DANIEL STUART decd, etc. Wit: WM POLK, LOT CLARK. Ackn 3 Nov 1784.

80 Deed, 28 Oct 1784, JOHN CANNON SR, JOHN CANNON JR, WITTINGTON CANNON, JAMES CANNON (s/o JOSEPH) & _____ his wife, HUDSON CANNON, CURTIS SMITH & SUSANNA his wife & GEORGE SMITH & SOPHIA his wife, all of Suss, sell to SOLOMON VINSON of Suss for £59+: 1/3 of 2 tr in Broad Creek Hund, CONSTANTINE NOPLE, 120 ac, & WOODEN MINE, 40 ac chiefly in a cypress swamp; originally granted to CONSTANTINE HUDSON decd. If heirs of CONSTANTINE HUDSON ever appear & claim land, then sellers will refund purchase price to VINSON. Wit: PETER RUST, JAMES SMITH. Proved 3 Nov 1784. (Signatures include LUERECY CANNON after JAMES CANNON.)

81 Deed, 2 Nov 1784, WM MADDOX of Little Creek Hund sells to AARON GORDY of same place for £80: tr CALLAWAYS NEGLECT, 62 ac, once purch/o EDWARD ELLES who purch it from FRANCIS ELLESS. Attys SAMUEL HALL & CAPT GEO SMITH of Suss. Wit: JOHN JAMES, SAMUEL HEARN. Proved 3 Nov 1784.

82 Deed, 3 Nov 1784, JAMES FISHER of Broadkiln Hund, yeoman, sells to JOHN ROWLAND of same place, tanner: land once owned by JOHN FISHER decd, f/o afsd JAMES, who in his will of 8 Feb 1770 devised it to JAMES: "land & marshes divided adj Broadkiln Creek at mouth of old ditch, Abraham's Pond & land of PARKER ROBINSON; to son THOS FISHER unless he die without issue, then to son JAMES FISHER". THOS FISHER & ALICE his wife sold land to JAMES FISHER on 24 Sep 1774, 150 ac; & PARKER ROBIN-SON quitclaimed to same 4 Feb 1778; land & marsh divided by JOHN FISHER betw his sons THOS & JAMES. JAMES FISHER now sells for £225. Wit: MARY TRAIN, DAVID TRAIN, WM BURCHER SR. Ackn 3 Nov 1784.

84 Conveyance bond, 22 Jan 1756, GRIFFITH JONES yeoman of Suss to MATTHEW REED yeoman of Suss for land assigned to JNO COVERDALE: 150 ac at head of Hills Branch. Wit: THOS OZBURN, JOHN SPENCER, MARY HAND. REED makes bond over to JOHN COVERDALL s/o SAML, 30 Jan 1770. Wit: PETER DAGMAN, MOSES WILLIAMS. Proved 3 Nov 1784.

84 Deed, 3 Nov 1784, PATRICK LINGO yeoman of Suss sells to ELIAS SHOCKLEY of Suss for £120: pt/o tr formerly sold by JEAN MULINIX? to PATRICK LINGO in Suss, 220 ac. Wit: WM SHOCKLEY, RICHARD HUDSON. Ackn 3 Nov 1784.

85 Deed, 3 Nov 1784, NEHEMIAH REED yeoman of Suss sells to JAMES REED of Suss for £25: tr in Broadkill Hund pt/o larger tr on which NEHEMIAH REED lives, adj county road & swamp, 10 ac. Wit: MANLA VERDIN, RHOADS SHANKLAND. Ackn same date.

86 Deed, 3 Nov 1784, RHOADS SHANKLAND surveyor of Suss sells to MANLOVE VIRDEN yeoman of Suss for £20: tr in forest of Broadkill Hund, pt/o grant to JOHN SHANK-LAND & JOHN MACKNIEL; MACKNIEL died before survey so SHANKLAND received whole tr; & he sold title to RHOADS SHANKLAND on 22 Mar 1762. Tr adj SAML TAM's survey, SOLOMON DODD's land & JOHN FOWLER's & THOS DODD's survey now owned by JOS TAM & BABLE DAVIS; 280 ac. Wit: NATHL WALLER, SAML HEARN. Ackn same date.

86 Deed, 28 Sep 1784, ZACHARIAH MADDOX of Little Creek Hund sells to RALPH LOW of same place for £50: tr PARRISH originally granted to THOS WALLER, then granted to _____? WALLER by MD, 30 ac. Attys JONATHAN HEARN SR & SAML HEARN s/o BENJN. Wit: WM LOW, NEHEMIAH NICHOLSON. Ackn 3 Nov 1784.

87 Power of Atty, 8 Oct 1784, WM JONES yeoman of Suss appts ELIAS SHOCKLEY of Suss to make over deed to RICHARD SHOCKLEY for land formerly belonging to my father JACOB JONES. Wit: WM TRUITT, WM SHOCKLEY. Proved 3 Nov 1784.

87 Deed, 7 Oct 1784, WILLIAM JONES yeoman of Suss sells to RICHARD SHOCKLEY of Suss for £77: tr in Cedar Creek Hund where JOSEPH BENNET dwells, 115 3/4 ac. Wit: WM TRUITT, WM SHOCKLEY. Proved 3 Nov 1784.

12.

88 Deed, 1782, THOMAS CROUCH yeoman of Suss sells to WM CHAMBERS yeoman of
Suss: tr in Cedar Creek Hund, adj JORAM GRIFFIN's land, 87½ ac. Wit: LEVIN SHAVER,
JOHN VENT. Ackn 3 Nov 1784.

89 Deed, 4 Nov 1784, JAMES FISHER of Suss sells to JOHN FISHER of Suss for 5
shillings: tr in Broadkill Hund pt/o tr owned by JAMES FISHER, adj land of
JACOB HAZZARD & land formerly of WM CRAIG now owned by HAP HAZZARD, 15 ac. Wit:
GEORGE WARD, ELIJAH WARRINGTON. Ackn same date.

89 Deed, 2 Nov 1784, ROBERT HART & ELIZABETH his wife yeoman of Suss sold to
JAMES POLLOCK merchant of Suss on 3 Aug 1784: tr in Suss RED OAK RIDGE, adj land
of NATHL HAYS & others, for £22, 11 ac pt/o tr RED OAK RIDGE. Attys WM OWENS,
JOHN POLK. Wit: NANCY HAYS, DAVID WILLIAMS, WM OWENS. Ackn 4 Nov 1784.

90 Deed, 4 Nov 1784, RICHARD BLOXOM & SARAH his wife farmer of Broadkiln Hund
sell to BENJAMIN YOUNG hatter of Cedar Creek Hund for £65 & 1 raccoon hat: tr in
Broadkiln Hund forest adj land of WM BLOXOM decd now owned by NICOLAS ABBITT, &
land of SOLOMON BACON;   whole tr 300 ac, 200 of which sold to HUGH BACON;
originally granted to THOS BAILY 5 Mar 1740, STUARTS FOLLY, 100 ac now sold.
Protect against claims of DANIEL STUART, THOS BAILY & HUGH BACON or their heirs.
Wit: JOHN LEUVENIGH, JOHN COLLINS. Testimony of SARAH BLOXOM to JOHN CLOWES.
Ackn same date.

91 Deed, 4 Nov 1784, JOSHUA COSTEN yeoman of Broadkiln Hund sells to MITCHELL
SCOTT yeoman of same place for £100: tr in Broadkiln forest pt/o tr COSTONS CONTENT
granted to afsd JOSHUA COSTON by his father BENTON COSTON yeoman late of Suss
decd, adj land of THOS PRETTYMAN, ELIHU JEFFERSON & adj WITCHES SAVANNAH, 100 ac.
Wit: MARY TRAIN, DAVID TRAIN. Ackn same date.

92 Deed, 4 Nov 1784, MITCHELL SCOTT yeoman of Broadkiln Hund sells to JOSHUA
COSTON yeoman of same place for £130: tr in on or near Green Branch in Broadkiln
Forest, 128 ac, pt/o tr surveyed for JOHN MORRIS, which ROBERT WATSON McCALLEY
sold to MITCHELL SCOTT on 4 Feb 1776; plus all cleared land formerly owned by
MITCHELL SCOTT adj said 128 ac. Wit: MARY TRAIN, DAVID TRAIN. Ackn same date.

93 Deed, 15 June 1783, STEPHEN MITCHELL planter & BETTY his wife (late BETTY
LACEY) of Suss, adminrs of WM BAGGS LACEY who died intestate, sell to ROBERT
WATSON McCALLEY planter of Suss for £99 in obedience to court: tr HOGG QUARTER
in forest of Broadkill Hund, 200 ac, granted by PA to THOS INGLISH 9 Jun 1743;
pt/o which by various conveyances became property of WM ROBINSON of Suss, who
sold it for £40 to NEHEMIAH REED & gave bond which then was transferred to afsd
WM BAGGS LACEY who died leaving a widow (now BETTY MITCHELL adminx) & 1 lame
child DIRECTOR. Orphans Court permits them to sell land (the smaller pt/o
whole tr) for maintenance of crippled child & settlement of debts, excepting 1/3
wid dower. Land adj BURTON WAPLES, ABRAHAM HARRIS & heirs of WM BAGGS LACEY:
100 ac. Wit: JOHN ENNIS, ELI COLLINS. Testimony of BETTY MITCHELL to JOHN
CLOWES. Ackn 4 Nov 1784.

94 Deed, 1 Aug 1783, ROBERT WATSON McCALLEY & ANTHALINA his wife of Suss sell
to STEPHEN MITCHELL planter of Suss for £99: same above tr. Wit: JOHN ENNIS, ELI
COLLINS. Testimony of ANTHALINA McCALLEY to WM POLK. Ackn 4 Nov 1784.

94 Deed of common recovery, 3 parties, 1 Nov 1784, between JAMES FISHER & JOHN
FISHER of Suss & RICHARD BASSETT of Kent Co DEL: 5 sh pd to JAMES FISHER by JOHN
FISHER for barring of estates etc in re pt/o tr in Broadkiln Hund owned by JAMES
FISHER adj JACOB HAZZARD & land formerly of WM CRAIGE now owned by HAP HAZZARD,
15 ac. With the intent that JOHN FISHER may be tenant, against common recovery to
be filed next Nov in which it is agreed RICHARD BASSETT shall be demandant, JOHN

FISHER tenant and JAMES FISHER vouchee, etc. Wit: JOHN ST LEUVENIGH, GEORGE WARD. Ackn 5 Nov 1784.

96 Deed, 28 Sep 1784, LYDIA WINDSOR, wid & adminx of JAMES WINDSOR yeoman, both of Suss, sells to ROBERT HOUSTON s/o JOHN of Suss, Esq, for £175: tr ROUND POND ENLARGED in Broad Creek Hund, 860 ac, originally granted by MD to JOHN HOUSTON, f/o afsd ROBT, who sold 153½ ac of it to JAMES WINDSOR (deed recorded Snow Hill, Worc Co) who then died intestate, so that Reg PHILLIPS KOLLOCK apptd LYDIA WINDSOR adminx, & ROBT HOUSTON JR testified for adminx that personal estate was insufficient to pay debts, so on 4 Feb 1784 court approved sale of land enough to cover debts: 133 ac of above land bought by afsd ROBT HOUSTON in Feb. Wit: JACOB BURTON, ISAAC GRAY. Attys PHILLIPS KOLLOCK, CORD HAZZARD. Ackn 5 Nov 1784.

98 Deed, 5 Nov 1784, JAMES MARTIN ESQ adminr of THOS GRAY of Suss decd sells to MARNIX VIRDEN of Suss for £180: tr in Lewes Hund pt/o tr TOWER HILL late owned by THOS GRAY, adj JOHN PRETTYMAN & JOHN WILTBANK, includes a beaverdam, 100 ac+. Permission of court of 5 Nov 1783 to sell land for debts. Wit: JAMES VENT, JOSEPH MORISON. Ackn 5 Nov 1784.

99 Deed, 3 Nov 1784, ANDERSON PARKER gentleman of Suss & ANN his wife sell to WM COLEMAN silversmith of Lewes & BETTY his wife for natural love & affection for ANDERSON & BETTY (their dau) PARKER: tr pt/o 4 ac lott in Lewes on n side of southernmost street of town joining the Blockhouse Pond, adj South St, adj land late of EDWARD STRETCHER decd now owned by WM BRERETON, adj Market St, adj burying ground, laid off by Dep Surveyor RHOADS SHANKLAND 27 Jul last for 3½ ac land & pond: the same land sold by JOSEPH CORD & JANE his wife on 30 Jul last to ANDERSON PARKER. Wit: JOHN CLOWES, JOHN HILL. Ackn 5 Nov 1784.

100 Deed, 4 Jul 1782, JOHN ADAMS pilot of Lewes sells to WM COLEMAN silversmith of Lewes for £25: tr adj Lewes, adj JOHN ADAMS f/o afsd JOHN ADAMS, adj land once owned by NATHL HALL decd of Suss now owned by DAVID HALL Esq of Lewes, adj 2 ditches & a road, 90+ square perches. Wit: D TRAIN, MARY TRAIN. Proved 6 Nov 1784.

101 Deed, 4 Sep 1784, JOSHUA FISHER & PETER HARMONSON of Lewes Rehoboth Hund, yeomen, sell to WM COLEMAN silversmith of Lewes for £103+: MARY ELDRIDGE late of hund afsd decd owned tr in afsd hund, adj WESTLEYS OLD FIELD, adj SAML ROWLAND, adj heirs of JACOB ART decd, adj ISAAC HOLLAND, 83 ac; she left land in her will to her 2 gr-sons THOS HARMONSON & JOSHUA FISHER, & THOS HARMONSON died intestate so land fell to PETER & LYDIA HARMONSON his bro & sis by the f/o his nearest of kin. JOSHUA FISHER sells now his part for £103, & PETER HARMONSON sells his part for £51+. Wit: DAVID TRAIN, MARY TRAIN. Proved 6 Nov 1784.

103 Petition, ABIGAIL JONES adminrx of ISAAC JONES decd, to sell land to JOHN COVERDALE, 7 Dec 1784: ABIGAIL JONES wid/o ISAAC JONES decd who was only child/o GRIFFETH JONES of Suss who d intestate; GRIFFETH JONES gave bond to MATTHEW REED yeoman of Suss on 2 Jan 1756 for £50 in guarantee of 150 ac at head of Hills Branch ; & MATTHEW REED sold bond to JOHN COVERDALE s/o SAMUEL on 30 Jan 1770; & GRIFFETH JONES d intestate without satisfying terms of bond; so ABIGAIL prays court's permission to give deed to JOHN COVERDALE. Granted 7 Dec 1784.

103 Deed, 7 Dec 1784, ABIGAIL JONES wid & adminrx of ISAAC JONES decd, yeoman, gives deed to JOHN COVERDALE s/o SAMUEL yeoman; money for land having been paid, sells for £25. Wit: NATHL MITCHELL, ELIAS JONES. Ackn 7 Dec 1784.

104 Deed, 8 Dec 1784, NEHEMIAH DAVIS s/o MARK of Suss buys from JOHN HICKMAN of Suss for £52+: 21 ac 95 perches land & marsh in Slaughter Neck of Suss, adj BLACK WALNUT HAMMOCK, adj NEHEMIAH DAVIS SR, adj former div line of HICKMAN & DAVIS, adj ditch out of HOGG ISLAND GUTT. Wit: JOHN PAYNTER, HERCULAS KOLLOCK.

14.

105 Deed 7 Feb 1785: EDWARD WILLIAMS, Sussex planter & MARY his wife, sells to
DANIEL POLK Esq of Sussex for 300£: BITERS BITT in NW Fork Hund, 214 ac 1 part
& 4 ac 2nd part; EDWARD WILLIAMS & MARY his wife seized of Absolute State of
Inheritance to afsd parts of land. Attys JOHN RODNEY, PHILLIPS KOLLOCK, WM
HARRISON of Lewes, gentlemen. Test WM POLK, BARTHOLOMEW TAYLOR. Exam WM POLK.
Ackn 9 Feb 1785.

106 Deed 8 Feb 1785: WM BUTCHER s/o ROBERT, Sussex housecarpenter, sells to
JEHU WAIT of Sussex: tr in Indian River Hund where WM ABDELL lives & heretofore
held by conveyance bond given by afsd ROBT BUTCHER to LITTLETON ABDELL f/o
afsd WM ABDELL, & now is assigned by WM ABDELL to JEHU WAIT; lying w of road
from Dorbridge to St Georges Chappell, adj land taken up by HUGH McINTUSH, & on
which LITTLETON ABDELL decd (lived?), called RED OAK RIDGE, 106 ac; for 3£.
Wit: MARY MUKLEVAIN, WM JOHNSON. Ackn 9 Feb 1785.

107 Deed 10 Aug 1784: ELVINGTON CALDWELL, joiner of MD, sells to JOHN GODDARD
of Suss for 55£: tr THIRD CHOICE in Little Creek Hund on a creek of Nanticoke R
called Little Creek ca ¼ mi above the new Indian Town, on e side of Little Creek,
50 ac. Attys PHILLIPS KOLLOCK, GEO WARD of Lewes. Wit RISDON MOORE, CHAS MOORE.
Signed ELVERTON CALDWELL. Ackn 9 Feb 1785.

108 Deed 31 Jan 1785: PLANNER SHORES of Suss sells to SOLOMON VINSON, BENJN
VINSON, THOS WELLS & JACOB JONES of Suss, and JOHN FARLOW, WM FARLOW, HEZEKIAH
MADDUX, JACOB EVANS & THOS McCLISH of Worcester Co for 2£ & divers other causes
& considerations: that pt/o tr PLEASENT GROVE, or GROVE, near the west line, 1 ac;
with the intent a preaching house or chapple for Methodist Preachers or Clergy
of Church of England that are friendly shall be erected, & that Trustees shall
always permit persons appointed by yearly Conference of the People called
Methodest held in America to preach Gods holy Word therein, & no others to injoy
the said premises for afsd purpose; provided always the said persons preach no
other docttring then is contained in the Revd W JOHN WESTLEYS notes on the New
Testament & his 4 Vollumes of Sermons; & that the Trustees always number nine.
Wit: SHADRACH SHORT, ISAAC SHORT. Ackn 9 Feb 1785.

108 Deed 1 Feb 1785: NEHEMIAH TUNNELL, of Accomack Co VA, farmer, sells to
JOSEPH HOUSTON, farmer of Suss: JAMES WATTSON formerly owned 100 ac pt/o patent
300 ac tr called LANES ADVENTURE on s side of Indian River ca ½ mi n of place
formerly called Blackfoot but now Dagberry, out of which he conveyed 5 ac to
JAMES GRAHAMS on 31 Oct AD 1761, 3 poles from public road from Blackfoot Town to
head of Indian R; GRAHAMS sold to WM TUNNELL who bequeathed it to his son NEHEMIAH
TUNNELL afsd; NEHEMIAH TUNNELL gave bond to the widow MARGARET GRAHAMS 31 Dec AD
1781, & she assigned it to JOSEPH HOUSTON; HOUSTON now pays TUNNELL 7£+ for the
5 ac. Atty JONATHAN NOTTINGHAM of Suss, friend. Wit: JOS DIRICKSON, SAML DIR-
ICKSON. Ackn 9 Feb 1785.

109 Deed 7 Feb 1785: DAVID MOORE, farmer of Suss, sells to JOSEPH HOUSTON,
farmer of Suss for 30£: HINMAN WHORTON owned tr patent LANES ADVENTURE & sold
part of it to THOS HARGIS who bequeathed it to his son GEORGE HARGIS, & to his
2 other sons THOS & WM HARGIS if GEO die without issue, which he did. Afsd THOS
HARGIS thus acquired 98 ac of LANES ADVENTURE & on 4 Nov 1772 sold it to DAVID
MOORE a part, 15 ac. Atty friend JONATHAN NOTTINGHAM. Wit: CALEB EVANS, JOHN
DARBY. Ackn 9 Feb 1785.

110 Deed 9 Dec 1784: ELIZABETH OLIVER wid of LewesTown sells to PETER HARMONSON
yeoman of Lewes Rehoboth Hund, 27£: tr in Lewes pt/o larger tr, adj lott formerly
of ROBERT GILL, se side of southernmost street of town, adj old line of patent
of ALEXANDER MOLLESTON, adj JOHN HALLs smith shop & his dwelling, adj JOHN RUS-
SELLs lott, 7 ac+. Attys JOHN HARMONSON, JOHN CLOWES of Lewes Rehoboth Hund.

Wit: D HALL, ELIZABETH HALL. Ackn 9 Feb 1785.

111 Deed 8 Feb 1785. JOSEPH CANNON planter of Suss sells to SHADRACH SHORT
planter of Suss for 75£: tr in Broad Creek Hund called GOLDEN LOTT, ¼ mi from
the Cypress Swamp, 33 ac; originally granted by MD to afsd JOSEPH CANNON by patent
of 8 Apr 1758. Wit: DAVID TRAIN, MARY TRAIN. Ackn 9 Feb 1785.

112 Deed 7 Jan 1785. ISAAC WILLIAMS of Suss sells to NATHANIEL WALLER of Suss
for £50: 50 ac pt/o tr WILLIAMS CHOICE (100 ac), adj WESTONS FOLLY, near tr surveyed for BENJN EASOM, on e side of Gravelly Branch. Attys JOHN WILTBANK ESQ,
JOHN RODNEY. Wit: THOS LAWS, THOS DUNCAN, JOHN O'DAY. Ackn 9 Feb 1785.

113 Deed 7 Jan 1785. ZADOCK LINDAL, REBECCA LINDALE, AVORY CLINDANIEL & ANNA
CLINDANIEL of Suss sell to JOSEPH MORRIS s/o JACOB yeoman of Suss for £50: JACOB
MORRIS f/o afsd REBECCA & ANNA owned while alive tracts in Sussex & died intestate
leaving 6 children to whom land descended, so afsd daus with their husbands have
legal power to sell their rights in same; refers to REBECCA LINDALE w/o ZADOCK &
ANNA CLINDANIEL w/o AVORY. (3rd spelling LINDALL.) Wit SOLOMON VEACH, JOHN
CLOWES, NANCY MORRIS. Ackn 9 Feb 1785.

113 Deed 3 Oct 1781. AMBROS GREEN yeoman of Suss states that STEPHEN GREEN owned
tr in Lewes Rehoboth Hund & in his will directed 100 ac be sold for debts, & by
death his circumstances had bettered so much it wasn't necessary; therefore AMBROS
GREEN for £50 doth remise, release & quitclaim to EDWARD CRAIG yeoman of Suss all
his right in any land in which he may have a claim & by power of atty do same for
brother WM GREEN & any brothers or sisters. Wit: RUSSELL & COMFORT HALL. Ackn
10 Feb 1785.

114 Deed 10 Feb 1785. NICHOLAS LITTLE & HESTER his wife of Suss sell to JOHN
FIELD yeoman of Suss for £190: tr on s side Kollock's millpond, same land conveyed
3 Mar 1767 by JOSEPH ATKINS to JOHN LITTLE f/o afsd NICHOLAS, adj ROBERT BURTON's
line, 76 ac. Wit: HENRY NEILL, RHOADS SHANKLAND. Ackn 10 Feb 1785.

115 Deed 9 Feb 1785. MITCHELL SCOTT yeoman of Broadkiln Hund sells to JOSHUA
COSTON yeoman of same place for £125: tr in forest of Broadkiln Hund, pt/o tr
COSTONS CONTENT, adj land of JOSHUA COSTON, 100 ac, being same land JOSHUA COSTON
sold to MITCHELL SCOTT last Nov. Wit: CALEB BALDING, SOMERSET DICKINSON. Ackn
10 Feb 1785.

116 Deed 10 Feb 1785. NICHOLAS LITTLE & HESTER his wife quitclaim for £125 to
WALTER HUDSON of Suss: land on s side of Loves Branch pt/o 2 deeds: one conveyed
by JOSIAH MARTIN to JOHN LITTLE f/o afsd NICHOLAS 15 Oct 1765; other conveyed by
JOSEPH HAZZARD to afsd JOHN LITTLE 10 Jan 1769, adj JONATHAN STEVENSONs land, adj
land of heir of WM ALLEN decd, adj Bundocks Bridge, 62 ac. Wit: HENRY NEILL,
RHOADS SHANKLAND. Ackn 1o Feb 1785. Exam WM POLK.

116 Bond 10 Sep 1783. WM CALAWAY of Suss to BETTY & JONATHAN CALLAWAY of Suss,
£1500; for all WM CALLAWAYS personal estate at decease to go to his children afsd
BETTY & JOHNNATHAN CALLAWAY. To dau Betty 1 negro woman FILLIS & 1 negro man KUFF.
Wit: JOHN ONIONS, SUSANNAH ONIONS. Ackn 11 Feb 1785.

117 Deed 9 Feb 1785. JOSHUA COSTON yeoman of Suss sells to MITCHEL SCOTT yeoman
of Suss for £100: tr in Broadkiln Hund granted by warrant 19 Feb 1776, laid out by
surveyor 25 Jun 1777, 100 ac, adj HOGG QUARTER, adj COLLIERS land, called SECOND
CHOICE. Wit: CALEB BALDING, SOMERSET DICKENSON. Ackn 10 Feb 1785.

118 Deed 2 Dec 1782. ZADOCK STAFFORD yeoman of Suss & MARGARET his wife sell to

16.

LEVI STAFFORD yeoman of Suss for £33+: 30 ac of STAFFORDS LOTT adj that pt/o
tr conveyed to NATHAN STAFFORD. Attys JOHN WILTBANK, PHILLIPS KOLLOCK. Wit:
ISAAC BRADLEY, HENRY SAFFORD. Ackn 10 Feb 1785.

118 Deed 14 Jun 1784. JOSHUA WRIGHT & SARAH his wife of Somersett Co MD sell
to JESSE GRIFFETH for £25: pt/o tr GRAPEVINE THICKET in Suss, 25 ac. Atty JOHN
RODNEY. Wit: JOHN TURPIN, JEREMIAH CANNON. Examr WM POLK. Ack 10 Feb 1785.

119 Deed 10 feb 1785. SMITH FRAME of Suss sells to GEORGE FRAME yeoman of Suss
for £150: ROBT FRAME yeoman of Suss decd owned trs in Suss & died intestate
leaving wid ISABELLA & 5 children: NATHAN, MARY, SMITH, GEORGE & WM who inherited,
& eldest son NATHAN ordered division of land on 14 Mar 1766 by BENJ BURTON, THOS
ROBINSON, BURTON WAPLES, JOSIAH MARTIN & WM PRETTYMAN who proceeded 7 May 1766,
in Indian River Hund; NATHAN's share at n end of bridge by mill intersecting mill
pond, 183 ac. On 29 May 1771, SMITH FRAME petitions to sell some of NATHAN's
land for debts (NATHAN decd), & sells afsd land to GEO FRAME. Wit: WM COULTER,
WM HARRISON. Cert 10 Feb 1785.

121 Deed of Mortgage 10 Feb 1785. WM KOLLOCK mariner of Angola & Indian River
Hund mortgages to GEORGE FRAME innkeeper of same place for £66+: tr in place afsd
on n side Indian R called ROCK HOLE where WM KOLLOCK lives, 136 ac. Wit: DAVID
TRAIN, MARY TRAIN. Ackn 10 Feb 1785.

121 Deed 1 Jan 1785. DAVID THORNTON of Suss sells to ELIPHAZ MORRIS yeoman of
Suss for £900: DAVID THORNTON has 2 warrants, one from SARAH & ALEXANDER DRAPER,
execs of NEHEMIAH DRAPER decd, one from COMFORT THARP of Suss: tr TWILLINGTON
granted to ROBT TWILLEY & resurveyed to him 4 Jul 1686; & tr surveyed for WM PAGE
& patented to WM CLARK 2 Jun 1684; & DAVID THORNTON has since sold 2 parcels of
afsd land, one to JONATHAN WILLIAMS, other to ALEXANDER DRAPER decd & given bond
to JOHN METCALF for remaining land, which bond has passed to afsd ELIPHAZ MORRIS:
adj se side of Cedar Creek, adj land of MARY DRAPER (a minor), near the Church,
217+ ac. Wit: STEPHEN REDDEN, RHOADS SHANKLAND. Ackn 10 Feb 1785.

123 Deed 4 Feb 1785. ELIPHAZ MORRIS & NANCY his wife of Suss sell to JOSHUA
BARWICK of Caroline Co MD for £400: ELIPHAZ MORRIS & NANCY his wife own TWILLINGTON
granted to ROBT TWILLEY 4 Jul 1686 & another tr surveyed for WM PAGE & patented
to WM CLARK 2 Jun 1684 which they now sell. Wit: JOHN TAM, EBENEZER WARREN.
Examr JOHN CLOWES. Ackn 10 Feb 1785.

124 Bond 4 Jun 1767. WM FIGGS of Somerset Co gives bond to JOSEPH FORMAN JR of
same place for tr SUMMER RANGE in Worcester Co, adj cypress branch falling into
Broad Creek near small road, 100 ac. Wit: A SPENCE, JONA VAUGHAN. JOSEPH FORMAN
assigns bond on 8 Nov 1770 to WM RICKARDS. Test SARAH COULBOURN. WM RICORDS of
Worcester Co assigns to LOUDA (Louder) SIRMAN on 31 Aug 1771. Test JNO WILLIAMS
JR, WM POLK.

124 Deed 30 Jan 1785. JOSEPH HALL planter of Suss sells to WM BLIZZARD SR of Suss
for £34: tr in Indian River Hund pt/o larger tr where afsd HALL now lives, adj
JOHN FILEMON's land. Wit: PETER ROBINSON, WM COULTER. Ackn 10 Feb 1785.

125 Deed 24 Jul 1784. JOHN SMITH yeoman of Worcester Co sells to JOHN JONES of
Suss Co for £100: tr COW QUARTER in Worcester Co now Suss Co, back in woods from
St Martins River, adj Pigpen Swamp on e side of Pocomoke R near tr formerly surveyed
for ARASMUS HARRISON, 100 ac. Atty JOHN RODNEY. Wit: WM MASSEY, MARY MASSEY.
Memo as to possession. Wit: JAMES MURRAY, WM MASSEY. Ackn 10 Feb 1785.

126 Deed 10 Feb 1785. JAMES THOMPSON farmer of Suss sells to SAMUEL PAYNTER of

Suss, housecarpenter, for £42: parcel of marsh pt/o larger island SHANKLANDS ISLAND in Lewes Creek formerly taken up by WM SHANKLAND, at fork of creek, 14 ac. Wit: JOS HALL, LEVIN DERICKSON. Ackn 10 Feb 1785.

127 Deed 22 Nov 1774. MARY OZBURN of Suss sells to LURANEY, ANN & MARY BANUM of Suss 180 ac for diverse good causes etc. Wit: THOS PARREMORE SR, GEORGE BENAM. To LURANEY BANUM various personal property. Deed of gift ack 10 Feb 1785.

127 Deed 3 Nov 1783. WM WAPLES sells to THOS WAPLES yeoman, both of Suss, for £83: tr in Indian River Hund pt/o larger tr BATCHELORS LOT, originally granted by patent to GRIFFITH JONES on 4th day of 6th mo 1684, & eventually descended to WM WAPLES SR who bequeathed it to his eldest son PETER WAPLES who died intestate, & it was accepted at the valuation by his eldest son WM WAPLES afsd; by the river, 67½ ac. Attys: DR JOSEPH HALL, JOSEPH WAPLES. Wit: WM PRETTYMAN (River), BENJN PRETTYMAN. Ackn 11 Feb 1785.

128 Deed 9 Mar 1785. JOSHUA COSTON yeoman of Suss sells to ROBT PRETTYMAN yeoman of Suss for £81: parcel in forrest of Broadkiln Hund pt/o COSTONS CONTENT & another tr LIBERTY laid out to JOSHUA COSTON afsd, 81 ac. Wit: THOS WATKINS, RHOADS SHANKLAND. Ackn 9 Mar 1785.

129 Deed 22 Feb 1785. MOSES ALLEN pilot of Lewestown & ELIZABETH his wife sell to JOHN BURTON of Indian River & Angola Hund yeoman for £60: tr pt/o larger tr ARCAIDED? in Indian River Hund, adj land of JOHN COULTER, adj ALLEN's land, adj road to Indian R, adj COULTERS RESURVEY, 13 ac+. Atty DAVID HALL of Lewes. Wit: JNO WILTBANK, JNO RUSSELL. Examr JNO WILTBANK. Ackn 9 Mar 1785.

130 Deed 8 Mar 1785. ROBERT MILLER carpenter of Cedar Creek & Slaughter Neck Hund & SARAH his wife sell to BAKER JOHNSON husbandman of same place for £176+: messuage, plantation & tr in Slaughter Neck, adj land lately sold by ISAAC KILLO to BRANSON LOFLAND, being a corner of afsd LOFLAND's & THOS CARLILE's land, adj land sold by JOHN BOWMAN, 100 ac+ , granted by patent to ROBT TWILLEY & resurveyed for him 4th day 7th mo 1686 by JOHN BARSTEAD Dep Surveyor to WM CLARK Chief Surveyor of Suss; & ALEXANDER DRAPER, merchant, later became part owner of afsd patent & sold to HENRY DRAPER & ROBT MILLER pt/o afsd patent & they divided it between them; & HENRY DRAPER deeded to ROBT MILLER 308 ac on 17 Feb 1729, surveyed by ROBT SHANKLAND Dep Surveyor, & MILLER devised same to his 2 sons JOHN & ROBT MILLER, 100 ac to JOHN & residue to ROBT, all in TWILLEYS PATENT; & ROBT MILLER sold his 208 ac to WM BOWNASS on 4 Nov 1752, & BOWNASS bequeathed to his son WM BONESS on 14 Jan 1762 afsd 205¼ ac; & on 18 Jul 1774 he sold it to ISAAC KILLO who sold 88 ac on 1 Oct 1774 to JOHN MILLER. JOHN MILLER died intestate leaving 6 children, & his eldest son ROBERT MILLER arrived at age 21 requested division but it was deemed undividable; resurveyed by WM POLK 8 Feb 1785. Wit: JOSHUA HICKMAN, WM HICKMAN. Ackn 9 Mar 1785.

131 Deed 1 Sep 1784. CHARLES COLLINS yeoman & one of sons of EZEKIEL COLLINS & HESTER his wife sells to DENNES MORRIS yeoman of Suss for £50: land & marsh in Cedar Creek Hund adj JOHN LOFLAND SR, WM COLLINS & plantation formerly belonging to GABRIEL LOFLAND, place where CHARLES TOWNSEND formerly lived, 350 ac. The £50 being 1/3 purch price, other 2/3 having been paid to ELIAS TOWNSEND. BAKER JOHNSON exec of estate of EZEKIEL COLLINS & HESTER his wife; land represents 5/8 of EZEKIEL & HESTER's dividend. Attys ELIAS TOWNSEND, BAKER JOHNSON. Wit: LUKE KILLINGS-WORTH, EUNICE KILLINGSWORTH. Ackn 9 Mar 1785.

132 Deed 9 Mar 1785. ROBERT MILLER yeoman of Cedar Creek Hund sells to BETTY MILLER spinster of same place for £48: JOHN MILLER f/o afsd ROBT & BETTY decd owned land TWILLEYS in Slaughter Neck & died intestate leaving ROBT, BETTY & sev-

18.

eral other children to whom land descended; eldest son ROBERT requested division
which was not feasible so denied; so on 3 Apr 1783 ROBERT petitioned for valuation
for sale of land which was done & reported on 28 Jul 1783, 30 shillings per ac
for 154 ac; now ROBT sells to BETTY for £48: pt/o tr TWILLEYS, adj RACHEL TURNER,
adj BRANTSON LOFLAND, 32 ac. Wit: D HALL, WM HARRISON. Ackn 9 Mar 1785.

133 Deed 9 Mar 1785. JOHN LOFLAND yeoman of Suss became bound on 24 Apr 1782
for £80 to ELIJAH BLOXOM for tr in head of Primehook Neck on n side of Sowbridge
Branch adj land where ABSALOM MOSELY now lives, adj MARY TURNER, 23 ac. ELIJAH
BLOXOM died intestate before conveyance was made leaving wid LEAH & one child
MARY BLOXOM (LEAH pregnant with another) to whom land descended; LOFLAND now dis-
charges bond by selling for £40 pd him by ELIJAH BLOXOM + more from LEAH, to MARY
BLOXOM d/o ELIJAH & to unborn child of LEAH; adj JOHN LOFLAND. Wit: WM WEST, DAVID
TRAIN. Ackn 9 Mar 1785.

134 Deed 25 Jan 1785. THOMAS WALKER, JAMES WALKER, WM WALKER, OWEN DAY & BETSEY
his wife, JOSHUA INGRAM & ESTHER his wife, & LUKE COVERDALE & MARY his wife, heirs
of JAMES WALKER of Suss decd sell to WM LOUGHLAND/LOFTLAND yeoman of Suss for £100:
tr LAYTONS NECK in Cedar Creek Hund forrest, 400 ac, granted to JOHN WEBB by warrant
of 19 Jun 1747; & WEBB sold it on 19 Sep 1752 to afsd JAMES WALKER decd (230 ac,
s side of neck adj HEZEKIAH DANELLY & DAVID MILLS, & by JOHN ELIOTTs millpond on
nw side) now property of afsd children of JAMES WALKER decd, 117 ac, adj JOHN
RECORDS & afsd pond now called Roberts Millpond. Attys CORD HAZZARD, JOHN RODNEY.
Wit: JOHN CLOWES, THOS LAVERTY, CHATTON SMITH. Ackn 7 Mar 1785.

136 Deed 9 Mar 1785. Tr in Broadkilln Hund on branch of Broadkiln Creek called
Pembertons Branch adj JOHN PONDER, JOHN WILSON DEAN & others, 113 ac pt/o 224 ac
which PETER MARSH late of Suss sold on 9 Aug 1735 to CHARLES PERRY late of Suss,
who sold 111 ac to his dau MARGARET late?, & CHAS PERRY on 15 Aug 1759 mortgaged
remaining 113 ac to JACOB KOLLOCK & RYVES HOLT of the General Loan Office for £60
And JOHN RODNEY ESQ late Trustee of General Loan Office but since Feb term 1779
in the Court of Common Pleas, recovered judgement against JOSEPH BAILY late pilot
of Suss & adminr of ELEANOR PERRY & WINNIFRED BAILY late WINNIFRED PERRY, execx
of will of CHAS PERRY: £220 to repay debt of PERRY to RODNEY; then High Sheriff
LUKE WATTSON was ordered to seize afsd land to satisfy debt, & it was sold to
JOSEPH BAILEY for £5000. And LUKE WATTSON was removed from his office of high
sheriff before deed was rendered to BAILEY, so BAILY petitioned that he had satisfied the debt & paid for the land without receiving deed; now present High
Sheriff CORD HAZZARD grants good & sufficient deed. Wit: WM POLK, DAVID TRAIN.
Ackn 9 Mar 1785.

137a Receipt 10 Jan 1785. Certificate of Resurvey made 30 Apr 1761 by WM HASKINS
Dep Surveyor of Dorchester Co for WM ADAMS s/o RICHARD: tr TAYLORS DESIRE containing with the vacancy added 220 ac, with endorsement dated 31 Jul 1766 "Maryld. I
hereby assign etc unto JACOB NUNER of Dorch my 100 ac vacant land added in
within Certificate lying w & sw of NUNER's pt/o TAYLORS DESIRE. Signed WILLI ADAMS."
Wit: THOS WHITE, ANDERTON BROWN. Certificate recd of WM DAWSON. And Nov 16 1767,
Maryld: " I hereby assign etc to DANIEL GODWIN of Dorch my 100 ac vacant land
added in within certificate lying w & sw of NUNER's pt/o TAYLORS DESIRE. Signed
JACOB NUNER. Wit: NEH? PRICE, JOSEPH GODWIN. Then 27 Mar 1774 WM ADAMS transfers
to MARK MERRELL of Caroline Co 93½ ac, wit; DANL GODWIN, GEO HARDY FISHER. And
on 6 Feb 1782 transfers 93½ ac pt/o TAYLORS DESIRE afsd to THOS ALCOCK FOWLER of
Caroline Co, wit: AMBROS GOSLIN, WM GOSLIN. Test to above document with endorse-
ments: WM RICHARDSON. Cert ZABDIEL POTTER, Justice of Caroline Co, 21 Apr 1785.
Cert by WM RICHARDSON that ZABDIEL POTTER is a Justice of Caroline Co, 30 Apr 1785.

137a Deed 20 Jan 1785. DANIEL GODWIN late of Suss but now of Dorch Co sells to
WILLIAM DAWSON SR of Caroline Co MD, for £157: On 30 Apr 1761 WM HASKINS, Dep
Surveyor of Dorch Co granted by resurvey tr TAYLORS DESIRE in Dorch Co to WILLIAM
ADAMS, s/o RICHARD, his part being 27 ac, adding 193½ ac of vacancy & reduced
whole into one entire tr ADAMS VENTURE, 220½ ac. WM ADAMS assigned on 31 Jul
1766 to JACOB NUNER of Dorch Co, 100 ac vacant land added in the resurvey lying w
& sw of afsd NUNER's pt/o TAYLORS DESIRE; & NUNER on 16 Nov 1767 sold same to
DANIEL GODWIN, 127 ac. WM & DANIEL POLK, attys. Wit: JAS HARRIS, JOSEPH GODWIN.
Ackn 5 May 1785.

138 Deed 26 Apr 1785. ROBERT KING SR of Suss sells to ROBERT KING JR planter of
Suss for £5 & good causes: tr POOR CHANCE granted to JAMES KING on 7 Sep 1723, 50
ac now in Little Creek Hund, Suss, with about 80 ac added by resurvey of afsd ROBT
KING SR, reserving only the fruit that may grow on the Old Orchard during ROBT SR's
lifetime. Attys: JOHN CLOWES, WM POLK, WM DONE. Wit: JOHN COLLINS, MITCHELL
LINTCH. Ackn 5 May 1785.

139 Deed 5 May 1785. JAMES BRATTAN/BRATTON, yeoman of Suss, sells to JAMES TRUSHAM
yeoman of Suss for £300: 1 moiety of tr TRUSHAMS CHOICE, 12 ac; same tr sold by
afsd JAMES TRUSHAM to afsd JAMES BRATTAN on 10 Jul 1784. Wit: NS HAMMOND, PETER
WHITE. Ackn 5 May 1785.

139 Deed 31 Aug 1784. JAMES TRUSHAM sells to ELIJAH WOOTTON for £182: 77 ac+ adj
afsd WOOTTON's orchard, also pt/o resurvey made by afsd TRUSHAM 67 ac adj afsd
patent, whole being 144 ac in Little Creek Hund; the former being pt/o tr HOUNDS
DITCH, the latter a resurvey called TRUSHAMS ADDN. Signed JAS & TRANY TRUSHAM.
Wit: WM BEVINS, WM LORD. Test of TRAIN TRUSHAM w/o JAMES. Ackn 5 May 1785.

140 Deed 30 Apr 1785. JEREMIAH WARWICK planter of Suss sells to JAMES TULL of
Suss for £500: 200 ac on Nanticoke R in Suss, COSTONS PURCHASE. Wit: JOSEPH LECAT,
JOHN PULLET? Ackn 5 May 1785.

140 Deed 16 Apr 1785. LEVIN IRVING & ISAAC HANDY of Somerset Co, execs of will of
GEORGE HANDY of same place decd, sell to BENJN WAILES of Somerset Co for £228: tr
in Broad Creek Hund, Suss, pt/o tr GOOD LUCK 73½ ac; also parcel pt/o tr COCKLAND
purch by GEO HANDY from DAVID PRITCHARD, also in Broad Creek Hund; also 407 ac of
resurvey by afsd GEO HANDY upon tr GOOD LUCK. HANDY purch GOOD LUCK from JOSEPH
PAREMORE, 486 ac with resurvey; COCKLAND 100 ac. Wit: ISAAC HENRY, WILL MOORE.
Attys JOHN RODNEY, PHILLIPS KOLLOCK. Ackn 5 May 1785.

141 Deed _____ 1785. JOSEPH BAILY pilot of Lewes sells to widow & heirs of ELIAS
MASON for £98+: tr in Broadkiln Hund on branch of Broadkiln Cr called Pembertons
Branch, adj land of JOHN PONDER, JOHN WILSON DEAN & JOHN INGRAM, 100 ac, pt/o 224
ac tr sold by PETER MARSH 9 Aug 1735 to CHARLES PERRY; PERRY sold pt/o tr to his
dau MARGARET CALE, 111 ac,& mortgaged remaining 113 ac to Genl Loan Office on 15
Aug 1759, & died leaving will appointing ELENOR his wife & WINIFRED his dau execxs;
& WINIFRED married afsd JOSEPH BAILEY & ELENOR died. Mortgage unpaid & JOHN RODNEY
obtained judgement against execs (sheriff LUKE WATSON). On 23 Dec 1773 JOSEPH
BAILEY made verbal agreement with ELIAS MASON to sell him the land (113 ac) and
MASON made part payment; then MASON died intestate leaving wid SARAH & 7 children:
DAVID (eldest), RHODA, JONATHAN, GEORGE, KEZIAH, ISAAC, & MARY, so right of land
descended to wife & children, subject to mortgage debt. Now BAILEY sells to SARAH
for remainder of price. Wit: JOHN CLOWES, DEBORAH ROWLAND. Attys PHILLIPS KOLLOCK
& CORD HAZZARD. Ackn 5 May 1785.

144 Deed 5 May 1785. MARGARET KOLLOCK wid/o Lewes sells to ISAAC TURNER housecarpenter of Lewes for £44: lot in Lewes, 60' on Front St & 200' back adj WM WEST,

adj land late of FRANCES CAHOON now of SAML THOMPSON, pilot,which HENRY FISHER & ABRAHAM WILTBANK, pilots of Lewes, sold to NEHEMIAH FIELD of Lewes on 3 Jan 1769, & which was possessed by state by Act of Free Pardon & Oblivion of 1778 & therefore was sold at public sale to HENRY FISHER for £173; & FISHER on 31 May 1779 sold to MARY FIELD: & MARY FIELD on 29 Jun 1780 sold to MARGARET KOLLOCK afsd. Wit JACOB KOLLOCK, DANL RODNEY. Attys WM BRERETON, SIMON HALL. Ackn 5 May 1785.

145 Deed 4 May 1785. JOHN POTTER yeoman of Suss sells to THOMAS GROVE house-carpenter of Suss for £150: 145 ac in Broadkill Hund, formerly conveyed to DAVID STEWART by THOS, SAML & SUSANNAH GROVES; & STEWART sold it to afsd JOHN POTTER who sold 70 ac to heirs of JACOB ADDESON adj Primehook Creek, remaining 75 ac adj JOHN & JONATHAN ADDESON on s side Primehook Cr, adj THOS GROVES' land. Wit: WM HAZZARD, JOSEPH DARBY. Ackn 6 May 1785.

146 Petition for leave to convey land,5 May 1785, by MARGARET TRUITT wid & adminx of JOHN TRUITT, yeoman of Suss: LEVIN CRAPPER decd of Suss recovered judgment against BENJN TRUITT, yeoman of Suss, for £80+; writ of Feb 1774 to PETER ROBINSON sheriff to sell lands of TRUITT in Cedar Creek Hund, 100 ac, est of BENJN TRUITT, but there were no buyers; so another writ of 1784 issued & ROBINSON sold land to JOHN TRUITT s/o BENJN for £45; but JOHN TRUITT died intestate before deed issued leaving wid MARGARET & 4 children: only son GEORGE, ESTHER, SARAH & LEAH: 2/5 to GEO, remainder to 3 daus of JOHN, subject to widow's dower; MARGARET now petitions for deed to sell land from new sheriff CORD HAZZARD. Ackn 5 May 1785.

147 Deed 5 May 1785. CORD HAZZARD issues deed to GEORGE, ESTHER, SARAH & LEAH TRUITT: tr SPITTLEFIELD in Cedar Creek Hund 'said to lie in the manner of Worming-hurst', adj BENJN TRUITT's land, adj ELIZABETH TRUITT, adj COVERDALE COLE's new ground, adj Waltons Mill Rd, adj fording place by old schoolhouse, adj ROBT HOUSTON, 160½ ac, surveyed 17 Apr 1776 by CALEB CIRWITHIN. Above history repeated. Wit: EDWD TILGHMAN JR, WM DONE. Test PETER ROBINSON. Ackn 5 May 1785.

149 Deed 8 Mar 1785. PHEBE VINING of Wilmington, wid, & BENJN WYNKOOP gentleman of Phila, surviving execs of ABRAHAM WYNKOOP decd of Suss, sell to JOSEPH SIMS gentleman of Phila for £615: ABRAHAM WYNKOOP directed in his will of 15 Nov 1763 that his land be sold to pay his legacies (THOS & MARY WYNKOOP also execs, now decd); & MARY & BENJN WYNKOOP & PHEBE VINING sold 1 moiety or ½ part on 10 Feb 1775 to JOSHUA FISHER of Phila; remaining ½ put up for sale by advertisemnet at old coffeehouse in Phila on 8 Jan last & JOSEPH SIMS was high bidder: tr in Cedar Creek Hund FARMERS DELIGHT, adj se side Herring Branch of Misspillion Creek, adj JOHN CRAPPER's land, adj county road, adj DANIEL DINGUS & JOHN DRAPER, adj THOS CAREY JR, adj late ABRAHAM WYNKOOP, 657 ac. Attys RICHARD BASSETT, GEO WARD. Wit: SAMUEL R FISHER, DYRE KEARNY; for PHEBE VINING: GUNN J BEDFORD JR, JOHN VINING. Ack 5 May 1785.

151 Deed 18 Apr 1785. JOSEPH SIMS merchant of Phila sells to BENJN WYNKOOP mer-chant of Phila for £617, land described above, as described in resurvey. Attys RICHARD BASSETT, GEO WARD. Wit: DANL RODNEY, SAMUEL R FISHER. Ackn 5 May 1785.

152 Deed 3 May 1785. JOSHUA WILLIAMS farmer of Suss & ESTHER his wife sell to WM TURNER blacksmith of Suss for 5 shillings: ISAAC WILLIAMS decd willed land MARTINS HUNDRED & DAVIDS HOPE to his 2 sons JOSHUA & SPENCER WILLIAMS equally divided. JOSHUA & ESTHER now sell their part where they lived in May 1784; adj SPENCER WILLIAMS. Atty GEO WARD. Wit: CHAS GRIFFITH, PRETTYMAN BOYCE, JNO WILT-BANK. Ackn 12 May 1785.

152 Deed 6 May 1785. ISAAC HOLLAND of Lewes & Rehoboth Hund & ELIZABETH his wife sell to WILLIAM HOLLAND yeoman of same place for £200: tr in Lewes Rehoboth Hund

adj ISAAC HOLLAND, adj large swamp, surveyed 20 May 1780, pt/o larger tr which
WM SHANKLAND high sheriff conveyed on 11 Mar 1750 to JAMES WALKER decd of Suss,
whose son JOHN WALKER obtained it by deed of 5 May 1778, & sold it to afsd
HOLLAND. Wit: JOHN CLOWES, WM HOLLAND. Ackn 6 May 1785.

154 Deed 21 May 1784. EDWARD CRAIGE yeoman of Suss & SARAH his wife sell to
LEVI ROACH housecarpenter & joyner of Suss & MARTHA his wife for natural love &
affection of EDWARD CRAIGE & SARAH (their neice): 1 ac pt/o parcel in Town of
Lewes on s side of southernmost street, adj JOHN HART, adj JOHN McCRACKIN. Wit:
JNO WILTBANK, JNO RUSSELL. Ackn 7 May 1785.

155 Deed 9 May 1785. JOHN CRAPPER yeoman of Suss & MARY his wife sell to DAVID
WALTON of Suss for £14: 200 ac pt/o 800 ac tr FARMERS DELIGHT patented 5 Jan
1687 by HENRY SKIDMORE, by sundry conveyances coming to ABRAHAM WYNKOOP decd who
sold afsd 200 ac to afsd JOHN CRAPPER on 4 Aug 1752. Attys JOHN RODNEY, JOHN
WILTBANK. Wit: BENJN OLIVER, MATTHEW STEEL, GEORGE WALTON. Ackn 7 Jun 1785.

155 Deed 18 Apr 1785. JACOB ADDISON/ADERSON yeoman of Suss sells to CORD HAZ-
ZARD High Sheriff of Suss for £64: HERMANUS WILTBANK, by warrant of Deal Court
of 10 Mar 1681/2, had surveyed to him on 12 Feb following by CORNELIUS VERHOOF
then surveyor tr NEWTOWN on w side Delaware Bay, on s side Primehook Creek, 580
ac; same divided by Orphans Court among afsd HERMANUS WILTBANK's then surviving
heirs JOHN, ABRAHAM (pilot) & ISAAC WILTBANK (hatter) on 22 Mar 1755 (WM SHANK-
LAND surveyor); & afsd ABRAHAM the Elder on 16 Aug 1755, with ABRAHAM JR & afsd
JOHN, obligated himself for £210 to convey 320 ac of afsd land to JACOB ADER-
SON; therefore NEOMY WILTBANK execx contracted with descendants of JACOB ADERSON;
his 3 sons JOHN, JACOB & JONATHAN ADERSON on 19 Feb 1783 agreed to division of
land among them. JACOB ADERSON now sells 32 ac of above land to CORD HAZZARD,
adj Groves Road, GROVES' land, adj WM HAZZARD's land, adj JOHN ADERSON. Wit:
JOHN HAZZARD, ELIJAH RICKARDS. Ackn 8 Jun 1785.

156 Deed 7 May 1785. LEVI COLLINS/COLLINGS of Suss sells to MATTHIAS AYDELOTT
of Suss for £50: 33 1/3 ac pt/o tr TIMBERLAND ENLARGED, surveyed 6 May 1760 for
JOHN DAGWORTHY; & on 29 Jun 1782, he deeded it to afsd LEVI COLLINS, adj ROBERT
McCREA, nearly joining said LEVI COLLINS where he dwells. Atty DAVID TRAIN,
URIAH HAZZARD. Wit: ISRAEL HOLLAND, JOHN AYDELOTT. Ackn 9 Jun 1785.

157 Deed 1 Jun 1785. JAMES MARTIN admin of THOMAS GRAY late of Suss sells to
MARNIX VIRDIN for £13: land in Lewes Hund granted to WM PRETTYMAN 13 Dec 1757;
& assigned by him to THOMAS GRAY, cooper of Suss, 15 Jan 1766; adj land "Tower
Hill", adj the beaver dam, 7½ ac. GRAY died intestate; land now sold for debts.
Wit: ROBT STEVENSON, JAMES VENT. Ackn 9 Jun 1785.

158 Deed 1 Jun 1785. MARNIX VIRDEN SR sells to JAMES MARTIN adminr of THOS GRAY
late of Suss for £193: land in Lewes Hund, pt/o tr "Tower Hill" late owned by
afsd THOS GRAY, adj JOHN PRETTYMAN & JOHN WILTBANK, crossing beaver dam, 100 ac+,
and also 20 ac adj DANIEL BROWN on e side of Beaverdam Branch in Rehoboth Hund,
granted to WM PRETTYMAN 13 Dec 1757 & assigned by him to THOS GRAY on 15 Jan 1766.
Wit: ROBT STEVENSON, JAMES VENT. Ackn 9 Jun 1785.

159 Deed 9 Jun 1785. JOSHUA HALL blacksmith of Lewes & COMFORT his wife sell
to JOHN WESTLY of Suss & MARY his wife for 5 shillings: DANIEL HOSMAN decd owned 2 lotts in Lewes, 11 ac+, & died intestate leaving a wid, since decd, & 2
sons & daus: STOCKLEY, JOSEPH, JANE & COMFORT HOSMAN to whom land descended, &
COMFORT mar afsd JOSHUA HALL. Land on Mulberry St, adj Market St & Fenwicks St,
near Blockhouse Pond, adj Ship Carpenter St; 2nd lott adj 1st on Market St, adj
PHILLIP RUSSELL SR decd; blacksmith's shop to remain. Wit: JOHN CLOWES, WILLIAM
HARRISON. Ackn 10 Jun 1785.

160 Deed 28 Jul 1785. AVERY MORGAN yeoman of Baltimore Hund sells to JOHN MASSEY JR yeoman of same place for £113+: tr in Baltimore Hund, pt/o tr "Stockeleys Adventure" devised by AVERY MORGAN the elder to afsd AVERY MORGAN his son, adj AVERY MORGAN's field by road, adj land of WM RILEY EVANS & JACOB BANKS formerly owned by HENRY SMITH & HENRY KILLUM, adj pt/o "Stockeleys Adventure" sold by AVERY MORGAN to GINNETHAN HARNEY late of Suss decd. Wit: DAV TRAIN, MARY TRAIN. Ackn 9 Jul 1785.

161 Cert of Resurvey 30 ___ 1761. WM HASKINS certifies he has resurveyed for WM ADDAMS his pt/o a tr & finds it to contain 7 ac, 25 ac the remainder of "Taylors Desire", & 93½ ac vacant land, & has reduced it all into one tr renamed "Addams Venture", being in Dorchester Co MD; by warrant granted ADDAMS 3 Nov 1760; containing pt/o tr "Taylors Desire" granted to WM TAYLOR 10 Dec 1740; resurveyed tr being on road from Hunting Creek to Marschehope Bridge, close on w side of Harpers Branch between ADDAMS' & JACOB NUNER's land, 220½ ac 'to be holden in the manor of Nanti-coke'.
31 Jul 1766, Maryland: WM ADDAMS assigns 100 ac of his vacant land in Dorchester Co to JACOB NUNER of Dorch Co, w & sw of NUNER's pt/o original tr "Taylors Desire" for value received. Wit: THOS WHITE, ANDERTON BROWN.
16 Nov 1767, Maryland: JACOB NUNER assigns to DANIEL GODWIN of Dorch Co his 100 ac afsd. Wit: NEH PRICE, JOSEPH GODWIN.
21 Jul 1785: JOSEPH GODWIN, wit afsd, testifies to EDWD WHITE, JP of Kent Co Del as to validity of above assignment. THOS WHITE testifies as to validity of 1766 assignment above.

161 Bond for conveyance of land. JONATHAN BELL of Suss binds himself to JAMES EDGER millwright of Suss for £200, 13 Apr 1775, for 100 ac, pt/o tr "Branch Side" granted by Maryland to JACOB ADDISON, 160 ac in 'the now purposed new County on Delaware', afsd land devised? by ADDISON to above bound JONATHAN BELL by record of Worcester Co. Wit: ROBT HOUSTON SR, JOHN COLLINS. Proved 4 Aug 1785.

162 Bond for conveyance of land. JOHN COLLINS planter of Suss binds himself to LUKE HUFFINGTON planter of Suss for £1200, 17 Feb 17778 (sic), to make over to Huffington an estate of inheritance for 200 ac, pt/o tr COXES PERFORMANCE, 1000 ac, being that part where afsd JOHN COLLINS plantation & dwelling house lies, in Broad Creek Hund, adj JOSHUA HALL, adj road from said COLLINS' mill to his house; pt/o tr conveyed by JOSEPH COLLINS late of Worcester Co,decd, to said JOHN COLLINS; but only after HUFFINGTON complys with a past bond to said COLLINS for payment of £544+. Wit: JOSHUA CATHELL, WM HARDY JR, WM CALDWELL JR. Proved 4 Aug 1785.

162 Deed 2 Nov 1784. DANIEL GODWIN planter of Suss sells to WM DAWSON of JONAS of Caroline Co for £157+: tr "Godwins Venture", 298½ ac, bounded by the beginning tree of the original "Lloyds Care" etc; mentions DANIEL GODWIN & SARAH his wife. Attys DANIEL POLK, JOSHUA POLK. Wit: JOHN DAWSON, HENRY SWIGGETT, SETH HILL EVITTS? Ackn 4 Aug 1785.

163 Quitclaim deed 18 Feb 1784. LOVEY WOOTTEN spinstress of Suss Co makes over title to her late father's estate to JAMES TRUSHAM planter of Suss for £40, being over 21 and eldest child of late father BENJN WOOTTON, therefore dispose of my equal part in manner aforesaid. Wit: WM BEVINS, ALEYFAIR BEVINS. Certified that LOVEY WOOTTON (now) eldest ch/o BENJN WOOTTON of Little Creek Hund, decd, etc 27 Feb 1784, by PHILLIPS KOLLOCK, clk, ROBT HOUSTON, JON BOYCE.

164 Deed ___ 1785. JOHN RODNEY ESQ recovered judgment in Aug 1771 against JOSEPH SHANKLAND merchant late of Suss Co for £100+; writ of 25 Apr 1772 commanded the sheriff deliver same the next Tues to court. JOHN RODNEY also recovered judg-ment against SAMUEL SHANKLAND merchant of Suss at same time for £100+; similar writ

issued. High Sheriff PETER ROBINSON seized among other things all estate, right
& title of afsd JOSEPH SHANKLAND to 5/6 Unity Forge & lands, 811 ac, & to 5/6
Unity Forge belonging to SAMUEL SHANKLAND with lands, 811 ac, in Cedar Creek
Hund. Inquisition decided lands had no clear annual value to settle debt in 7
years, & lands remained in sheriff's hands for lack of buyer; writ of 10 Nov
1772 commanded him to hold public sale; JOSEPH SHANKLAND's 5/6 Unity Forge & land
sold to CHAS POLK JR, RHOADS SHANKLAND & SAMUEL LAVERTY for £165 which settled
debt. ROBINSON removed as sheriff before deed issued, so on 4 Aug 1785 new owners
petition for deed from new sheriff, equally divided, 1/3 to each. Present High
Sheriff CORD HAZZARD makes deed. Wit: JAMES COOPER, RICHARD LITTLE, JACOB WHITE.
Test PETER ROBINSON. Ackn 4 Aug 1785.

166 Deed 2 Aug 1785. JOSHUA INGRAM of Suss sells to PHILLIP MARVEL of Suss for
£100: tr "Ingrams Chance", 50 ac, taken up by ROBT INGRAM under MD 5 Apr 1684,
who devised it to his son JOSHUA INGRAM by his will: on n side of Lone Pine Savannah, sw of county rd from Indian River to Gravell Branch, now in Del by new state
division line. Wit: JNO RUSSEL, WM FITCHET. Ackn 5 Aug 1785.

166 Deed 6 Aug 1785. PENELOPE HOLT JONES, gr-dau & sole heir of RYVES HOLT,
both of Lewes, she wid, sells in trust to JOHN HAZZARD shipcarpenter of Suss &
MARY his wife, gr-dau & one of heirs to MARY TOWNSEND decd of Lewes for 5 shillings:
lott in Lewes on Mulberry St, 60' front x 200' back, adj land once of ROBT PERRY,
adj WM GODWIN, granted 3 Sep 1695 to NEHEMIAH FIELD who sold it 1 Aug 1704 to
JAMES SANGSTER, who sold it 4 Feb 1723 to JOHN TOWNSEND who died intestate, & his
adminx MARY TOWNSEND his wid after administering estate (request of Orphans Ct)
sold it to JOHN BOYD 3 Aug 1736, & he on same date reconveyed it to her; & MARY
TOWNSEND on 4 May 1741 sold it to RYVES HOLT ESQ who gave bond of £40 for conveyance to MARY, SARAH, THOMAS & CATHARINE, children of afsd MARY TOWNSEND, all now
decd?,bond lost. Said MARY HAZZARD dau of MARY TOWNSEND along with SARAH, THOS &
CATHARINE. Wit: JNO RUSSELL, WM ARNAL. Ackn 6 Aug 1785.

167 Deed 3 Aug 1785. ROBERT CRAIG yeoman of Angola & Indian R Hund sells to
GEORGE WALTON s/o GEO yeoman of same & MARY his wife for £5: tr in Rehoboth Neck
once owned by HARMON HARMONSON of Suss, & after his death it descended to his dau
MARY, late MARY CRAIG w/o HAMILTON CRAIG late of Suss decd; & MARY died leaving
ch/o HAMILTON CRAIG: EDWARD, JOHN, RUTH who mar THOS WALKER, ELIZABETH aka BETTY
w/o WM PRETTYMAN, afsd MARY WALTON, ROBERT CRAIG afsd, & ESTHER CRAIG to whom
land descended, 30 ac. Wit: RHOADS SHANKLAND, DAVD TRAIN. Ackn 4 Aug 1785.

168 Deed 3 Aug 1785. WM COLWELL/CALDWELL of Suss sells to SOLOMON VINSON of
Suss for £50 pd by GEO THOMPSON to THOS COLWELL: tr "Poplar Neck" formerly in
Worcester Co, now in Suss, taken up by afsd THOS COLWELL under MD, 100 ac. Attys
ISAAC HENRY, SAMUEL HEARN. Wit: WM OWENS, JOHN WINGATE, WM PARKS. Ackn 4 Aug 1785.

169 Deed 4 Aug 1785. URIAH HAZZARD & SARAH his wife of Suss sell to JOHN MASSEY
SR of Suss for £80: parcel, 89 ac, pt/o tr "North Pathernton" on seaboard side
in Muddy Neck, adj salt pond, 500 ac, granted by MD on 8 Jan 1688 to MATTHEW
SCARBOROUGH, & on 8 Oct 1702 he sold it to RODGER THOMAS, & by many conveyances
it came to URIAH HAZZARD, & on 8 Jun 1770 he sold it to JOHN MASSEY; adj JOHN
EVANS cornfield (to whom HAZZARD sold 11 ac of tr on 4 Feb 1779),dividing line
of JOHN MASSEY f/o afsd JOHN MASSEY & JOHN EVANS SR who at that time owned afsd
land together, adj "Atkins Lott" in 1747, adj FOX SWAMP, adj JOHN EVANS Resurvey.
Wit: LEVIN DERICKSON, LITTLETON TOWNSEND. Ackn 4 Aug 1785.

170 Deed 29 Jul 1785. CORD HAZZARD ESQ High Sheriff of Suss issues to ELISHA
DICKERSON blacksmith of Suss: in Feb 1783 ELISHA DICKERSON recovered judgment
against WM GODWIN yeoman of Suss for £40+; writ issued directing RHOADS SHANKLAND

High Sheriff to collect amount of debt in lands & goods, so Sheriff seized tr
in Broadkiln Hund, 100 ac, but rents insufficient to satisfy debt, so court
ordered land sold. ELISHA DICKERSON highest bidder at £60, & sale satisfied afsd
debt plus another of WM GODWIN to ELISHA DICKERSON for £13+, but RHOADS SHANK-
LAND's term as sheriff ended before deed issued to DICKERSON, & DICKERSON now
petitions for deed from current sheriff, CORD HAZZARD, which is granted. Tr
granted 9 Jun 1743 to PRETTYMAN DAY, who sold it 5 May 1752 to JOHN GRAY, who
sold it 17 Feb 1753 to NATHAN BRITTINHAM, who sold it 30 Apr 1759 to afsd WM GOD-
WIN, in forrest of Broadkiln Hund about 15 mi sw of Lewes, adj ABRAHAM HARRIS &
ROBERT TALBERT, 200 ac. Wit JNO WILTBANK, D HALL. Ackn 29 Jul 1785.

172 Petition 29 Jul 1785. ELISHA DICKERSON's petition to court for deed, as
mentioned above; repeats same information.

173 Deed 30 Jul 1785. BENJAMIN STEEL yeoman of Suss sells to WM WILSON of Suss
for £60: parcel in forrest of Suss, pt/o tr sold by EZEKIEL GREEN to DANL STEEL
who devised & deeded it to his son BENJN STEEL afsd, 98 ac. Wit JOHN ENNES,
PHILLIPS KOLLOCK. Ackn 29 Jul 1785.

173 Bill of Sale 30 Jul 1785. SIMON KOLLOCK of Suss sells to JOHN AYDELOTT for
£20 & in consideration of AYDELOTT keeping 2 Negro children, CHARLES & (girl)
AMORET, free of charge until they both reach 6 years of age, the boy now being 4
and the girl 2: one Negro woman named DAFF, mother of above children, age 40.
Wit JOHN HAZZARD, MAGDALENE PERRY. Ackn 30 Jul 1785.

174 Certificate of Discharge 26 Jan 1788, Phila. JOSEPH SAPP certified unfit for
further duty as soldier of Del, in field or garrison, from wound received in
service. Signed WALTER STEWART, Colo Insp Northn Army. Discharge signed by W
JACKSON, Asst Secy at War, attest JOS CASLETES, Secy. Papers judged genuine by
WM PERRY & JOSEPH HAZZARD, JPs for Suss, 7 Oct 1785; instructions to pay SAPP
£1 17 shillings 6 pence per mo from time of discharge. Recorded JNO RUSSELL, recdr.

174 Deed 30 Jul 1785. DANIEL STEEL yeoman of Suss & MARGARET his wife & ELIZABETH
STEEL wid/o DANIEL STEEL (f/o afsd DANIEL) decd yeoman of Suss sell to JOHN ENNES
yeoman of Suss for £120: tr in forrest of Broadkiln Hund, 110 ac, pt/o tr sold by
EZEKIEL GREEN to afsd DANIEL STEEL the Elder decd, who by his will devised it to
his son DANIEL, giving ELIZABETH estate therein for life. Wit DAVD TRAIN, MARY
TRAIN. Examr JOHN CLOWES. Ackn 30 Jul 1785.

175 Deed 30 Jul 1785. NATHANIEL STEEL yeoman of Suss & SARAH his wife sell to
JOHN ENNIS yeoman of Suss for £111: tr in forest of Broadkiln Hund, 95 ac, pt/o
tr sold by EZEKIEL GREEN to DANIEL STEEL decd who bequeathed it to his son NATHAN-
IEL afsd. Wit: D TRAIN, MARY TRAIN. Ackn 30 Jul 1785.

176 Deed 10 Aug 1776. CATY STUART execx of WM STUART (will 7 May 1776) sells to
DAVID RANKIN planter of Suss for £75: parcel in Broadkiln Hund pt/ o tr granted
to CHRISTOPHER SANDRESS in 1686, 800 ac in Cave Neck about 1 mi s of main prong of
Broadkiln Creek, on nw side of Mill Creek; Mill Pond being pt/o parcel owned by
JOHN STUART the Elder who bequeathed pt/o his lands to his gr-son WM STUART afsd,
who directed in his will that said land be sold; adj DAVID RANKIN, adj JONATHAN
STEVENSON; divided in Mar 1773 by WM PERRY by consent of parties, 86 ac. Wit ANN
JONES, JOSEPH HALL. Ackn 4 Aug 1785.

177 Deed 12 Nov 1784. WILLIAM HICKMAN (TURNER) of Suss sells to JOHN HUBBERT of
Suss for £27+: tr "Hickmans Lot", 21½ ac. Attys JOSHUA & DANIEL POLK. Wit SETH
HILL EVITTS, SOLOMON HUBBERT, JOHN DAWSON. Ackn 4 Aug 1785.

177 Power of Atty. JOHN CLIFTON of Martin Co North Carolina, yeoman, appoints friend WM CLIFTON of Kent Co DEL atty to demand, recover & receive of ROGER ADDAMS of Caroline Co MD all his claims & accounts against estate of ROGER ADDAMS decd; 14 Nov in the year of our sovereign Lord George III, by the Grace of God King of Great Britain, 1774. Wit FRANCIS JESTER, ELIZABETH CLIFTON. Proved 4 Aug 1785.

178 Deed 4 Aug 1785. JOHN COLLINS yeoman of Broad Creek Hund sells to THOMAS ONEAL & WM ONEAL yeomen of same place for £30: tr "Addition", on n side of Broad Creek back in woods, in the head of Parsons Neck, n of tr now or formerly belonging to WM & PAUL WAPLES, 50 ac, granted by patent of MD on 20 Aug 1747 to JAMES ONEAL, f/o afsd THOS ONEAL, devised by JAMES to THOS his son, who sold it to afsd JOHN COLLINS. Wit SYDENHAM THORNE, DAVD TRAIN. Ackn 4 Aug 1785.

179 Deed 6 Mar 1784. AMBROSE GREEN yeoman of Suss sells to EDWARD CRAIG yeoman of Suss for £150: pt/o tr in Lewes Rehoboth Hund which STEPHEN GREEN the Elder, f/o afsd AMBROSE GREEN, owned when he died but laid off with consent of AMBROSE to RICHARD HOWARD, but never conveyed by deed to him, & RICHARD HOWARD sold or swapped the land to EDWARD CRAIG afsd, on mill road at fork of Old Road, adj JOHN HARMONSON, adj BAILEYs fence, 53 ac, laid off by RHOADS SHANKLAND surveyor. Wit ROBERT WEST, JOHN LITTLE. Ackn 4 Aug 1785.

180 Petition of CHARLES POLK JR, RHOADS SHANKLAND & SAMUEL LAVERTY, yeomen of Suss: same information as contained in #164.

180 Petition 4 Aug 1785. ROBERT HOUSTON JR of Dagsberry Hund execr of JONATHAN BELL of Suss petitions for leave to make deed to JAMES EDGAR for tr owned by BELL in Broad Creek Hund, 100 ac, conveyed to BELL by JACOB ADDISON 29 Mar 1760, for which BELL on 13 Apr 1775 gave his bond to sell to JAMES EDGAR, millwright of same place, £200, tr being 100 ac pt/o tr "Branch Side" granted by MD to JACOB ADDISON (160 ac) now in the proposed new county of Sussex in Delaware. BELL died intestate without issuing deed to EDGAR though EDGAR paid purchase price in full.

181 Deed 4 Aug 1785. ROBERT HOUSTON JR issues deed to JAMES EDGAR: same information as above; "Branch Side" patented to JACOB ADDISON 29 Sep 1752, in Worc Co Deed Book Lib E ff 26, 27. Wit ROBT HOUSTON SR, JAMES POLLOCK, LEVIN WAILES. Ackn 4 Aug 1785.

182 Deed 6 Sep 1785. AVERY MORGAN of Suss sells to JOHN WEST planter of Suss for £20: small parcel pt/o tr in Indian River Hund on e side/o Blackwater Creek, adj Wests recovery , adj "Marsh Point Inlarged", adj gut once dividing THOMAS & GEORGE WEST's pastures, adj creek to Broad Branch. "Marsh Point Inlarged" formerly surveyed by AVERY MORGAN decd; part sold being 10 ac. Wit D HALL, JOSEPH MILLER. Ackn 6 Sept 1785.

183 Deed 16 Feb 1785. RICHARD & WM HUDSON yeomen of Suss sell to ELIAS VEACH yeoman of Suss: 500 ac in Cedar Creek hund surveyed for JERIMA GRIFFIN 2 Jun 1743 (decd), who sold it to JOHN HUDSON, cooper, decd, & 101 ac thereof became property of RICHARD & WM HUDSON, who sold same for £101 to COVERDALE COLE & at same time gave their bond for conveyance to COLE who sold it to JOHN POLK who let ELIAS VEACH afsd have said land as swap; RICHARD & WM sons of JOHN HUDSON. Land adj road from Ingrams Rd to Drapers Rd, adj JEHU CLIFTON, adj Mill Road. Wit ELIAS JONES, WM COTMAN GUM, BENTON SMITH, BENJN HUDSON. Ackn 6 Sep 1785.

183 Deed 8 Sep 1785. WOODMAN STOCKLEY yeoman of Suss & ELIZABETH his wife sell to heirs of ANDERSON PARKER JR for £200: tr in Angola & Indian R Hund, on n

side of ROBINSONs Millpond, adj Braceys Branch (on n side of branch), adj heirs
of SOLOMON STOCKLEY decd, 250 ac; being land which JOSEPH STOCKLEY devised in his
will to afsd WOODMAN STOCKLEY his son, pt/o tr granted to RICHARD LAW who sometime
after sold it to JACOB KOLLOCK the Elder of Suss decd, who devised it to his 7
children: SIMON, HANNAH, JACOB, JANE, MAGDALEN, HESTER & CORNELIOUS. MARY wid/o
JACOB KOLLOCK Elder, dau HANNAH WILTBANK widow, dau JANE HERONS, HESTER w/o
JACOB PHILLIPS, SIMON, JACOB sold same to WOODMAN STOCKLEY the Grandfather, yeoman of Suss, who devised it in his will to afsd JOSEPH STOCKLEY. WOODMAN STOCKLEY
the devisee, gave his bond for conveyance of said land to ANDERSON PARKER JR (then)
of Suss on 10 Oct 1776; & afsd ANDERSON PARKER JR died intestate before deed was
made leaving wid RUTH (since mar to WM GRICE) & 2 children, PETER (eldest son) &
DAVID, & land descended to them; deed now made for conveyance. Wit DAVD TRAIN,
MARY TRAIN. Ackn 8 Sep 1785.

185 Deed 8 Sep 1785. WM COLEMAN silversmith of Lewes & BETTY his wife sell to
JOHN STAFFORD barber of same place for £65: Sir EDMOND ANDROS granted by patent
of 15 Jan 1675 to JOHN KIPHAVEN then of Suss: tr 69 ac on s side Lewes; & KIPHAVEN
assigned it on 9 Feb 1680 to WM CLARK then of Suss; who on 12 Apr 1681 assigned it
to Capt NATHANIEL WALKER; who by his will devised it to Maj WM DYER; & at his death
his son WM DYER, exec, sold it 6 Jun 1699 to THOS FINWICK; who sold pt on 29 Jan
1707, part adj Meeting House, to JOHN HEPBURN; who by his will of 2 Mar 1707 devised it to his sons-in-law EDWARD STRETCHER & ROBT CLIFTON, pt between JOHN HEP-
BURN's lot (afsd) & JACOB KOLLOCK's fence, with half of the savannah; & EDWARD
STRETCHER & MARGARET his wife & ROBERT CLIFTON & ANNE his wife sold 1 Nov 1715 to
NATHANIEL HALL; who sold pt on 16 Aug 1731, 90 sq perches+, to HANNAH, MARY, JOHN
& PETER ADAMS as joint tenants; & JOHN ADAMS who has survived others sold 4 Jul
1782 to afsd WM COLEMAN. Adj land of JOHN ADAMS, f/o afsd JOHN ADAMS, decd; adj
land once of NATHANIEL HALL decd, now owned by heirs of DAVID HALL of Suss, decd.
WM COLEMAN after gave his bond for conveyance of land to ROBT PRETTYMAN on 9 Jul
1785 (cordwainer), a part of above tr; COLEMAN now sells to STAFFORD all but pt/o
tr committed by bond to PRETTYMAN. Wit DAVD TRAIN, JOHN CLOWES. Ackn 8 Sep 1785.

186 Deed of Common Recovery 9 Sep 1785. DAVID HALL pays 5 shillings to SAMUEL
WILLIAMS, both of Suss, for the docking, barring etc of all estates & remainders
in tail, & setting of same for purposes described, & WILLIAMS sells to HALL tr
"Hoopers Chance", 100 ac, and that pt/o tr "Martins Hundred" owned by WILLIAMS,
175 ac; with intent HALL become perfect tenant of the freehold, & may stand seized
thereof until a perfect common recovery may be had; & it is agreed that DAVID HALL
will permit WM HARRISON to sue & prosecute against him a writ demanding said lands
& HALL will vouch to warranty afsd SAMUEL WILLIAMS, who will enter into warranty
& afterwards default & depart in contempt of court so that judgment may be given
for afsd WM HARRISON to recover lands from HALL & HALL to recover value from afsd
SAMUEL WILLIAMS, & WILLIAMS to recover value from the common voucher; to the end of
one perfect common recovery, & WM HARRISON shall own lands at end. Wit WM DONE,
WM BRERETON. Ackn 9 Sep 1785.

187 Deed 5 Aug 1785. JONATHAN WOOLF of Lewes Rehoboth Hund & RUTH his wife sell
to JOSEPH HEPBURN of same place, hatter, for £40: tr in Lewes Rehoboth Hund adj
afsd JONATHAN WOOLF's land conveyed to him by DAVID HALL ESQ, decd, adj road from
Lewes to Phila, 600 ac+, pt/o tr "St Martins" which DAVID HALL sold to afsd JONA-
THAN WOOLF 178_, Lib M Fol 457. Wit D HALL, JNO WILTBANK. Ackn 9 Sep 1785.

188 Bond 16 Nov 1785. PETER FRETWELL WRIGHT ESQ, high sheriff of Suss & RHOADS
SHANKLAND, PHILLIPS KOLLOCK & REECE WOOLF gentlemen of Suss give their bond to
Delaware State for £700 to serve & execute all writs without delay according to
law, etc. Wit JNO RUSSELL, JNO RUSSELL JR.

188 Deed 17 Oct 1783. WILLIAM MANLOVE of Roan Co North Carolina, atty in fact for MANLOVE WHEELER & heirs of KEZIAH WHEELOR late of Suss decd, sells to JAMES JOHNSON yeoman of Suss for £217+: tr in Cedar Creek Neck, pt/o "Harts Tract", 101 ac, adj JOHN CLINDANIEL & WM BELL ?, adj GEORGE WALTON, adj JOHN PLOWMAN. Land was recovered May 1758 by suit of WM MANLOVE, KEZIAH WHEELER & MARGARET CHIPMAN against JOSEPH HICKMAN, & 75 ac after deeded to JOHN & JONATHAN WHEELER by afsd WILLIAM MANLOVE, PARIS CHIPMAN & MARGARET his wife, the other part belonging to afsd KEZIAH WHEELER who died intestate. Land after devolved to her heirs: WILLIAM MANLOVE & MARY, JOHN, JONATHAN & MARGARET WHEELER. Said JOHN & MARY being of full age they sold their part to afsd JOHN PLOWMAN on 3 Oct 1774, valued at £3 per ac 16 Feb 1775 but not paid by PLOWMAN so afsd WILLIAM MANLOVE in behalf of heirs of KEZIAH WHEELER accepted land at valuation; now sells to JAMES JOHNSON. WILLIAM POLK, WILLIAM HAZZARD attys. Wit GEORGE BLACK, GEORGE HAZZARD. Ackn 9 Nov 1785.

189 Deed 9 Jan 1773. WILLIAM GODWIN planter sells to ABRAHAM HARRIS housecarpenter, both of Suss, for £16: tr "Hog Quarter" in forrest of Broadkiln Hund on Kenneys Savana, 200 ac, granted by warrant of PA to THOMAS INGLISH 9 Jun 1743; & pt/o afsd tr became by various conveyances property of afsd WILLIAM GODWIN, adj ABRAHAM HARRIS, adj heirs of WILLIAM BAGGS LACEY, adj BURTON WAPLES, adj LUKE THOMAS' dividend (24 ac); 76 ac. Wit JAMES LAWLESS, STEPHEN MITCHELL, SAMUEL SHANKLAND. Ackn 9 Nov 1785.

190 Deed 10 Aug of 10th year of American Independence, 1785. ISAAC BENSON of Suss sells to ELIHU JACKSON of Suss for £100: JAMES BENSON wheelwright decd owned 50 ac "Lott" in Suss but formerly in Summerset Co, on main road from Saulsberry to Broad Creek Bridge; & afsd ISAAC BENSON as heir at law now owns same & sells. Wit ROBT HOUSTON s/o R?, COLLINS CAREY, JOHN HOUSTON. Ackn 9 Nov 1785.

191 Deed 1 Nov 1785, 10th year of Independence of Delaware State. LOWDER CALLAWAY, soulder of Suss, sells to WILLIAM HURT, farmer of Suss for £100: 95 ac, pt/o tr "addition" in Broad Creek Hund (250 ac), devised to CALLAWAY by his father ISAAC CALLAWAY in his will. Wit ROBT HOUSTON, s/o R?, ISAAC CALLAWAY. Attys PHILLIPS KOLLOCK, PETER WRIGHT. Ackn 9 Nov 1785.

192 Deed _____ 1785. ISAAC McDOWEL of "Broadwater Contention" in Suss sells to JOSEPH MELSON: MARGARET KOLLOCK of Lewes execx of JACOB KOLLOCK decd who owned 2 tr in Indian River Hund. One tr "Broadwater Contention", 212 ac, surveyed for JOHN DAY 12 Feb 1735/6. At his death land descended to his son WILLIAM DAY who sold it for debts of JOHN DAY to JACOB KOLLOCK 14 Feb 1767 (RHODE SHANKLAND sheriff) (Lib K, fol 249). Other tr "Little Broadwater", 75 ac, surveyed for JOHN WARRINGTON 20 Aug 1744, also sold to JACOB KOLLOCK by WILLIAM DAY. Now Margaret KOLLOCK sells to ISAAC McDOWELL for £136+ (yeoman); & McDOWEL by power invested in him sells to JOSEPH MELSON same for £250. Wit WM KOLLOCK, HERCULAS KOLLOCK. Ackn 9 Nov 1785.

193 Deed 7 Nov 1785. JACOB MESSICK yeoman of Suss sells to JOHN COLLINS/COLLINGS yeoman of Suss for £96+: tr in Broadkiln Forrest granted by warrant to MARY WEST who became w/o JOSEPH LUFTON, who sold it (except for 100 ac on ne side) to OBEDIAH MESSICK who bequeathed it to afsd JACOB MESSICK, 103½ ac; adj LEVI MESSICK's division line, adj JOHN ROSS' pt/o land, adj afsd COLLINGS' pt/o land. Atty CORD HAZZARD late high sheriff of Suss. Wit JOHN CLARK, STEPHEN REDDEN, GEORGE POLK. Ackn 9 Nov 1785.

194 Deed 10 Nov 1785. PETER FRETWELL WRIGHT ESQ high sheriff of Suss issues to HENRY LINGO: SHEPARD KOLLOCK of Suss decd sold to JOHN REGUA of Suss on 1 May 1753

28.

148½ ac, pt/o tr granted to JOHN PRETTYMAN, SIMON KOLLOCK & CORD HAZZARD, late of Suss, surveyed by Dep Surveyor WILLIAM SHANKLAND of Suss, on se end of whole, adj ROBERT BURTON's land (decd) called the "1100 Acre Tract", e of land surveyed for JOHN HOLMES, on s side of land of WILLIAM PRETTYMAN, w of the fork of Swan Creek, n of division line of afsd CORD HAZZARD. On 6 Aug 1754 CORD HAZZARD sold to JOHN REGUA parcel in Indian River Hund, 147 ac, pt/o afsd tr granted to PRETTYMAN, KOLLOCK & HAZZARD, adj ROBERT BURTON's "1100 Acre Tract", adj JOHN REGUA, adj GEORGE DAY, adj JOHN PRETTYMAN decd. THOMAS & PETER ROBINSON recovered judgment against afsd JOHN REGUA for £75+, writ issued 4 May 1785 for seizure of land to pay judgment (sheriff CORD HAZZARD), seized tr in Indian River Hund, 260 ac, being same 2 parcels described above; at public sale of Oct 15 HENRY LINGO was high bidder at £95+; sheriff now issues deed. Wit D HALL, JOSEPH MILLER, JACOB KOLLOCK, DAV TRAIN. Ackn 10 Nov 1785.

195 Deed 12 May 1780. LEVIN DERICKSON ESQ Commissioner of Act of Free Pardon & Oblivion to dispose of forfeited lands sells to COLONEL HENRY NEILL of Suss for £3000: tr in Indian River Hund adj Braceys Branch, adj ANDREW McELVAIN & JOHN LITTLE, 220 ac, on which St Georges Chapel stands, formerly belonging to ROBERT McKEY. And parcel in same hundred on n side Braceys Branch, opposite Chapel, 2 ac laid off for mill built on afsd branch. THOMAS ROBINSON of Suss owned ½ both tr, late of Suss, on 16 May 1778, & being one of offenders named in afsd Act & not having surrendered to JP for trial for treason by that date he forfeited lands. HENRY NEILL highest bidder. Wit ANDREW McILVAIN, LEONARD McILVAIN. Ackn 10 Nov 1785.

196 Deed 10 Nov 1785. JOSHUA COSTON yeoman of Suss sells to STEPHEN MITCHEL yeoman of Suss for £50: tr in Broadkill Hund surveyed by warrant for afsd JOSHUA COSTON 6 Jun 1776, adj RICHARD JEFFERSON near Waterhole Swamp, adj "Costons Content", 50 ac. Wit JONA NOTTINGHAM, RHOADS SHANKLAND. Ackn 10 Nov 1785.

197 Deed 9 Nov 1785. GAMAGE EVANS HODGSON/HOG of Suss sells to JOHN MASSEY SR of Suss for £17+: 20 ac, pt/o tr "Addition' which is pt/o resurvey surveyed for MOSES DAZEY, patented to DAZEY 24 Jun 1761 (298 ac). Later DAZEY sold GAMAGE EVANS HOG 20 ac afsd, on seaboard side in Muddy Neck, adj "Bettys Lott", adj tr taken up by DAVID WHORTON. Wit N WAPLES, NATHL YOUNG, WM POLK. Ackn 9 Nov 1785.

198 Deed 18 Jun 1784. JOHN RUST of Westmoreland Co VA sells to CURTIS BROWN of Suss for £300: 150 ac which afsd RUST purch of JOSEPH DAWSON 8 Nov 1777, pt/o tr "Second Addition To Canaan", which JOSEPH DAWSON afsd patented 21 Jun 1776. Attys JOHN RUSSELL, DANIEL POLK. Wit PETER RUST, SALLY RUST, FANNY JACKSON, THOMAS LAWS. Ackn 9 Nov 1785.

198 Deed ___ Nov 1785. WILLIAM KENDRICK cordwinder of Slaughter Neck in Cedar Creek Hun & LYDIA his wife sell to JACOB HICKMAN cooper of same place for £142+: plantation & tr in Slaughter Neck sold by SARAH CLARK, late SARAH HODSON, adminx of ROBERT HODSON blacksmith late of Suss who died intestate. ROBERT HODSON owned tr in Slaughter Neck, pt/o Bowmans Farms, sold by JOSEPH HICKMAN to afsd ROBERT HODSON 6 Aug 1747 (Lib H no 47, fol 153); adj afsd HICKMAN, adj JAMES WHITE, adj WILLIAM HICKMAN's fence where his father lived: 50 ac, pt/o lands left to afsd HICKMAN by his father who purchased same from HENRY BOWMAN decd. And tr adj afsd tr, purch by JAMES KENDRICK from MARGARET WHITE wid/o JAMES WHITE, which JAMES WHITE bequeathed to his 2 daus ISBAL & SOPHIA WHITE, reserving to wid for her lifetime; & wid & 2 daus on 12 Oct 1767 sold to JAMES KENDRICK by conveyance bond, 10 ac; adj land surveyed for JACOB HICKMAN & ROBERT HODGER's, surveyed 2 Dec 1767 by WILLIAM SHANKLAND Dep Surv; & JAMES KENDRICK left in will to his son WILLIAM KENDRICK afsd. Wit DAVID WATTSON, WM CHAMBERS. Examr JOHN CLOWES. Ackn 10 Nov 1785

200 Deed 10 Nov 1785. WILLIAM CHAMBERS & ANNE his wife of Suss sell to WILLIAM KENDRICK cordwainer of Suss for £200: tr in Suss 132 ac, surveyed 7 Nov 1785 by WM JOHNSON DS, adj ABSOLAM WARREN, ALEXANDER WARREN, RICHARD BLOXOM & several others. Wit DAVID WATTSON, JACOB HICKMAN. Examr JOHN CLOWES: ANNE CHAMBERS of full age, 10 Nov 1785. Ackn 10 Nov 1785.

200 Deed 22 Sep 1785. EZEKIEL ONEAL planter of Suss sells to JOHN MITCHELL merchant of Suss for £51+: tr "Snow Hill" in Suss near Broad Cr, 100 ac, granted by Maryland to JOHN ONEAL. Wit JAMES BRATTAN, JAMES SAFFORD, CYRUS MITCHELL. Atty ISAAC HENRY. Ackn 10 Nov 1785.

201 Deed 31 Aug 1785. EZEKIEL JACKSON planter of Suss sells to JOHN MITCHELL merchant of Suss for £60: tr "Now or Never" in Suss near the wading place on Broad Creek (nb: Laurel), on south side Broad Cr near afsd JNO MITCHELL's pond, 4½ ac, granted by Maryland to EZEKIEL JACKSON. Wit JESSE BOUNDS, JONATHAN JACKSON, JOS BRATTAN. Atty ISAAC HENRY. Ackn 10 Nov 1785.

202 Deed 22 Nov 1784. JOHN CLARK yeoman of Broad Cr 100 sells to STEPHEN TOWNSEND yeoman of Cedar Cr 100 for £54+: tr in Slaughter Neck in Cedar Cr 100, adj ALEXANDER DRAPER, surveyed by WM POLK 15 Apr last past, 81 ac+, which NEHEMIAH CLARK late of Suss owned at death, which his adminr JOSHUA CLARK sold for debts to JOHN CLARK late of Suss (deed of 5 Mar 1760), and JOHN CLARK died intestate leaving a widow and 2 children named MEIRS CLARK and JOHN CLARK the afsd to whom the tr descended; MEIRS CLARK the eldest recd 2/3 & JOHN CLARK 1/3 agreeable to widows rights of dower, said widow MARY now the widow of ANDREW COLLINS late of Suss; and JOHN CLARK now sells his 1/3 share of the tr; defend from claims of afsd MARY COLLINS and also from claims of heirs of JAMES WHITE and MARGARET WHITE. Attys PHILLIPS KOLLOCK & CORD HAZZARD, sheriff. Wit DAVID WATTSON, WM HIFFERNAN? Ackn 23 Nov 1785.

203 Deed 8 Aug 1785. JESSE LEWIS, PHEBE VIRDIN, JOSEPH KILLS & MARGARET his wife & NAOMI POOR sell to WM POLK of Suss for £37 (all are of Suss): tr in Cedar Cr 100 called "Widows Contrivance" 400 ac, on the main branch called Church Br of Cedar Cr, in a fork with a small branch called Burrobung Br or Turks Br making into it, granted to ELIZABETH POOR who was mother to ROSOMAN LEWIS & NEHEMIAH POOR; ROSEMAN POOR was mother of JESSE LEWIS afsd & NEHEMIAH POOR was father of PHEBE VIRDIN, MARGARET KILLS and NAOMI POOR afsd; ELIZABETH POOR died intestate as did ROSOMAN LEWIS & NEHEMIAH POOR; adj HENRY PENNINGTON's land now in possession of JESSE WATTSON, adj JAMES REED. Attys HENRY NEILL ESQ & DR JOSEPH HALL of Suss. Wit COLLINGS TRUITT, PEGGY POLK, JOHN CLOWES, SARAH CLOWES. Examr JOHN CLOWES: MARGARET KILLS of age. Ackn 22 Nov 1785.

204 Deed 7 Nov 1785. HENRY NEILL merchant of Lewes & MARY his wife sell to PETER ROBINSON of Angola & Indian River Hund , merchant, for £240: tr in Indian R Hund on s side of Braceys Branch adj ANDREW McILVAIN & JOHN LITTLE, 220 ac, on which St Georges Chapel stands, formerly owned by ROBERT W KEY late of Suss; and tr in Indian R Hund on n side afsd br opposite Chapel, cont 2 ac laid off for mill; LEVIN DERICKSON ESQ commissioner for sale of forfeited estates by virtue of Act of Pardon & Oblivion seized ½ of both tracts from THOMAS ROBINSON late of Suss (he being named in Act) & sold them with grist mill on 16 May 1778 to HENRY NEILL afsd for £3000. Wit DAV TRAIN, HEBRON DOD. Examr JNO WILTBANK. Ackn 22 Nov 1785.

205 Deed 30 Jul 1785. SARAH WILSON/WILLSON execx of DANIEL STUART late of Suss sells to DAVID SMITH for £35: tr at head of branches of Broadkiln in forest of Broadkiln Hund, 100 ac, pt/o tr "Stuarts Folly" granted 5 Mar 1740 to THOMAS BAILY who assigned his warrant to afsd DANIEL STUART who sold 200 ac of it to HUGH BAKER on 4 May 1752; adj RILEYs & ABBOTTs lands, adj WM CARPENTER, near Sow-

bridge Branch; on 18 Apr 1785 sold to SMITH afsd for 7 shillings twopence per ac (total £35+). Wit JOSEPH HALL, JOHN PAYNTER. Ackn 23 Nov 1785.

206 Deed 1 Aug 1785. DAVID SMITH taylor of Broadkiln Hund & IBBIE his wife sell to SARAH WILLSON of Lewes Town for £35+ (same amt as in deed on p 205): tr near head of branches of Broadkiln in Broadkiln Hund, being pt/o tr "Stuarts Folly" granted 5 Mar 1740 (Phila) to THOMAS BAILY who assigned it to DANIEL STUART who sold 200 ac of it on 4 May 1752 to HUGH BAKER; same description as in deed on p 205; DANIEL STUART appointed his dau SARAH WILSON execx. Attys Dr JOSEPH HALL & PHILLIPS KOLLOCK ESQ. Wit J MAXWELL, HUGH PATTERSON. Examr JOHN CLOWES. Ackn 23 Nov 1785.

208 Deed 9 Nov 1785. PETER FRETWELL WRIGHT High Sheriff of Suss sells to JOHN GIBBONS yeoman of Suss for £200: JOHN CLOWES ESQ conveyed to LEVIN MILBEY yeoman of Suss on 3 May 1780 tr in Indian R Hund on sw side Beverdam Cr above the old bridge at head of Indian R, near GOSLING's land, adj Tusaky Br & Cowbridge Br, 300 ac; MILBEY sold it to CONSTANTINE MARINER who became indebted to JOHN ENNIS & ELI COLLINS for £1200 so he made over 100 ac of above tr to them, the 100 ac called "Cowbridge Branch", along with a millstream dwelling; and this bond was later made over to LEVIN ENNIS. JOHN ENNIS obtained a judgment against LEVIN ENNIS for £616+ on 5 Aug 1784; so the said Sheriff seized 131 ac of LEVIN ENNIS' land including ½ a mill in Indian R Hund and sold it to GIBBONS afsd to satisfy debt. Said Sheriff CORD HAZZARD was removed from office before deed was made & GIBBONS now petitions for deed which is granted. Wit HERCULAS KOLLOCK, WM HARRISON. Ackn 23 Nov 1785.

209 Deed of Mortgage 18 Nov 1785. RICHARD BLOXOM yeoman of Suss mortg to BETTY MELSON of Suss for £20: tr in Broadkill forrest s/o WM LAUGHLAND lands, e/o WM KENDRICKS lands, w/o ELIAS PARKER & n/o SAMUEL HEAVERLO lands, 140 ac; if BLOXOM pays w interest before Dec 1 1789 mortgage terminates. Wit DAVID THORNTON, DANIEL THORNTON. (Also spelled BLOCKSOM here.)

210 Deed 29 Nov 1785. JAMES HICKMAN planter of Suss & MARGARET his wife sell to CALEB NUTTER planter of Suss for £34: pt/o tr "Saplin Ridge" in NW Fork Hund adj main road, 24 ac; also pt/o tr "Hickmans Conclusion" adj the main county road, adj THOMAS HICKMAN, adj "Clearance" taken up by CHARLES BROWN the Elder, 10 ac. Attys JOHN RODNEY & PHILLIPS KOLLOCK of Lewes Town. Wit WM POLK, DANIEL POLK. Examr WM POLK. Ackn 16 Dec 1785.

211 Deed 3 Dec 1785. JOHN RICHARDS planter of Suss sells to his son DAVID RICHARDS his son for £10 and natural love and tender affection: pt/o tr "Dublin" where DAVID now lives, 209 ac, ref deed from WM NUTTER to THOMAS NUTTER & from THOMAS NUTTER to afsd JOHN RICHARDS; also tr "Delight" 57 ac; also tr "Rich Ridge" 50 ac according to patent; also tr "Tough Bottom" 50 ac with a resurvey for same for 159 ac added to the patent land 10 May 1776; also tr "Poplar Level Improved" 152 ac in NW Fork Hund. Attys JOHN WILTBANK & PHILLIPS KOLLOCK ESQ of Lewes Town. Wit WM POLK, DANIEL POLK. Ackn 16 Dec 1785.

212 Deed 8 Dec 1785. ROGER ADAMS SR planter of Suss sells to his son ROGER ADAMS JR for £10 and natural regard & affection: tr "Regulation" 264 ac; also pt/o tr "Bite the Bitter" adj JAMES ADAMS, adj division line intended betw ROGER ADAMS JR & his bro ENNALLS ADAMS. Wit D HALL, JOSEPH MILLER. Ackn 16 Dec 1785.

213 Bill of Sale 4 Jan 1786. JONATHAN NOTTINGHAM of Suss sells to ROBERT HOUSTON for £300: one new sloop now launched & laying in Indian R opposite my plantation called "The Porpus", 40 tons; also ½ another sloop now on the stocks at the said landing called "The Fly", building with me JONATHAN NOTTINGHAM & JOSHUA INGRAM 20 tons, together with all the materials to complete her. Wit JOSEPH HOUSTON, POLLY HOUSTON.

31

213 Certificate of Discharge. THOMAS HOLDSON soldier of Del found to be unfit for further duty in field or garrison by reason of wound received in service of US and is recommended for discharge 26 Jan 1783; granted by W JACKSON ajutant secy at war. Attest Jos? CARLETON secy. Adjudged genuine by JPs of Suss 7 Feb 1786, signed by WILLIAM PERRY?,SIMON KOLLOCK. Pay unto THOMAS HOLDSON citizen of this state £1 17 shillings sixpence per? month, signed WM PERRY?, SIMON KOLLOCK. (To the State Treasurer.)

214 Deed of Gift. RACHEL MACKLIN wid/o THOMAS MACKLIN of Suss gives to her daughter ANNES (and ANNESS) MESSICK now w/o ISAAC MESSICK, & after her decease to gr-dau SALLIE MESSICK, 50 ac in Broadkill Hund on the narrow west side of a bever dam branch, pt/o tr "Dobsons Folly", woodland; 6 Feb 1786. Wit JOHN WALTON, SARAH MESSICK.

214 Deed 3 Nov 1785. ABDIL WILLIAM SIMPLER & his wife LITTLETON & JEHU WYATT all of Suss sell to NATHANIEL WAPLES ESQ of Suss: tr in Indian R Hund on w side of county road from Doe Bridge to Lewes Town by way of St Georges Chappel, 1½ mi from Doe Bridge, called "Red Oak Ridge", granted by warrant of 5 Oct 1749 to ROBERT BELCHER & surveyed unto him 4 Jun 1756 for 106 ac by WM SHANKLAND dep surveyor; & ROBERT BELCHER gave conveyance bond on 4 Sep 1759 & sold to LITTLETON ABDIL but no deed was made & on 13 Mar 1778 LITTLETON ABDIL died intestate leaving ALIC his wid and 3 children: ELIZABETH who had mar WM SIMPLER, WILLIAM & LITTLETON; & the heirs divided the tr into 2 equal parts, & WILLIAM ABDIL the eldest son took the west half & ALIC the wid, WM SIMPLER & ELIZABETH his wife & LITTLETON ABDIL took the east half; & WILLIAM ABDIL sold the right to his half to JEHU WYATT along with his interest in the conveyance bond; & afsd JEHU WYATT applied to WILLIAM BELCHER the eldest son of afsd ROBERT BELCHER for a deed & recd it on 8 Feb 1785 for £3 & it is recorded in Lib N13 fol 106. Said tr adj land resurveyed to SAMUEL CARY on 7 Jul 1741, stands in small glade or savannah, adj land resurveyed to HUGH MACINTOSH on 10 Nov 1743, adj land of NATHANIEL WAPLES, SAMUEL CARY's resurveyed land now in possession of JOSEPH ROBINSON; now sell to WAPLES for £20+. Attys Col HENRY FISHER, Maj WM PERRY, Dr JOSEPH HALL, ROBT SHANKLAND, WM BURTON? all of Suss. Wit THOMAS SIRMAN, ISAAC ATKINSON, JOHN M? Mc? IVER?, WM PRETTYMAN. (A drawing of the plat is shown.) Ackn 4 Nov 1785.

216 Deed 12 May 1780. LEVIN DERICKSON/DIRRICKSON ESQ Commissioner by Act of Pardon & Oblivion to sell forfeited estates sells to NATHANIEL WAPLES ESQ of Suss: tr in Indian R Hund, originally (granted?) to WILLIAM KENNY who conveyed part of it to GEORGE YOUNG, which part was executed & sold for a debt due CORNELIUS WILTBANK & JANE his wife to WILLIAM BURTON, being 216 acres of which THOMAS ROBINSON late of Suss owned half on 16 May 1778; and ROBINSON being one of the offenders described in the above Act & not having surrendered himself to abide his trial for treason all his right in afsd tr became forfeit & was seized by LEVIN DIRICKSON & sold at auction to NATHANIEL WAPLES for £960. Wit ANDREW McELVAIN, LENARD McIVAIN (also written McILVAIN). Ackn 11 Feb 1786.

217 Deed 7 Feb 1786. HENRY SMITH of Suss sells to JOHN RICHARDS of Suss for £13: pt/o tr "Fox Harber" 36 ac. Attys JOHN WILTBANK, WM POLK ESQs. Wit ISAAC BRADLEY, CALEB NUTTER. Ackn 20 Feb 1786.

218 Deed 16 dec 1785. CHARLES WILLIAMS, JOB SMITH, WILLIAM RICHARDS & TAMSEY his wife, HENRY RICHARDS & ESTHER his wife, DAVID RICHARDS & TAMSEY his wife, ELIJAH ADAMS & JANE his wife, JOSEPH BRADLEY & ELIZABETH his wife all planters in Suss Co sell to JOHN RICHARDS of Suss for £400: JAMES RICHARDS died intestate & his sundry lands in Suss fell to his brothers & sisters to be equally divided & they contracted with JOHN RICHARDS to sell all the lands, now sell him tr "Smiths Lott" 100 ac; also tr "First Purchase" 110 3/4 ac surveyed 9 Apr 1776; also tr "Batcheldors Ridge" surveyed for JAMES RICHARDS 100½ ac; all in NW Fork Hund. Attys JOHN RODNEY, PHILLIPS KOLLOCK of Lewes Town. Wit WM POLK, ISAAC BRADLEY, CALEB NUTTER. Examr WM

POLK. Ackn 20 Feb 1786.

219 Deed 7 Feb 1786. JOHN RICHARDS of Suss sells to DAVID RICHARDS for £75: tr "First Purchase" 110 ac in NW Fork Hund taken up by JAMES RICHARDS in 1776. Attys JOHN WILTBANK, WM POLK ESQs. Wit ISAAC BRADLEY, CALEB NUTTER. Ackn 20 Feb 1786.

219 Deed 11 Jan 1786. ELIJAH COLLINGS & ABERILLA his wife & SHEPHERD COLLINGS of Suss sell to JOHN COLLINGS of Suss for £150: will of ISAAC INGRAM dated 26 Feb 1776 devised to his dau ABERILLA COLLINGS w/o ELIJAH COLLINGS all his lands west of a dividing line & after her death to his gr-son SHEPHERD COLLINGS s/o ABERILLA, pt/o INGRAM's manner plantation in Nanticoke Hund on headwaters of Collings Mill Pond on Gravelly Br, 133 ac. Attys STEPHEN REVEL, PETER FRETWELL WRIGHT WSQ. Wit JOHN CLOWES, JOHN LINCH. Examr JOHN CLOWES. Ackn 20 Feb 1786.

220 Deed 12 May 1780. LEVIN DERICKSON Commissioner for Act of Pardon & Oblivion sells to SIMON KOLLOCK ESQ: tr in Indian R Hund on n side Herring Br which proceeds out of Middle Cr, 232 ac, adj land formerly of JOHN RUSSELL, adj TUCKBERRY's land; also tr in Indian R Hund 70 ac, pt/o "The Irish Tract"; both formerly owned by THOMAS ROBINSON late of Suss one of the offenders named in the afsd Act, so his lands were seized, these being one moiety or half, and sold to SIMON KOLLOCK at auction for £2570. Wit ANDREW McILVAIN, LEONARD McILVAIN. Ackn 20 Feb 1786

221 Deed 28 Dec 1785. ELIZABETH ALEXANDER & CLARKSON CANNON of Suss sell to NATHANIEL MORRIS of Suss for £195: £195 pd to WILLIAM CAWSEY of Caroline Co MD by reason of CLARKSON CANNON & ADAMS ALEXANDER selling land to CURTIS JACOBS of Suss & giving conveyance bond for same, & afsd JACOBS assigning bond to WM CAWSEY; now ELIZABETH ALEXANDER & CLARKSON CANNON sell to NATHANIEL MORRIS tr in forrest of Misspillion on s side of road leading from Owenses Bridge to Marshope Bridge near "Taylors Chance" now in possession of heirs of DANIEL MORRIS, 130 ac. Attys JOHN MORRIS, FRANCIS WRIGHT of Suss. Wit CURTIS JACOBS, NEHEMIAH NICOLLS, JOHN MORRIS. Ackn 20 Feb 1786.

222 Deed 4 Feb 1786. EBENEZER JONES planter of Suss & ANN his wife sell to JOHN DARBY planter of Suss for £200: tr in Suss, 76 ac, pt/o "Good Hope" on n side Sheep Pen Br which issues out of head of Indian R in Dagsberry Hund where afsd EBENEZER JONES dwells, patented to SIMON KOLLOCK SR by Maryland by virtue of assignment of certificate of survey by JOHN CALWELL to afsd SIMON KOLLOCK; & SIMON KOLLOCK sold to LAZARETH KENNY (deed in Wocester Co) sold "Good Hope" to EBENEZER JONES SR who died intestate (the land then being in MD) descended to his son THOMAS JONES; & THOS JONES for fatherly love & £50 deeded 76 ac of "Good Hope" to his son EBENEZER JONES JR on 20 Jan 1780; adj ZACHARIAH JONES. Also tr in Dagsberry Hund "Jones First Choice" granted by PA to said EBENEZER JONES at Phila 12 Mar 1776 & surveyed by RHOADS SHANKLAND dep surveyor under JOHN LUKENS ESQ surveyor genl & recorded 16 Mar 1776, adj ZACHARIAH JONES division line, 100 ac on n side Sheep Pen Br. Wit JOHN WALKER, PETER HALL. Ackn 20 Feb 1786.

223 Deed 4 Feb 1786. ZACHARIAH JONES planter of Suss & MARGARET his wife sell to JOHN DARBY planter of Suss for £200: tr in Suss, 100 ac, "Dispute" granted by Maryland to WILLIAM PHILLIPS by patent 3 Jul 1741; & PHILLIPS sold to HENRY WALLER on 16 Aug 1760; & WALLER sold to ZACHARIAH JONES the Elder on 18 Mar 1763 (deed in Worcester Co); & ZACHARIAH JONES devised by his will of 25 May 1780 to his son ZACHARIAH JONES along with a resurvey to same of 200 ac called "Dispute Disputed"; on n side Shialoes Br which issues out of head of Indian R near Buck Glade, adj small house belonging to ZACHARIAH JONES; resurvey 12 Mar 1776 Phila by RHOADS SHANKLAND, on n side Deep Cr Rd, adj "Double Purchase", adj "Hay Savanah", on s side Broad Cr Co Rd; ZACHARIAH JONES & PEGGY his wife. Wit JOHN WALKER, PETER HALL. Ackn 20 Feb 1786.

33

224 Deed 4 Feb 1786. EBENEZER JONES planter of Suss & ANN his wife sell to JOHN
DARBY planter of Suss for £50: tr in Suss Co, 70 ac, pt/o tr now in possession of
ROBERT INGRAM, on s side Sheep Pen Branch issuing out of head of Indian R in Dagsberry Hund, granted to ROBERT INGRAM by warrant to resurvey a tr he now dwells on
called _____ by PA, dated in Phila ____1776, surveyed by RHOADS SHANKLAND depty
surveyor; ROBERT INGRAM by deed of 19 Jan 1780 conveyed afsd 70 ac to afsd EBENEZER
JONES; adj ZACHARIAH JONES' resurvey, adj Sheep Pen Br, adj EBENEZER JONES' corn
house, to a stake on the hill. Wit JOHN WALKER, PETER HALL. Ackn 20 Feb 1786.

225 Deed 8 Feb 1786. AVERY MORGAN planter of Suss sells to JOHN MASSEY JR yeoman
of Suss for £100: tr in Baltimore Hund "Stockleys Adventure", adj JONATHAN WHARTON's
fence, adj JOHN WEST's old field near the going over place of a branch betw MORGAN's
house & the fork field, adj WILLIAM RILEY EVANS' line, adj land of said JOHN MASSEY,
adj Widow HARNEY's line, 160 ac. Wit LEVI COLLINS, WATSON WHARTON, JONA. BOYCE.
Ackn 20 Feb 1786.

226 Deed 19 Jan 1780. ROBERT INGRAM sells to EBENEZER JONES both yeomen of Suss
for £30: pt/o tr on Sheep Pen Br in Dagsburrah Hund, taken up & surveyed for said
INGRAHAM by warrant of Phila; adj ZACHARIAH JONES' resurvey to a stake in cripple
of Sheep Pen Br, adj ABENEZER JONES' corn house, 70 ac +. Wit THOMAS JONES, SAMUEL
SHANKLAND. Ackn 20 Feb 1786.

226 Deed 20 Jan 1780. THOMAS JONES sells to EBENEZER/ABENEZER JONES, both yeomen
of Suss, for £50 and fatherly love: pt/o tr "Good Hope" on n side of a br issuing
out of the Indian R, alias Baltimore R, called the Great Cypress Br, patented to
SIMON KOLLOCK by assignment of a certificate from JOHN CALDWELL, conveyed by KOLLOCK
to LAZARUS KENNY, & by KENNY to ABENEZER JONES, & by death of ABENEZER JONES descended to afsd THOMAS JONES; adj ZACHARIAH JONES' dividend of afsd larger tr, 76½ ac,
including also all that land described that falls into tr called "Pippers Chance"
patented to WILLIAM PIPPER & now belonging to THOMAS JONES which somewhat interlocks.
Wit SAMUEL SHANKLAND, ROBERT INGRAM. Ackn 20 Feb 1786.

227 Deed 19 Jan 1780. ROBERT INGRAM sells to ZACHARIAH JONES, both yeomen of Suss,
for £50: pt/o tr on Sheep Pen Br in Dagsburrah Hund, taken up by & surveyed for
said ROBERT INGRAHAM by warrant of Phila; adj corner of afsd JONES' resurvey, adj
division line of ABENEZER JONES, 76 ac +. Wit THOMAS JONES, SAMUEL SHANKLAND.
Ackn 20 Feb 1786.

227 Deed 8 Feb 1786. THOMAS MARVEL yeoman of Suss sells to PHILIP MARVEL yeoman
of Suss for £100: 100 ac pt/o tr in Broadkiln Hund originally granted by warrant
to RICHARD PETTYJOHN late of Suss decd who devised by his will to his son JOHN
PETTYJOHN who sold 100 ac to NEHEMIAH REED giving a bond for same; and & REED after
assigned the bond to JAMES REYNOLDS to whom the said JOHN PETTYJOHN afterward conveyed the land; & REYNOLDS sold to THOMAS MARVEL afsd; adj fork in road from Lewes
Town to EVANS sawmill & Green Br, adj edge of swamp, adj HARRIS' fence. Wit JNO
WILTBANK, JOS MILLER. Ackn 20 Feb 1786.

228 Deed 8 Feb 1786. PHILIP MARVEL yeoman of Suss sells to JONATHAN CAHOON yeoman
of Suss for £108: tr in Broadkill Hund pt/o tr granted by warrant to RICHARD PET-
TYJOHN late of Suss decd, who devised to his son JOHN PETTYJOHN who had entered a
written obligation to sell 100 ac of said tr to NEHEMIAH REED, & REED sold to JAMES
REYNOLDS who consents that PHILIP MARVEL now sell it to JONATHAN CAHOON; same description as in deed above. Wit JNO WILTBANK, JOS MILLER. Ackn 20 Feb 1786. Deed
of JOHN PETTYJOHN to JAMES REYNOLDS in Lib N11 fol 274 at Lewes. Deed of JAMES
REYNOLDS to THOMAS MARVEL in Lib N11 fol 456 Lewes.

229 Deed 6 Feb 1786. NATHANIEL WALLER SR yeoman of Suss sells to NATHANIEL WALLER JR, JOHN WALLER & JAMES WALLER yeomen of Suss for £75: tr in Broad Cr Hund on w side of Pokeomoke R, adj SOLOMON VINCENT's lands on west, on the east by tr "Worlds End" in the Cypress Swamp taken up by THOMAS & NATHANIEL WALLER SR, on the south by Green Branch and on north by Green Branch; patented by THOS WALLER SR, 50 ac; also a resurvey made by NATHANIEL WALLER SR, s/o afsd THOS WALLER & party to this deed who inherits the whole by deed of sale, containing in the whole 201 ac called "Swamp Ridge". Atty JOHN WILTBANK ESQ of Lewes Town. Wit ELIJAH LECAT, THOS GRAY. Ackn 20 Feb 1786.

229 Deed 19 Oct 1785. THOMAS COPES of Suss gives to his son JOSEPH COPES of Suss for natural love and affection and his better maintenance: tr "Cherry Garden", 100 ac in Broad Cr Hund; also "Collins Luck", 17 ac in Broad Cr Hund; also 1/3 of sawmill in partnership with THOMAS ONEAL & SMITH WINGATE. Wit JESSE BOUNDS, JOHN BENSON of WM. Ackn 20 Feb 1786.

230 Deed 1785. THOMAS COPES of Suss gives to his dau SUCKEY/SUKEY WINGATE for natural love and affection and her better maintenance: half of 100 ac of land conveyed to THOMAS COPES by EDMOND HITCHENS lying nw of tr "Collins Industry", bounded on n by 50 ac deeded by THOMAS COPES to UNICE WINGATE and on w by tr "Chery Garden". Wit JESSE BOUNDS, JOHN BENSON. Ackn 20 Feb 1786.

230 Deed 19 Oct 1785. THOMAS COPES of Suss gives to his dau UNICE WINGATE for natural love and affection & her better maintenance: 50 ac "Security Enlarged", bounded on w by tr "Last Of All" and on e by tr "Collins Industry" and on s by other parts of "Security Enlarged" containing 500 ac granted by Maryland to EDMOND HITCHENS. Wit JESSE BOUNDS, JOHN BENSON. Ackn 20 Feb 1786.

231 Deed 4 Feb 1786. LEVI COLLINS sells to JOHN AYDELOTT bricklayer & THOMAS HARNEY SR of Suss for £1 7 shillings: 1 ac for use of the body of Indian R Meeting House or Ceciety of the Prisbytering Meeting or Congregation, pt/o tr whereon Meeting House now stands called "Chance", on n side Blackwater Branch nigh the going over said branch on e side of road. Wit JOHN EVANS s side, WILLIAM HALL. Ackn 20 Feb 1786.

232 Deed 1 Feb 1786. WILLIAM CARY of Suss & ANN his wife sell to SAMUEL CARY br/o WILLIAM CARY of Suss for £69+: tr in Indian R Hund pt/o tr granted by warrant to afsd WILLIAM CARY 28 Nov 1755, surveyed to him 19 May 1756, adj tr surveyed to ROBERT BURTON 13 Dec 1723 called "Rock Hole" now owned by NATHANIEL WAPLES ESQ, on s side JOHN COLLINGS plantation surveyed for HUGH McINTUSH 10 Nov 1743 called "Scotlands Barrons", adj road called Robinsons Road, adj pt/o afsd tr laid off to ELIZABETH CARY now owned by BENJAMIN BENSTON?, adj BENSTONs? house & plantation, adj tr surveyed to SAMUEL JOHNSON GREEN now owned by afsd BENJAMIN BENSTON, adj tr resurveyed to JOSEPH CARTER 10 Jul 1735 called "The Vineyard"; 200 ac+ surveyed by WILLIAM PRETTYMAN surveyor. Attys WILLIAM PERY ESQ, Dr JOSEPH HALL, HENRY NEILL & SIMON KOLLOCK ESQ all of Suss. Wit THOS CARY JR, JONA NOTTINGHAM, N WAPLES. Drawing of land. Ackn 20 Feb 1786.

233 Deed 7 Feb 1780. TRAVOUS TAYLOR, WILLIAM RILEY EVANS & WILLIAM EVANS s/o JOHN of Mudy Neck for JOHN HOPKINS, all of Suss, yeomen, sell to HENRY SMITH late of Somerset Co MD for £3000: JOHN HOPKINS late of Suss & CATY his wife gave power of atty to above three persons on 18 Mar 1779 to sell 2 tracts called "Stockleys Adventure" & "Marsh Point" both near s side Indian R, 200 ac, by Blackwater Br, adj JOHN WEST's fence, adj Broad Br. Wit ISRAEL HOLLAND, WILLIAM BELL. Ackn 20 Feb 1786.

234 Deed 3 May 1785. THOMAS FOWLER & MARTHEW his wife of Suss sell to LEVIN MILBFY yeoman of Suss for £432: tr in Broadkiln Hund, pt/o plantation where JOHN FOWLER died seized & devised to afsd THOMAS FOWLER by will, adj CLOWES' five Natch survey, a corner of WILLIAM CAHOONs land bought of afsd JOHN FOWLER, adj JOHN SHARP's land

adj JAMES PETTYJOHN's land, intersecting main Ditch at the savannah leading ne into the branch, adj a road, dividing line of LEVIN MILBEY & land RHOADS SHANKLAND bought of JOHN & THOS FOWLER, adj JOHN WRIGHT's survey, 293 ac land & swamp. Wit WILLIAM STEEL, RHOADS SHANKLAND. Wife examined by JNO WILTBANK, JOSHUA FISHER. Ackn 20 Feb 1786.

235 Conveyance bond 7 Mar 1772. WM DRAPER, CHARLES DRAPER, ALEXANDER DRAPER & JOSEPH DRAPER all gentlemen of Suss bound to JOHN CAMPBELL of Worcester Co gentleman in amount of £3800; excused if they make over deed to all land and marshes on which CHARLES DRAPER now dwells, also lands and marshes on which WILLIAM DRAPER now dwells with 27 ac woodland purchased by CHARLES DRAPER from THOMAS RILEY, being all the lands and marshes they own except 150 ac sold to JOHN HICKMAN by WM & ALEXANDER DRAPER, and all their right to island "Wynkoops Island" adj Cedar Cr, and the burying ground; reserved that JOSEPH DRAPER may put his creatures in the marsh pasture during his life, 1100 ac; the DRAPERS agree to convey same at any reasonable request after half the purchase money is paid & then bond will be void. Wit LEVIN CRAPPER, LITTLETON TOWNSEND, ALEXR DRAPER. Nov 19 1785 LITTLETON TOWNSEND testifies he witnessed WM DRAPER, CHARLES DRAPER, ALEXANDER DRAPER & JOSEPH DRAPER deliver this bond to CAPTN JOHN CAMPBELL & called on him and LEVIN CRAPPER to subscribe as evidences which they did. Feb term of court LITTLETON TOWNSEND appeared and swore to truth of above affidavit, 1786. Ackn 19 Feb 1786.

235 Conveyance bond 13 Sep 1759. SAMUEL TRUITT of govt of New Castle, Kent & Suss on Dillaware, planter, bound to JEHU TRUITT of county afsd in amt of £40; void if SAMUEL TRUITT convey deed to tr "Pole Cat Tract" concluding (sic) the whole unsold to MILMAN, at Court of Quarter Sessions at Lewes on first Tues Nov 1761. Wit JNO JOHNSON, ELIE PARKER. Jan 2 1760, JEHU TRUITT assigns bond to JONATHAN MILMAN; wit JOHN JOHNSON, THOS J? SINDALL. Feb 9 1786 afsd bond proved in court by oath of ELI PARKER; ackn 20 Feb 1786.

236 Deed 17 Dec 1785. SAMUEL HANDY planter of Suss sells to his brother JOHN HANDY planter of Suss for £50; tr "Handys Chance" in NW Fork Hund on nw side division line of SAMUEL & JOHN HANDY, adj "Millers Mistake", adj JOHN TENNENT's land, 75½ ac. Attys JOHN WILTBANK, PHILLIPS KOLLOCK. Wit HUGHIT CANNON, DANIEL POLK. Ackn 20 Feb 1786.

237 Deed 31 Dec 1785. MATTHEW WILSON clerk, PETER MARSH yeoman & POLLY his wife all of Lewes Town sell to PETER WHITE merchant of Lewes Town for £174: pt/o tr in Lewes & Rehoboth Hund formerly the maiden right of HESTER WILSON decd late wife of said MATTHEW WILSON & mother of the said POLLY MARSH, adj land of RHOADS SHANKLAND, on nw side road to Coolspring, adj ELIZABETH DRAIN's pt/o same tr, adj land of heirs of DAVID HALL ESQ decd, 58 ac plotted by RHOADS SHANKLAND 10 Mar 1785 from deed from DAVID GRAY to said MATTHEW WILSON in trust for POLLY MARSH late POLLY WILSON. Wit JOHN CLOWES, ELIZABETH DRAIN. Examr JOHN CLOWES. Ackn 8 Feb 1786. POLLY MARSH of full age, also called MARY MARSH. Atty Col HENRY NEILL. Ackn 20 Feb 1786.

238 Deed 9 Feb 1786. WILLIAM POLK ESQ of NW Fork Hund recovered judgment against DORMAN LOFLAND yeoman of Suss at turn of May 1786 for promise and assumption made and not performed; CORD HAZZARD then High Sheriff of Suss seized 100 ac from DORMAN LOFLAND in Slaughter Neck in Cedar Cr Hund but they were not worth the amount of the damages and remained unsold for want of buyers; then NEHEMIAH HILL of Suss recovered another judgment against DORMAN LOFLAND for £28+, & sheriff levied the amount on surplus of sale of afsd land should there be one; sheriff CORD HAZZARD sold lands to NUTTER LOFLAND for £45 so that WM POLK who had the prior judgment was paid, but he was removed from office before deed was made & NUTTER LOFLAND now petitions for deed which is granted by PETER FRETWELL High Sheriff for tr "White Oak Tract". Wit D HALL, WM DONE. Ackn 20 Feb 1786.

239 Deed 8 Feb 1786. JOHN CLOWES & CATHARINE YOUNG of Sussex sell to JOHN SHELDON
DORMON of Sussex for £500: tr on Mill Creek in Broadkill Hund 227 ac formerly owned
by JOHN FISHER who died intestate; Orphans Court divided it among heirs; heirs sold
to EDWARD LAY: 3 heirs owned 177 ac on sw side of Fishers Landing, another heir WM
FISHER was a minor not of age til 2 Nov 1736 at which time his part was conveyed
which was the remainder of the parcel: on se side of fork in branch of Mill Creek,
50 ac. EDWARD LAY died intestate & Orphans Court sold his land for debts to THOS
STATON (conveyed by ANN LAY adminr). Will of THOS STATON dated 11 Apr 1751 bequeathed to son HILL STATON; HILL STATON sold to DAVID CLOWES by deed of 4 Feb 1767. Will
of DAVID CLOWES dated 13 Apr 1770 bequeathed to dau HANNAH CLOWES but if HANNAH die
without issue then land to revert to DAVID CLOWES' brother JOHN CLOWES and 2 sisters
CATHARINE and MARY CLOWES equally divided. HANNAH CLOWES died a minor without issue
so land reverted to brother and sisters of DAVID as stated, MARY CLOWES now MARY
DORMON and CATHARINE CLOWES now CATHARINE YOUNG. Now JOHN CLOWES & CATHARINE YOUNG
sell their 2/3 to JOHN SHELDON DORMON. Wit JA'S FERGUS, ELIJAH RICKARDS. Ackn 10
Feb 1786.

240 Deed 10 Feb 1786. JAMES BEVINS of Slaughter Neck in Cedar Cr Hund, yeoman,
sells to WM ARNALL of Lewes, house carpenter, for £12+: lott in Lewes fronting Ship
Carpenters Street, 60' front &200' back, adj on ne lott formerly owned by ROBERT
PERRY but now owned by ADAH BOYD, adj on sw lott claimed by SARAH WILTBANK, originally
granted by Sussex court to NEHEMIAH FIELD who by deed of 1 Aug 1704 conveyed to JAMES
SANGSTER, who in his will dated 5 May 1705 devised to MARY his wife who afterward
married CORNELIUS BEVINS by whom she had issue: afsd JAMES BEVINS, her eldest son,
and CORNELIUS BEVINS; and she later died intestate so lott was divided with 2/3 to
JAMES BEVINS and 1/3 to CORNELIUS BEVINS. Wit PETER ROBINSON, EDMOND DICKERSON.
Ackn 10 feb 1786.

241 Deed 9 Nov 1785. JOHN COLLINS of Sussex to WILLIAM, JOHN & JOSIAH POLK sons of
JOHN POLK ESQ late of Broad Cr Hund decd. JOHN COLLINS acquired grant from Maryland
for 2 ac "Chance" and "Likewise" in 1776, included in his survey containing about 18
more acres called "Runing Meade", lying west of tr "Coxes Performance", 20 ac in
Broad Creek Hund near Broad Creek Bridge, owned by he & his late wife. In 1779 they
agreed to sell same 20 ac to JOHN POLK decd for £2500 then current money of Del of
the intended value of £125 specie, and JOHN POLK in his lifetime satisfied £81+
specie of the debt and his adminr has paid agreed upon £43+ with interest, so deed
is now given to JOHN POLK's heirs as stated above. POLLEY, JEANY & PEGGY COLLINS,
daus of afsd JOHN COLLINS release any right therein. Wit WM POLK, DANIEL HOSEA.
Ackn 10 Feb 1786.

241 10 Feb 1786. JAMES MURRAY yeoman of Susses, MARY his wife & MAGDALIN HOUSTON
wid of Sussex (MARY MURRAY & MAGDALIN HOUSTON daus of ROBT PRETTYMAN yeoman late of
Sussex decd) sell to ROBERT PRETTYMAN cordwainer of Sussex (son of afsd ROBERT PRET-
TYMAN decd) for £95 gold & silver coin: Will of ROBERT PRETTYMAN decd dated 22 Mar
1769 devised to son THOMAS PRETTYMAN 50 ac on head of bank of land adj Long Neck Rd
51 ac; to 2 sons WM & ROBERT PRETTYMAN rest of lands equally divided; eldest son WM
to have his part on the east side of land adj Back Creek; ROBT to have his part on
west side creek called Cabbin Neck. Afsd sons WM & THOS PRETTYMAN afterward died
intestate & without issue afsd lands descended to afsd ROBT PRETTYMAN, MARY MURRAY
late MARY PRETTYMAN, MAGDALIN HOUSTON & ELIZABETH PRETTYMAN in equal parts. MARY
& MAGDALIN now sell their shares to ROBERT. Wit D TRAIN, NATHL WALLER. Ackn 10
Feb 1786. WM POLK examr.

243 11 Feb 1786. JOSEPH DARBY adminr of ELIZABETH DARBY late of Suss, wid, decd,
and of unadministered chattels of SAMUEL DARBY yeoman late of Suss decd who in his
lifetime was adminr of afsd goods & chattels etc, sells to WM BICKNALL. Said JOSEPH
DARBY preferred petition to Orphans Ct on 8 Sept 1785 for sale of ELIZABETH DARBY's
undivided right in a resurvey granted to JOHN CREW and others to settle her debts:
land and marsh in Lewes & Rehoboth Hund, of which intestate sold the residence in

37

her lifetime. Sold to WM BICKNALL of Lewes & Rehoboth Hund on 14 Jan 1786 £15.
Wit JOHN COLLINS, D TRAIN. Ackn 11 Feb 1786.

243 Petition of JOHN CLOWES for leave of court to the present Sheriff to convey
land, 6 Mar 1786: at Aug term 1783 JOHN CLOWES obtained an attachment against
the estate of NEWNEZ? DEPUTY directed to RHOADS SHANKLAND ESQ High Sheriff of Sussex, & at 6 Nov term 1783 Sheriff returned that he had taken the lands of said
NEWNEZ? DEPUTY & appointed WM POLK, WM PERRY ESQ & THOS EVANS Gentleman auditors,
& at Aug term 1784 Sheriff returned that he had sold lands on 19 Jul last, 140
ac, to JOHN CLOWES ESQ for £55; other creditors of DEPUTY gave up claim in this
sale; and since SHANKLAND is no longer Sheriff petitioner implores court to order
new Sheriff PETER F WRIGHT ESQ to make a deed for afsd 140 ac.

244 Deed 7 Mar 1786. PETER FRETWELL WRIGHT High Sheriff of Sussex to JOHN CLOWES
ESQ of Suss, for £55: as above, NEWNEZ DEPUTY indebted to JOHN CLOWES for 40 shillings
and upwards, CLOWES obtains attachment of his land and when it is sold CLOWES buys
it , 140 ac in Broadkill Forrest. Inquiry shows DEPUTY is indebted to CLOWES for
£94, therefore Sheriff grants deed. Wit WM POLK, HAP HAZZARD. Ack 7 Mar 1786.

245 Deed 6 Mar 1786. ZADOC/ZADOCK SINDAL & REBECKA his wife yeoman sell to JOHN
WILLICE blacksmith, all of Suss, for £105: tr "Bashan" in Nanticoke Hund in the
Great Neck, surveyed 1756 for 530 ac at request of WARREN BURROUGHS by virtue of
Propretors warrant granted to JOHN PADMORE at Phila 14 Dec 1740, assigned by PADMORE
on 20 Nov 1749 to CHARLES PERRY, who on 12 Dec 1749 assigned same to JOHN TRUITT,
who on 14 Jul 1751 assigned same to WARRING BURROUGHS. WARREN BURROUGHS sold to
JOHN WHITE who sold 300 ac of the ne side to 3 of his sons. On 3 Mar 1773 JOHN
WHITE sold remainder 230 ac to afsd ZADOCK SINDAL & REBEKA his wife: adj land of
WM TALMAN, JAMES DUGLASS, THOMAS LAFFERTY & GEORGE WHITE, now to JOHN WILLIS. Wit
ROBT JONES, WM OWENS. Examr JOHN CLOWES states REBECCA SINDAL is aged about 32
years. Ackn 7 Mar 1786.

246 Deed of Common Recovery, 1 Feb 1786. THOMAS DAVIS (s/o HENRY) of Slaughter
Neck in Cedar Creek Hund yeoman sells to WM HARRISON yeoman of Lewes; PHILLIPS KOL-
LOCK ESQ of Sussex party of the third part. Afsd THOS DAVIS, for docking, barring
etc of all estates tail etc in the lands, hereditaments etc herein mentioned, ac-
knowledges receipt of £5 paid to him by afsd WILLIAM HARRISON & conveys tr of land
and marsh, 150 ac in Slaughter Neck, pt/o larger tr "Good Luck" or "Good Looke";
also tr of land & marsh 140½ ac betw Indian Br and Log House Branch, adj se side
of Log House Br in Slaughter Neck; also land & swamp 115 ac in Slaughter Neck pt/o
afsd larger tr "Bowmans Farms"; also 31 ac land & marsh in Slaughter Neck, pt/o
larger tr originally granted by patent to EDWARD FURLONG for 400 ac called "Edward
Furlongs Patent"; also 55 ac being one moiety of Persimons Island and of 25 ac addi-
tional marsh adj in Slaughter Neck; all of which lands were property of HENRY DAVIS
f/o afsd THOS DAVIS; agreed by all parties that afsd PHILLIPS KOLLOCK ESQ shall
sue out one or more Writs of Entry etc returnable at Lewes Court of Common Pleas on
____ Feb inst whereby the said KOLLOCK shall demand against said HARRISON all the said
tracts herein; and said HARRISON shall appear gratis and vouch to warranty the said
THOMAS DAVIS who shall likewise appear gratis and enter into warranty and vouch over
etc for the said PHILLIPS KOLLOCK to recover all the said tracts against WM HARRISON
and for him to recover in value against THOS DAVIS etc. Wit D TRAIN, JOSEPH DRAPER.
Ackn 7 Mar 1786.

247 Deed 7 Feb 1786. THOMAS DAVIS (s/o HENRY) of Slaughter Neck in Cedar Creek
Hund yeoman sells to JOHN METCALF yeoman of same place: HENRY DAVIS (the father)
late of Slaughter Neck left will devising his lands to his son afsd THOMAS DAVIS,
reference to above Deed of Recovery; one of the parcels referred to in Deed of Common
Recovery was pt/o larger tr "Bowmans Farms" 115 ac in Slaughter Neck adj land of
JOHN METCALF which was also pt/o "Bowmans Farms": now THOS DAVIS sells same for £115
to METCALF, adj small parcel 5+ ac sold by LUKE DAVIS late of Suss to HENRY DRAPER

late of Suss, adj land JOHN METCALF purchased of SAMUEL DRAPER; tr now conveyed containing 50 ac. Wit PETER ROBINSON, DAVD TRAIN. Ackn 7 Mar 1786.

248 Deed 6 Feb 1785. SAMUEL DRAPER ship carpenter of Suss sells to JOHN METCALF farmer of Suss for £475: AVERY DRAPER purch'd from ISAAC DRAPER on 26 Feb 1774 4 tr land and marsh, and in his will devised to his son SAMUEL DRAPER afsd the following: adj "Furlongs Pattent", adj CHARLES DRAPER,, adj Long Point Gutt, 124 ac "My Fortune"; adj Log House Br, adj "Furlongs pattent" & Long Point Gutt, 100 ac; 50 ac adj afsd 100 ac adj "My Fortune", adj land that was GABRIEL HENRY's, adj HENRY DRAPER's land, adj LUKE DAVIS' land, adj "Drapers Pattent"; also 5+ ac adj the above described lands, adj DRAPER's land, adj "My Fortune"; also 40 ac in Slaughter Neck a little to the west of the above described lands, adj a swamp, adj GABRIEL HENRY's land, adj Log House Br; 200 ac totally, in Slaughter Neck. Wit THOS DAVIS, AVERY DRAPER. Ackn 7 Mar 1786.

249 Deed 7 Mar 1786. ISAAC McDOWELL & NAOMI McDOWEL his wife of Suss sell to LEVIN ELLIS of Suss: ISAAC McDOWEL on 17 Jun 1769 was due by deed 45 ac pt/o tr originally surveyed for THOMAS WALLER called "The Round Savannah", then in Maryland but now in Suss, described in 2 deeds THOS WALLER to JOHN McDOWELL of 8 Feb 1759 and 20 May 1761, on record in Somerset Co. ISAAC McDOWELL now sells for £132+. Wit JONATHAN HEMMONS, W HARRISON. Ackn 7 Mar 1786.

250 Deed 7 Mar 1786. JOHN SMITH of Cedar Cr Hund sells to JEAN TRUITT & NANCY BLACK of same place: conveyance bond of 23 Mar 1770, JOHN SMITH to MITCHEL BLACK, tr in Slaughter Neck, and before execution of bond MITCHEL BLACK the obligee died, so now McDOWELL conveys to WILLIAM BLACK, JEAN TRUITT & NANCY BLACK, heirs of MITCHEL BLACK: adj ALEXANDER DRAPERs land & Wid WILLIAMS' land which REYNEAR WIL-LIAMS purch'd of DAVID THORNTON, 87 ac. Wit DANIEL ROGERS, JOSEPH MILLER. Ackn 7 Mar 1786.

251 Deed 18 Feb 1786. PETER HARMONSON yeoman of Suss sells to ADAM HALL taylor of Lewes for £27: one undivided moiety pt/o larger tr on s side of Lewes, formerly owned by JOHN HALL blacksmith of Lewes who died intestate -----(NB: clerk has en-tered dashes here)---the undivided estate of ELIZABETH OLIVER (late ELIZABETH HALL), one of the daus of JOHN HALL decd as by her deed of sale for same recorded in Lib N No 13 fol 110, Rolls Office. Purchase of PETER HARMONSON was of a division ordered by Orphans Court among heirs of JOHN HALL, assigned to HARMONSON by ELIZABETH OLIVER and ADAM HALL: adj JOHN RUSSELs Lott, adj JOHN HALLs part, 60' x 120'. Wit WALTER HUDSON, WM A PARKER. Ackn 7 Mar 1786.

251 Petition 9 Mar 1786. MARGARET KOLLOCK petitions court for deed from Sheriff: writ issued 3 Aug 1785 to CORD HAZZARD ESQ late High Sheriff to take lands of AARON & THOMAS PETTYJOHN & return to render to MARGARET KOLLOCK afsd for her debt. Lands duly sold to MARGARET KOLLOCK afsd on 18 Oct for £120, but HAZZARD died before is-suing deed, now requests deed of new SheriffPETER FRETWELL WRIGHT.

252 Deed 9 Mar 1786. PETER FRETWELL WRIGHT High Sheriff of Suss to MARGARET KOLLOCK. Reference to above petition, AARON & THOS PETTYJOHN owe MARGARET KOLLOCK £235+, Sheriff seized 2 parcels of their land in Broadkill Hund which MARGARET KOLLOCK bought; WRIGHT now grants deed: 2 parcels adj each other, on southern prong of Long Bridge Br, 250 ac, and pt/o larger tr adj first on nw, 50 ac. Wit ELIAS SHOCKLEY, JOSEPH MILLER, CHARLES DRAPER, W HARRISON. Ackn 9 Mar 1786.

253 Deed 10 Mar 1786. STEPHEN BAILY yeoman of Somerset Co & ELIZABETH his wife (she one of surviving issue of LEVI ROBINS of Suss yeoman decd sell to NATHANIEL HICKMAN yeoman of Suss: WILLIAM ALLEN late of Philadelphia decd sold on 14 Dec 1768 to LEVI ROBINS a tr in Suss sw of road from Lewes to Broadkiln Drawbridge, adj land sold by afsd WM ALLEN to PARKER ROBINSON (since decd), 262 ac, pt/o tr "Taylors

Hill", recorded in Sussex Rolls Office Lib K No 10 fol 35? (351?), of which LEVI
Robins sold 50 ac to JOSHUA BURTON; and another tr in Broadkiln Hund where LEVI
ROBINS dwelt at death, adj "Newcombs Barrens", Maidenhead Thickett", & "Collesons Choice", adj a glade of marsh, 140 ac, pt/o tr _____(nb left blank).
LEVI ROBINS died intestate leaving wid PHEBE, now w/o NATHANIEL HICKMAN, and
6 children: ELIZABETH afsd, JOSEPH, JOSIAH, CHARLES, MARY & JAMES, and 30 ac of
above land was sold to HAP HAZZARD for debts, that part where HAP HAZZARD now
dwells; PHEBE had her widows thirds of both tracts, 61 ac of first & 42 3/4 of
the last; JOSEPH the eldest son & JOSIAH the next eldest son died intestate &
without issue, so remainder except 30 ac sold & widows thirds went to afsd
ELIZABETH, CHARLES, MARY & JAMES, surviving issue, in equal parts. Orphans Court
directed RHOADS SHANKLAND, JOHN SHELDON DORMAN, JACOB HAZZARD, JOHN ABBOTT WAR-
RINGTON & MIERS CLARK to partition same. ELIZABETH's portion, tr adj PHEBE &
JAMES afsd, 78 ac, + tr adj PHEBE's thirds & glade of marsh, 9 ac, totalling 87
ac, assigned to STEPHEN BAILY & ELIZABETH his wife afsd. And PHEBE died so that
ELIZABETH received ¼ of the lands PHEBE had received as her widows thirds, to
wit ¼ of 102 ac. Now STEPHEN BAILY & ELIZABETH his wife sell for £160 all the
lands described above that belonged to ELIZABETH. Examr JOHN CLOWES: ELIZABETH
of the full age of 21 years. Wit: DAVD TRAIN, PETER F WRIGHT. Ackn 10 Mar 1786.

256 AWARD BETWEEN JAMES MILLER, WILLIAM RICKARDS & LUKE TOWNSEND, 17 Jan 1785.
Greetings from LEVIN DERICKSON, WM JORDAN HALL, JACOB ROGERS, JOHN STEPHEN HILL
& ISRAEL HOLLAND (& signed by them). Whereas divers controversies and disputes
have lately arisen between JAMES MILLER of Suss of the one part and WM RICK-
ARDS & LUKE TOWNSEND of Suss of second part, regarding boundary of tr "Cow
Quarter", parties bound themselves to arbitration on 6 Nov 1784 in amt of £800.
Arbiters (abovenamed) determine bounder line & describe it: tr adj the Old Ditch,
adj Assawoman Bay, adj JONES RICKARDS line.

257 Deed of Gift 13 Apr 1786. WINIFRED BAILY of Pilot Town, seamstress daughter & only heiress of JOSEPH BAILY pilot of same place decd, gives to SARAH LUNDY
seamstress of same place, for love and special request of her decd father: lott
on Pilot Town Bank, with 60' on Lewes Creek, 250' deep, adj land of JOHN MAUL
where his dwelling stands, being pt/o lands JOSEPH BAILY owned when he died intestate. Atty JOHN RUSSELL. Wit JNO WILTBANK, JOHN MAULL. Ackn 6 May 1786.

257 Deed 3 May 1786. WILLIAM GREEN mariner of Lewes sells to WILLIAM BICKNALL/
BIGNALL yeoman of Lewes for £12: by an award lately signed to settle a boundary
dispute between afsd WM GREEN & EDWARD CRAIG of Lewes & Rehoboth Hund, 4¼ ac adj
the plantation of the said EDWARD became vested in WM GREEN, GREEN now sells to
BICKNALL, land in Lewes Rehoboth Hund, adj the Mill Road, adj "Bailys Patent",
adj MARSH's pretended line of "Timber Neck". Wit JOSEPH MILLER, LUKE WATTSON.
Ackn 3 May 1786.

258 Deed 29 Apr 1786. HENRY SMITH of Suss sells to ARCHABALD/ARCHABLE W SPAREN
of Kent Co Del for £200: tr on s side Indian R, pt/o 2 tracts, near Blackwater
Meeting House, formerly purch'd by WM HOLLAND from HAMPTON HOPKINS & sold by
HOLLAND to SACKER MUMFORD, & sold by MUMFORD to HENRY SMITH; adj road from sea-
board to Blackwater Meeting House, adj road north to the beverdam, adj
land of JOHN MASSEY JUNR purchased of AVERY MORGAN: "Stockleys Adventure" &
"Marsh Point", adj HENRY SMITH's property, on n side of road from seaside to
Blackwater Meeting House. Attys ISRAEL HOLLAND, DAVID TRAIN. Wit MILES HARNEY,
JNO MASSEY JUNR, JOHN EVENS. Ackn 3 may 1786.

259 Deed 16 Mar 1786. EBENEZER EVENS/EVANS yeoman of Suss to ISRAEL HOLLAND
ESQ of Suss: EBENEZER EVANS had, by patent from Maryland of 22 Apr 1773, tr "Bear
Trap Ridge" formerly in Worcester Co but now in Suss, which he sold by bond to
WILLIAM HOLLAND of county & state afsd on 16 Apr 1773, £120 current money of
Maryland, 122½ ac. WM HOLLAND died leaving ISRAEL HOLLAND his heir. WM HOLLAND

Attys GEORGE MITCHELL, Esqr, RHOADS SHANKLAND Esqr, PHILLIPS
KOLLOCK Esqr and Mr. DAVID TRAIN. Wit: WILLIAM LOCKWOOD, JOHN R.
HAZZARD, ELIHU BREDELL. Ackn 3 May 1786.

259 Deed BENJAMIN HUDSON from PETER FRETWELL WRIGHT, High
Sheriff of Suss. Whereas THOMAS EMORY of the Feb term 1785
recovered a judgment agnst BENJAMIN TRUITT of Suss, yeoman, for
150 pounds the sheriff seized a tr in Cedar Creek Hund, Suss, 101
ac and caused an inquisition thereon by two men who determined
the debt could be paid from 7 yrs use of the property. Whereas
ANN CATHARINE HOLMES of the Feb term 1785 recovered a judgment
agnst said TRUITT for sum of 103 pounds, 2 shillings, 2 pence.
Land was sold to BENJAMIN HUDSON for 30 pounds, 10 shillings, 101
ac - adj line along JOSEPH TRUITT's land, pt of a larger tr containing 200 ac originally granted unto BENJAMIN TRUITT Senr.,
warrant dated 9 Jun 1737 lying within the bounds of the manor
Warninghurst (?) and called Spittle Field. Ackn 3 May 1786.

261 Deed 3 May 1786. THOMAS MARVEL, Junr of Suss, yeoman from
MATHIAS JONES, Suss, yeoman. 200 pounds, parcel of land on s
side of branch called Green Branch in Nanticoke Hund, Suss, pt of
a larger tr called Support to Double Purchase and the remaining
part thereof being pt/o large tr lately taken up by GEORGE ADAMS
and by him conveyed to afsd MATHIAS JONES. 200 ac. Wit: W.
HARRISON. Ackn 3 May 1786.

261 Deed 28 Oct 1785. ZADOC CRAPPER, Suss, from SOLOMON
HAMBLIN and ELISABETH his wife, Wor Co, MD, for 131 pounds, 11
shillings, 6 pence, parcel in Suss, Cedar Creek Neck on Delaware,
being his pt/o the land falleth to SOLOMON HAMBLIN by the death
of his father, which said land was conveyed from JOHN READ and
MATHEW his wife unto WILLIAM DRAPER on 6 May 1773, it being pt/o
a larger tr by patent to JOHN HOMS and by him conveyed 8 Aug 1770
unto JOHN READ. 117 1/2 ac in the whole, SOLOMON HAMBLIN's part
being 1/2 of that. Attys: THOS. BATSON, Esqr or JOHN EVANS.
Wit: JOHN W. BATSON, JOHN CRAPPER. Ackn 28 Oct 1785.

262 Deed 26 Apr 1786. JONES RICKARDS from Wm EVANS (son of
Walter) admr of MICHAEL ROBINSON, Suss. Parcel on n side of a
creek in Suss beginning at a corner post near point called Sloop
Point, runs to a beginning post of Rickard's Choner(?), 12 ac,
being pt/o the property of WILLIAM ROBINSON decd, the father of
said MICHAEL ROBINSON, decd, and by virtue of the Orphans Court
on 8 Feb last. 12 pounds. Atty GEORGE MITCHELL, Esqr, JOHN
AYDELOTT,Bricklayer, WILLIAM LOCKWOOD. Wit: JOHN EVANS, MATTHIAS
AYDELOTT, ISAAC TUNNELL. Ackn 26 Apr 1786.

263 Deed 3 May 1786. MATTHIAS JONES, Suss, bricklayer, from
ABRAHAM ADAMS, Suss, planter, parcel in Nanticoke Hund on sw side
of branch called Green Branch being pt/o a larger tr lately taken
up by sd ADAMS beginning at corner post being the northernmost
corner of said JONES land whereon he now dwells on nw side of
Green Branch running along a division line between said JONES and
ELIAS JOHNSON to a oak in the line of ISAAC MASSEY's Resurvey.
161 ac. Wit: JOHN GIBBINS, THOS. GRAY. Ackn 3 May 1786.

263 Deed 14 Apr 1786. GABRIEL LOFLAND, Suss, yeoman, from DAVID
WARREN of New Jersey, yeoman, a parcel in Cedar Creek Hund, being

pt/o larger tr surveyed and taken up by JOHN WEBB. 32 ac, 51 3/4 perches. 25 pounds. Wit: JOSEPH TRUITT, NATHAN CLIFTON. Atty JOHN HUDSON.

264 Deed 14 Apr 1786. JOHN HUDSON son of Wm, Suss, yeoman, from DAVID WARREN, New Jersey, yeoman, a parcel of land in forrest of Cedar Creek Hund being pt/o larger tr of land surveyed for JOHN WEBB by virtue of a warrant which said parcel begins at stone on side of the Old Draper Road. 36 ac, 12 perches. Ackn 14 Apr 1786. Wit: JOSEPH TRUITT, GABRIEL LOFLAND.

264 Deed 14 Apr 1786. NATHAN CLIFTON, Suss, yeoman, from DAVID WARREN, New Jersey, yeoman, tr in Cedar Creek Hund, being pt/o larger tr surveyed by JOHN WEBB by virtue of a warrant beginning at a stone bounder of GABRIEL LOFLAND and JOSEPH LAIN. 47 ac, 2 perches. 67 pounds. Atty JOHN LAWS, Esq. and JOHN HUDSON. Wit: JOSEPH TRUITT, GABRIEL LOFLAND. Ackn 14 Apr 1786.

265 Deed 14 Apr 1786. Bennet WARREN, Suss, yeoman, from DAVID WARREN, New Jersey, yeoman, for 25 pounds, parcel in forrest of Cedar Creek, being pt of larger tr surveyed and taken up by JOHN WEBB by virtue of a warrant and JOHN WEBB sold the same to DAVID WARREN. 22 ac, 34 1/2 perches. Atty JOHN LAWS, Esqr and JOHN HUDSON son of WILLIAM. Wit: JOSEPH TRUITT, GABRIEL LOFLAND. Ackn 14 Apr 1786.

265 Deed 14 Apr 1786. ALEXANDER WARREN, Suss, from DAVID WARREN, New Jersey, yeoman. Parcel in Forrest of Cedar Creek Hund, being pt/o larger tr surveyed for JOHN WEBB by virtue of a warrant, 35 ac 27 perches. 37 pounds. Attys JOHN LAW and JOHN HUDSON son of WILLIAM. Wit: JOSEPH TRUITT, GABRIEL LOFLAND. Ackn 14 Apr 1786.

266 Deed 29 Apr 1786. ZADOC POWELL, Worcester Co, MD, from BAILY HICKMAN, Suss, planter, and his wife MARY, for 110 pounds, a tr called Drusile, beginning a marked oak standing at a piece of flat ground near the head of a tr surveyed for Capt. JOSEPH MILLER of the s side of a plantation whereon SAMUEL GRAY lived on on e side of a road leading from Capt. MILLER to Cedar Neck - 55 ac. Atty THOS. BATSON Esq. Wit: STEPHEN STYER, JACOB ROGERS, RACKLIFFE CONNER. Ackn 29 Apr 1786.

267 Deed 30 Mar 1786. TRUIT THOMPSON, Suss, from SOLOMON CARY and NANCY his wife, Suss, 45 ac, being pt/o a resurvey made to a tr called First Choice granted to JOHN THOMPSON by the Lord Proprietary of MD, which resurvey is called Second Choice, in Dagsburry hund, on a branch called Comforts Branch that issueth out of Shealo's Branch, which empties itself into the head of Indian R, the original tr and resurvey taken and secured by afsd JOHN THOMPSON ca. 1760. JOHN THOMPSON by his will dated 27 May 1768 bequeathed said 45 ac to his grandson, afsd SOLOMON CARY and whereon said SOLOMON CARY now resides. 44 pounds. Atty WILLIAM NEWBOLD, JOHN THOROGOOD, JOSEPH MELSON. Wit: PETER HALL, SIMON KOLLOCK. Ackn 30 Mar 1786.

267 Deed 3 May 1786. JOSEPH DARBY from WILLIAM BICKNALL of Lewes and Rehobeth Hund, Suss, same Hund, yeoman. Whereas ELIZABETH DARBY late of the same place, widow, decd, in her

lifetime was seized and possessed of undivided right in a Resurvey granted unto JOHN CREW and others for a qty of land and marsh
in Lewes and Rehoboth Hund, pt/o which she sold in her lifetime,
the residue thereof she died intestate, seized and possessed of.
JOSEPH DARBY adminr of sd ELIZABETH DARBY unadministered by
SAMUEL DARBY late of the sd hund, yeoman, decd, did sell the
residue for 15 pounds as recorded in Orphans court. Ackn 3 May
1786. Wit: JOS. MILLER, JOHN WALKER.

268 Deed 25 Mar 1786. JOSEPH MELSON from WILLIAM PIPPER and
ELIZABETH his wife, Suss, tr in Broad Creek Hund, 40 ac, pt/o
larger tr of 150 ac called Third Choice which was granted by Lord
Proprietary of MD to JOHN PHILLIPS patented on 8 Apr 1755, on w
side of Wimbesocom Branch and near the head thereof. JOHN
PHILLIPS by his will bequeathed sd 150 ac to his two daus, RACHEL
WINDSOR and ELIZABETH PHILLIPS, the land on the nw side of said
branch to RACHEL and remainder on the s and e side of said branch
to ELIZABETH wife of afsd WILLIAM PIPPER, being the part the said
PHILLIPS resided on at the time of his death and the part whereon
the said WILLIAM PIPPER now dwells and is supposed to be 40 ac.
The remainder on nw side being before sold to said JOSEPH MELSON
by said RACHEL WINDSOR and now in his possession. Attys SIMON
KOLLOCK, WOOLSEY BURTON. Ackn 25 Mar 1786. Wit: ROBERT HOPKINS,
JOHN MELSON.

269 Deed 26 Apr 1786. THOMAS HARNEY from AVERY MORGAN, Suss,
for 40 pounds. - 17 ac being pt/o tr granted to sd. AVERY
MORGAN by his father and known as Stockleys Adventure. Wit:
LITTLETON TOWNSEND, JONATHAN NOTTINGHAM, LEVI COLLINS. Attys
ISAAC WEST, WILLIAM LOCKWOOD, SAMUEL DIRICKSON and JAQUESH
HUDSON. Ackn 3 May 1786.

269 Deed 29 Apr 1786. JAQUESH HUDSON, Suss, planter, from JOHN
EVANS and CATHARINE his wife of Muddy Neck, Suss, 5000 pounds, tr
called Hopkins Discovery, s side of Indian R near head of Black
Water Creek that issues out of the said Indian R. JOSIAH HOPKINS
and JOHN HOPKINS did obtain right unto this tract, 360 ac, JOHN
HOPKINS deceased w/o making a will and by the laws of MD the tr
fell to his eldest son, EZEKIEL. On 23 Sep 1778 EZEKIEL HOPKINS
and his wife SARAH sold the land not already sold or taken away
by elder surveys, which is estimated to be 170 ac to said JOHN
EVANS. Attys ISRAEL HOLLAND, SAMUEL DIRICKSON and GEORGE PARKER
and WILLIAM LOCKWOOD. Wit: LITTLETON TOWNSEND, WATSON WHARTON.
Ackn 3 May 1786.

270 Deed 27 Apr 1786. JAQUESH HUDSON, farmer, Suss, from AVERY
MORGAN, and his wife HANNAH, Suss, for 100 pounds, pt/o tr called
Marsh Point Enlarged, on s side of Indian R between two branches
known as Blackwater Branch and Broad Branch, each issuing out of
said Indian R beginning at the second bounder of a tr called
Stockley Adventure adj lines of a mill pond and along the lines
of the mill lot now belonging to HARVEY WHARTON, 43 3/3 (?) ac.
Said land was taken up in a Resurvey by AVERY MORGAN, father to
above said AVERY MORGAN which by his will bequeathed said land to
his son AVERY MORGAN. Attys ISRAEL HOLLAND, SAMUEL DIRICKSON,
GEORGE PARKER, WILLIAM LOCKWOOD. Wit: LITTLETON TOWNSEND,
JONATHAN NOTTINGHAM, LEVI COLLINS. Ackn 3 May 1786.

271 3 Nov 1785. Deed JOSIAH MITCHELL, Suss, from JOSHUA ROGERS,
Wor Co, MD for 300 pounds, trs called Mattapany and Addition to
Brotherhood, both trs formerly lying in Wor Co, MD, but now in
Suss. on the Seaboard side near the head of Saint Martins Sound.
Mattapany beginning at a point on n side of Herring Creek near a
corner tree of tr formerly surveyed for ABRAHAM WHITE called
Happy Entrance, 300 ac. The other tract, Addition to Brotherhood, on the s side of Mattapany, north of the creek, originally
granted unto afsd JOSHUA ROGERS for 20. Wit: THOS. BATSON,
EDWARD DINGLE. Attys WILLIAM DONE. Certified that the land in
dispute with heirs of WILLIAM WOODCRAFT and said JOSHUA ROGERS
took possession and claimed it as his own and executed the within
deed and left HINACY LAWRANCE in possession of the premises at
the house of ANN ACKER and also said JOSHUA ROGERS entered on
that pt/o the conveyed land called Mattapany which is now in the
possession of AUTHUR WILLIAMS and at the front door of the
mansion house the said JOSHUA ROGERS there claimed it as his
property. Wit: THOS. BATSON, EDWARD DINGLE. Attys WILLIAM DONE.
Ackn 4 May 1786.

272 Bond for conveyance of land, JOSHUA RIGGIN from CHARLES
RIGGIN, Suss, planter. 300 pounds. If the bounded CHARLES
RIGGIN shall and do at the request of said JOSHUA RIGGIN 150 ac
in a neck of land called Wimbo Sockom Neck in two tracts, one
called Walters Land, 100 ac on afsd, the other called Pusle, 50
ac excepting the dwelling house and 75 ac during the natural life
of said CHARLES and his wife ANNE. Wit: JOHN COLLINS, TEGUE
RIGGIN. Ackn 5 May 1786.

272 Deed 5 May 1786. ELISHA LONG, Suss, yeoman, from WM. POLK,
Esq, Suss, exr of will of EDWARD VAUGHAN late of Suss, Gentleman,
decd, tr formerly lying in Som Co, now in Suss, patented by Lord
Proprietary of MD on 24 Feb 1767 unto JONATHAN VAUGHAN and Company, 137 ac known as Stony Branch or Charles Tindals Branch.
Said JONATHAN VAUGHAN died intestate in Wor Co, possessed of this
land, leaving ANN his widow and EDWARD VAUGHAN his eldest son and
sole heir. The land is now situate in Nanticoke Hund, Suss.
Said ANN VAUGHAN and EDWARD VAUGHAN on 29 Dec 1779 for 20,000
pounds bound themselves to ELISHA LONG; however EDWARD VAUGHAN
died before conveying the land. Said EDWARD VAUGHAN left a will
appointing above named WILLIAM POLK exr of land adj land of
SAMUEL TINDAL and lands of JOHN SMITH and also adj lands of
ELISHA LONG. Wit: D. HALL, D. TRAIN. Ackn 5 May 1786.

274 Deed 5 May 1786. Allin SMITH, Suss, shipwright, from MARTHA
MUNKS widow of ISAAC MUNKS decd, Suss, for 100 pounds, parcel in
Broadkill Hund, being pt/o a larger tr called Griffiths Pond
Land, surveyed and laid off to GRIFFITH JONES, decd and after was
the property of ISAAC JONES who died intestate and after division
made on the said ISAAC JONES intestate lands according to law the
above piece of land became the property of above said MARTHA
MUNKS. 175 ac Wit: D. HALL, W. HARRISON. Ackn 5 May 1786.

274 Deed 9 May 1786. NOAH COLLINS, Suss, planter, from
ELIZABETH COLLINS widow, LEVI COLLINS and MARY COLLINS wife to
the said LEVI COLLINS of Suss, for 120 pounds, tr called Chance,
being part whereon Blackwater Meeting house stands. 60 ac Wit:

JOHN EVANS, JOHN LIGGET, ISAAC WEST. Attys PHILLIP KOLLOCK.
Ackn 7 Jun 1786.

275 Deed 7 Jun 1786. JOHN ROWLAND from MARY BURTON, widow, admr
of WM. BURTON, decd., late of Broadkiln Hund, yeoman, who died
intestate. Whereas GEORGE WALKER late of Suss by Indenture dated
8 Nov 1780, recorded in Book M.N. 12, folio 371, conveyed to
WILLIAM BURTON, a grist mill on the Coldspring Branch in Broadkiln Hund and 2 ac on the w (or nw) side and 1/2 ac on the e or
se side of the branch. Said 2 ac on the w pt/o a large tr called
Abrahams Lott, the two acs among other things seized and taken in
execution at the suit of PETER MARSH and sold at public vendue by
RHOADS SHANKLAND then high Sheriff as estate of WM. PRETTYMAN,
late of Suss decd, and afterward conveyed unto said GEORGE WALKER
by PETER ROBINSON by indenture dated 29 Feb 1772, recorded in
Liber L.W. 11, folio 201. And whereas the said WILLIAM BURTON
afterwards died intestate seized of the Mill and lands thereunto
and w/o personal estate sufficient to pay his debts an order of
the Orphans Court on application of afsd MARY BURTON admrs, was
made to sell said real property. Sold for 65 pounds. Wit: DAVID
TRAIN, JOSEPH STOKLY. Ackn 7 Jun 1786.

276 Mortgage 30 Jan 1786. PHILLIPS RUSSEL, town of Lewes,
house carpenter, from MOSES ALLEN, town of Lewes, pilot, for 60
pounds, 5 shillings, 3 pence, mortgages parcel of land in Angola
and Indian R Hund, 7 miles from Lewes adj the w side of the
Indian R Road, 300 ac, being the same devised to said MOSES ALLEN
by his grandfather JOHN ALLEN, decd, and the greater part thereof
by his uncle JOSEPH ALLEN, decd, by their last wills and testa-
ments. Wit: JOHN RUSSEL, ELIZABETH RUSSEL. Ackn 8 Jun 1786. On
8 Nov 1786 appeared RUTH RUSSELL admr of PHILLIPS RUSSEL and ackn
to have received full satisfaction from MOSES ALLEN the mortgager
and thereby releases and quit claims.

277. Deed. JOSEPH STOCKLEY from MARY BURTON admr of WM. BURTON,
Broadkiln, decd. Whereas there is a tr on nw side of Coldspring
Branch in Broadkiln Hund called Abraham Lott, originally granted
by patent from proprietary of Penn., to ABRAHAM POTTER for 300 ac
which after sundry conveyances and descents in law became the
right and property of ROBERT CRAIG late of Suss, who died seized
thereof intestate, leaving ISAAC HAMILTON CRAIG, JOHN CRAIG, MARY
WHITE (then the wife of JACOB WHITE) and RUTH then the wife of
PARKER ROBINSON, and a grandson ROBERT CRAIG, a minor, son of
ALEXANDER CRAIG, decd, to whom the lands descended and whereas
HAMILTON CRAIG, JOHN CRAIG, JACOB WHITE and MARY his wife by deed
of sale of 5 Aug 1763, conveyed their rights to PARKER ROBINSON
who preferred a petition to the Orphans Court to have land
evaluated. This was done by commission of WILLIAM STEPHENSON,
SAMUEL ROWLAND and PETER PARKER who reported the value of the
land was 300 pounds. Whereas PARKER ROBINSON and his wife RUTH
on 6 Dec 1774 sold to WILLIAM MATHEWS for 379 ac exclusve of 2 ac
condemned for a mill. See L.N. 11, folio 460. WILLIAM MATHEWS
and his wife ANN sold on 24 Feb 1776 (See M.N. 12, folio 76) to
above named WILLIAM BURTON who afterward died intestate. MARY
BURTON appointed admr 1785 and applied to sell sufficient of the
land to pay debts of decd. On 17 Dec 1785 JOSEPH STOCKLEY of
Suss, Blacksmith, purch 148 ac for 170 pounds, 4 s Wit: HAP
HAZZARD. Ackn 7 Jun 1786.

278 Deed 8 Jun 1786. JOSEPH CANNON, Suss, yeoman, from PETER
FRETWELL WRIGHT, High Sheriff, Suss., tr called Waller's Lane,
100 ac in Broad Creek Hund, originally granted by patent by
proprietary of MD, to THOMAS WALLER, 5 Aug 1755 beginning at a
tree in the Neck called Wimbosockam Neck and whereas there is one
other tr called Pusle in the hund afsd on the e side of the
Nanticoke R at the head of Broad Creek in Wimbosockam Neck
originally surveyed by virtue of a warrant to JOHN CALDWELL who
assigned the said land, the certificate of survey thereof unto
PHILLIP KING to whom it was confirmed by the Proprietor of MD by
virtue of patent dated 10 Jun 1734. This tr begins at a bounder
of tr formerly laid out for ALEXANDER ADAMS, 75 ac. And whereas
CHARLES RIGGON, late of Worc Co, planter, on 29 Oct 1773 being
seized of 100 ac called Wallers Lane and also 50 ac, pt/o afsd tr
called Pusle by his bond was held bound to JOSHUA RIGGON of the
same place. And afterward CHARLES and his wife ANN both died
whereby the said JOSHUA RIGGEN died, seized of the land under the
condition of the bond afsd mentioned. Suss court ordered sale of
land now in the hands of ISABELLA RIGGEN admr of JOSHUA RIGGIN,
Suss, yeoman, decd, to cover debts owed to PETER and ISAAC
WICKOFF. Sale sold by High Sheriff PETER FRETWELL WRIGHT to
JOSEPH CANNON. Ackn 8 Jun 1786.

280 Deed 8 Jun 1786. ROBERT PRETTYMAN, cordwainer, from WILLIAM
COLEMAN, town of Lewes, Silversmith. Whereas Sir EDMOND ANDREWS
by patent dated 15 Jan 1675 granted to JOHN KIPSHAVEN then of
Suss parcel of 69 ac on s side of the town of Sussex [Lewes?]
which sd KIPSHAVEN on 90 Feb 1680 assign to WILLIAM CLARK then of
sd co who on 12 Apr 1681 assigned his right to land to Capt.
NATHANIEL WALKER who by his will devised to Major WILLIAM DYER
who died seized thereof. WILLIAM DYER his son and exr by his
deed of sale dated 5 Jun 1699 sold to THOMAS FENWICK who on 29
Jan 1707 conveyed all that parcel thereof joining to the meeting
house lott extending in front 90 feet unto JOHN KIPSHAVEN and by
his will dated 2 Mar 1707/8 devised to his son in law, EDWARD
STRECTHER and ROBERT CLIFTON all that parcel of land, pt/o the
above mentioned 69 ac between JOHN HEPBURN lot afsd and JACOB
KOLLOCK's fence with the half of the Savanah near Lewes Town; the
said EDWARD STRETCHER and MARY his wife, ROBERT CLIFTON and ANNE
his wife by their deed of sale dated 1 Nov 1715 sold the lands so
devised to NATHANIEL HALL who by his deed of sale dated 16 Aug
1731 a pt/o the land adj lot afsd conveyed as afsd unto afsd JOHN
HEPBURN containing 90 square perches and 1/3 of a perch of land
unto HANNAH, MARY, JOHN and PETER ADAMS joint tenants. And the
JOHN ADAMS who hath survived HANNAH, MARY and PETER ADAMS, by his
deed of sale of 4 July 1782 sold same to WILLIAM COLEMAN. 11
pounds 5 shillings. Wit: D. TRAIN, NATHANIEL BOWMAN. Ackn 12
Jun 1786.

281 Deed 9 Jun 1786. JOSEPH WALTON from PETER FRETWELL WRIGHT,
High Sheriff. There is a tr in Cedar Creek Neck in Cedar Creek
Hund, 101 ac, being pt/o a tr called Harts Tract, 75 ac whereof
was conveyed by WILLIAM MANLOVE late of Kent Co, Del, and PARIS
CHIPMAN of said co and MARGARET his wife unto JOHN and JONATHAN
WHEELER, both late of Suss, yeomen, and to the remaining title to
25 ac of the 101 ac then being in KERIAH WHEELER late of Suss
afsd who afterward died intestate whereas title to said 25 ac
descended to afsd WILLIAM MANLOVE, MARGARET CHIPMAN, JOHN and

JONATHAN WHEELER and MARY WHEELER, to the said WILLIAM MANLOVE
two shares or two undivided sixth parts. An whereas JOHN WHEELOR
and JAMES CALDWELL junr who married MARY WHEELOR, and said MARY,
sold on 3 Oct 1774 to JOHN PLOWMAN then of Suss, bricklayer,
their rights to said land. And whereas there is one other parcel
of land lying Cedar Creek Neck of 96 ac joining above described
land, being pt/o a larger tr called Harts Tract, or called ROBERT
HART's nine hundred acre Tract, being the the same which GEORGE
BLACK and SARAH his wife sold to JOHN PLOWMAN 5 Nov 1771 and
whereas said JOHN PLOWMAN was seized and possessed when he died
intestate and whereas THOMAS BOWMAN an assignee of WILLIAM DRAPER
lately in the court of Common Pleas recovered judgment agnst
JAMES JOHNSON and MARY his wife late MARY PLOWMAN admr of JOHN
PLOWMAN (who had incurred a debt of 467 pounds, 6 shillings, 6
pence). And whereas THOMAS BOWMAN assignee of WILLIAM DRAPER
lately recovered judgment agnst JAMES JOHNSON and MARY his wife;
and whereas the sheriff had seized a parcel of land of 129 ac
late the estate of JOHN PLOWMAN. On 27 Dec 1785 the land was
sold for 260 pounds to JOHN WALTON. Whereas CORD HAZZARD was
removed from his said office of high Sheriff w/o having made or
executed any deed. Wit: D. TRAIN, MARY TRAIN. Ackn 9 Jun 1786.
[In subsequent action Walton petitioned to have property properly
conveyed.]

284 Deed of Gift 9 Aug 1786. TRANY and RACHAL JONES from
MATHIAS JONES. MATHIAS JONES, bricklayer, Suss, for 5 shillings.
To TRANEY JONES 1 cow and calv, 1 bed and furniture, 1 black
walnut desk, 1 chest, half a dozen new pewter plates and 3
chairs. To RACHEL JONES 1 negro girl named WINEFRED, 1 cow and
calf, 1 bed and furniture, 1 chest and 3 chairs.

285 Deed 11 Aug 1786. JOHN COLLINS from PETER FRETWELL WRIGHT,
High Sheriff, for 52 pounds. Whereas JOHN COLLINS of Broad Creek
Hund of the term of August 1785 recovered a judgment agnst ROBERT
HOUSTON adminr of JONATHAN BELL late of Suss for 150 pounds. The
sheriff seized 287 ac, pt/o a tr called Cypress Swamp whereon the
sd JONATHAN BELL formerly dwelt, 100 ac pt/o tr called Partnership originally granted to said BELL and JOSEPH COLLINS by the
proprietary of MD, the whole of which (25 ac) Bell was entitled
to by virtue of his surviving said COLLINS, in Broad Creek Hund
on n side of main branch of Broad Creek; also the unexpired term
of a lease which said BELL had in one moiety of SAMUEL SCROGINS'
sawmill and utensils - which said trs contained in the whole 412
ac. Wit: ISAAC HENRY, D. HALL. Ackn 11 Aug 1786.

286 Deed 3 Sep 1785. JOSEPH TURPIN, planter, Suss, from HENRY
FLOWERS, bricklawyer, Suss. In consideration of monies spent as
follows: 1 pound, 15 shillings advanced towards building a
sawmill on Muddy Creek, a small branch of Nanticoke R at the
place where JOHN FLOWERS decd formerly had a grist mill. Plus 50
pounds by JOSEPH TURPIN - for 1 ac pt of Cannons Regulation in
Suss, adj JOSHUA TULL's land and near Turpin's land and at the
side of the Old Road that formerly led from Capt. JAMES BROWN to
Cannon's Ferry, and road that leads from Northwest fork Bridge to
Cannons Ferry, near Turpin's smith shop. Attys JOHN RODNEY, Esq.
and ANDERSON PARKER, Esqr. Wit: JEREMIAH CANNON, THOMAS CANNON.
Ackn 31 July 1786.

287 Deed 5 Jul 1786. ROBERT PRETTYMAN, cordwainer, son of afsd ROBERT PRETTYMAN, from JAMES MURRAY, yeoman, of Suss, and his wife MARY, late MARY PRETTYMAN, the d/o ROBERT PRETTYMAN late of Suss, decd, for 10 pounds. ROBERT PRETTYMAN by his will dated 22 Mar 1769 devised to his son THOMAS 50 ac near Long Neck Road, and to sons WILLIAM PRETTYMAN and ROBERT PRETTYMAN the residue of his lands. Eldest son WILLIAM to have his part on the e side of the land, binding on Back Creek and son ROBERT to have his part on w side of land binding on the Cabbin Creek. If WILLIAM or ROBERT died w/o issue then ROBERT, MARY MURRAY late MARY PRETTYMAN, MAGDALENE HOUSTON and ELIZABETH PRETTYMAN to receive property in equal portions and if ELIZABETH died w/o issue the other three to receive her share. And whereas the said ELIZABETH did die intestate, unmarried and w/o issue and whereby her said undivided right descended to ROBERT, MARY and MAGDALEN. Attys Phillip KOLLOCK and WILLIAM HARRISON of Lewes. Ackn 2 Aug 1786.

288 Deed 10 Aug 1786. Deed JESSE GRIFFIN, Suss, yeoman, from JOHN COLLINS of Broad Creek Hund, Gentleman, for 97 pounds, 10 shillings, 194 ac, a tr in Nanticoke Hund on Tusiky [Tusseky] Branch called Cronys Folly originally granted by patent on 20 Dec 1741 by the proprietary of MD unto JAMES CRONEY beginnning on n side of Tusiky Branch that issueth out of the e side of northeast fork of Nanticoke R and on e side of CRONEY's Dwelling plantation. Wit: JONATHAN BOYCE, JAMES BLYCE. Ackn 10 Aug 1786.

288 Deed 8 Jun 1786. RATLIFF POYNTER, Suss, from SEDGWICK JAMES, yeoman, Hartford [sic] Co, MD. Whereas a tr in Forrest of Cedar Creek Hund on nw side of Jumping Branch which said land was willed to said SEDGWICK by THOMAS HILL in Chester Co which land was sold from JEHU STAYTON to THOMAS POINTER and after many yrs said SEDGWICK JAMES came and took the said land from the said THOMAS POINTER by the will of THOMAS HILL which said land was sold to THOMAS HILL by HENRY BISHOP in Suss, it being pt/o Worminghurst Mannor in Suss, surveyed for above said HENRY BISHOP on 17 Feb 1725 it being pt/o a tr of 205 ac for which tr SEDGWICK JAMES obtained a warrant in 1776, lying on the nw side of Herrin branch one of the branches that runs into Mispillion Creek - near boundaries of THOMAS POINTER, WILLIAM WILLIAMS and MARGARET TRUITT. 102 ac 175 pounds. SEDGWICK JAMES of Kent Co, MD appoints Attys DAVID TRAIN and NEHEMIAH CARY. Ackn 10 Aug 1786.

289 Deed of mortgage 16 May 1786. EDWARD ROSS, Suss, from CURTIS BROWN, Suss, planter, for 72 pounds, 15 shillings, 8 pence, land whereon said CURTIS BROWN now dwells called Second Addition to Canaan, 140 ac Wit: JAMES BROWN Junr, JOHN HANDY, Ackn 10 Aug 1786.

290 Bill of Sale. EDWARD ROSS from CURTIS BROWN, Suss, for 72 pounds, 15 shillings, 8 pence, slaves: one called ISAAC, one negro woman called HANNAH and three negro boys, HESSE, JACOB and JACK. Wit: JAMES BROWN, Junr, JOHN HAND. Ackn 10 Aug 1786.

290 Deed 7 Jan 1786. JOHN BAYNARD, Kent Co, Del., from THOMAS LAYTON, carpenter, and REBECCA his wife, Suss, for 339 pounds, tr called Turpins Addition and tr called Turpins Conclution, in Suss, being the tracts which were bequeathed REBECCA wife of said THOMAS LAYTON by the will of SOLOMON TURPIN father of said

REBECCA LAYTON, 206 1/2 ac. Attys JOHN WEBB, JOHN LAWS, WM.
POLK. Wit: ISAAC BRADLEY, JOHN LAWS, DAVID NUTTER. Ackn 9 Aug
1786.

291 Bond. 7 Dec 1785. JOHN BAYNARD from THOMAS LAYTON.
Whereas THOMAS LAYTON, carpenter is held and firmly bound unto
JOHN BAYNARD of Kent Co, in the sum of 1000 pounds [security to
title of the land]. Wit: ISAAC BRADLEY, JOHN TENNENT. Ackn 9
Aug 1786.

292 Deed 5 Aug 1786. JOHN GOBY ANDERSON from ROBERT HOUSTON and
MARY WAILES, executors of will of JOHN HOUSTON, for 105 pounds, a
tr patented 4 Dec 1757 to JOHN CALLAWAY called Whitefield, in
Little Creek Hund; now contains 50 ac. JOHN CALLAWAY sold the tr
to JOHN HOUSTON on 8 Apr1765. 105 pounds. Wit: LEVIN WAILES,
WILLIAM ELLEGOOD, SARAH HITCHINS. Attys JOHN RODNEY and PHILLIPS
KOLLOCK. Ackn 9 Aug 1786.

292 Deed 5 Aug 1786. LEVIN WAILES, Suss, from JOHN GOBY
ANDERSON, Suss. 105 pounds, tr called Whitefield in Little Creek
Hund which was patented to JOHN CALLAWAY, 50 ac. Wit: ROBERT
HOUSTON, WILLIAM ELLEGOOD, SARAH HITCHINS. Attys JOHN RODNEY,
PHILLIPS KOLLOCK. Ackn 9 Aug 1786.

293 Deed 5 Aug 1786. ISAAC HORSEY, Suss, from LEVIN WAILES,
Suss, for 105 pounds, a tr called Whitefield in Little Creek Hund
which was granted to JOHN CALLAWAY, 50 ac. Wit: ROBERT HOUSTON
son of JOHN, G. ANDERSON, WILLIAM ELLEGOOD. Ackn 9 Aug 1786.

293 Deed 7 Aug 1786. ISAAC HORSEY, Suss, from JAMES WALLER,
Little Creek Hund, planter, 63 ac, pt/o a tr called Moore Lott
originally granted to JOSHUA MOORE and also 20 1/4 ac, pt/o tr
called Round Savanah originally granted to THOMAS WALLER, the two
tracts contiguous to each other in Little Creek Hund. - And have
been heretofore the property of WILLIAM WALLER who conveyed the
same 83 1/4 ac to JAMES WALLER. Attys JOHN RODNEY and PHILLIPS
KOLLOCK. Wit: ROBERT HOUSTON, NATHANIEL HORSEY. Ackn 9 Aug
1786.

294 Deed 9 Aug 1786. THOMAS ROSS, carpenter, Suss, yeoman,
from NAOMI POWER, Suss, maiden, a tr in forrest of Cedar Creek,
being pt/o larger tr surveyed and taken up for WILLIAM DONOLY,
late of Suss, decd, by virtue of a warrant, and after sd DONALY's
death the land became the property of his wife Morp(?) and 3 daus
MARY, JEMIMA and KEZIAH DONOLY. Daughter MARY married NEHEMIAH
POWER by whom she had the above named NAOMI POWER which by her
last will she devised and gave her dau NAOMI POWER. The parcel
is near Draper Road. 42 pounds. Wit: EDWARD POLK, WILLIAM
BRADLEY. Ackn 9 Aug 1786.

295 Deed 9 May 4 o'clock p.m. 1785. JOHN WINGATE, Suss, farmer,
from JOB INGRAM, Suss, farmer, a tr on s side of Indian R called
Chance, first granted to SUTHEY WITTINGTON by patent, 150 ac,
afterwards sold to JOSHUA ROBINSON who on 31 Aug 1764 sold to JOB
INGRAM, 1 ac out of the tract. 30 pounds for 1 ac. Also a
parcel for which part of the above sum is a consideration, which
JOB INGRAM surveyed and layed out in 1776 and called Mill Lot.

Attys SOLOMON WILLEY, ROBERT HOUSTON, WOLSEY BURTON, PHILLIPS
KOLLOCK. Wit: THOMAS WEST, THOMAS KELLUM. Ackn 9 Aug 1786.

296 Deed 2 Feb 1786. JOHN WINGATE, Suss, yeoman, from JOSHUA
ROBINSON, Senr, Suss, yeoman. Whereas SUTHEY WITTINGTON was
seized of a tr called Chance, patented to him by the proprietor
of MD, dated 21 Oct 1737 in formerly Wor Co, MD but now Suss on s
side of Indian R surveyed for 150 ac which SUTHEY WITTINGTON sold
to WILLIAM LEWIS and WILLIAM LEWIS on 31 Oct 1747 sold to JOSHUA
ROBINSON, Senr. Beginning at a fork between two creeks called
Duck Harbour to a creek called Duck head ... intersecting a line
of the tr called Exchange... 4 ac Attys HINMAN WHARTON, WOLSEY
BURTON, WILLIAM WAPLES. Wit: GEORGE WHARTON, JEREMIAH DARTER(?).
Ackn 9 Aug 1786.

296 Deed 23 Mar 1786. JOHN WINGATE, Suss, from PHILIP PARKER,
Suss, yeoman. Whereas PHILIP PARKER, father of afsd PHILIP
PARKER was seized of tr called Cabbin Ridge by proprietor of MD,
survey dated 22 Mar 1759, 100 ac. Said PHILIP PARKER father of
above PHILIP PARKER by his bond dated 25 Feb 1773 in the sum of
100 pounds sold to the above PHILIP PARKER the tr Cabbin Ridge
who now sells to JOHN WINGATE for 62 pounds. Attys HINMAN
WHARTON, WILLIAM WAPLES of Piney Neck. Wit: SOLOMON WILLEY,
BARNET DOWNS. Ackn 9 Aug 1786.

297 Deed 27 Feb 1786. ISAAC ATKINSON, cordwainer, from WILLIAM
WELCH, Suss, and RACHEL his wife, a tr in the Forrest of Broadkill Hund joining the road leading over Doe Bridge to Philadelphia on w side of road on Hairfields Branch being the n end of
parcel conveyed by deed of sale HUGH STEVENSON and WILLIAM
STEVENSON unto ELIZABETH OAKEY dated 3 May 1780. 106 ac. And
the said ELIZABETH OAKEY by deed dated 26 Feb 1784 conveyed one
moiety or half pt/o afsd land to afsd WILLIAM WELCH which deed is
recorded Liber B, folio 254. Land adj Harfields Branch. 53 1/2
ac for 31 pounds. Attys Colonel SIMON KOLLOCK, HENRY NEILL,
HENRY FISHER, Doctor JOSEPH HALL, RHOADS SHANKLAND. Wit: POLLEY
WOLLEY WOOLF, WILLIAM WOOLF, N. WAPLES. Ackn 10 Aug 1786.

298 Deed 8 Aug 1786. WILLIAM JONES, Suss, from MATHIAS JONES,
Suss, bricklayer, for 200 pounds, pt/o larger tr called Good
Will adj land sold of said tr to THOMAS MARVEL and ELIAS JOHNSON,
173 ac Wit: JONATHAN BOYCE, JOHN WINGATE. Ackn 9 Aug 1786.

298 Deed 25 Feb 1785. JOSEPH HOUSTON, Suss, farmer, from JOHN
DARBY, Suss, yeoman. Whereas HINMAN WHARTON was seized of a tr,
by patented from proprietor of MD called Lanes Adventure, on s
side of Indian R, north of a place formerly known as Blackfoot
now Dagsberry out of which said tr HINMAN WHARTON sold 100 ac to
URIAH WATSON, who the said URIAH WATSON dying, his son, JAMES
WATSON, as heir at law became seized of said 100 ac and sold to
JOHN DARBY 75 ac. And whereas JOHN GROOMS was seized of a tr
called Poor Chance on s side of Indian R and north of place
formerly known as Blackfoot now Dagsberry out of which tr JOHN
GROOM sold 23 ac to afsd JAMES WATSON by bond which sale was
confirmed by deed from CHARLES WHARTON as heir at law to said
JOHN GROOM (Groom then being decd) and said JAMES WATSON together
with the afsd 75 ac conveyd same to DARBY. Attys PETER WHITE,

50

PHILLIPS KOLLOCK and JONATHAN NOTTINGHAM. Wit: SIMON KOLLOCK, ROBERT HOUSTON. Ackn 10 Aug 1786.

299 Deed 7 Aug 1786. JOHN MOSLEY, Suss, planter, from ISAAC MOORE and SARAH his wife, Suss, 50 ac, a tr in Nanticoke Hund and Forrest on the sw side of Raccoon Swamp that empties into Nanticoke R which land was surveyed to afsd ISAAC MOORE by virtue of proprietary warrant dated at Philadelphia 1776 which warrant was layed on and surveyed for him the said MOORE by RHODES SHANKLAND, Deputy Surveyor. For 50 pounds. Attys WILLIAM DAVIS, THOMAS JONES, WILLIAM NEWBOLD, SIMON KOLLOCK. Wit: ROBERT HOPKINS, SIMON KOLLOCK. Ackn 10 Aug 1786.

300 12 Aug 1774. Articles of Agreement 12 Aug 1774. Between ROBERT HOUSTON of Wor Co, MD, planter, to JOHN COLLINS, Wor Co, planter. ROBERT HOUSTON for consideration will build and erect a saw mill on the place below where Boyces Mill Branch and Mirey or Taylors Branch meet in Wor Co and on ne branch of Broad Creek to be completed on or before 1 Dec next (the dam excepted). JOHN COLLINS will erect a dirt dam at the place afsd of 10 feet high and 12 feet wide to extend from point of land called the Parsons Point to above narrow Point on said HOUSTON's side the branch afsd to be finished by 1 Dec next. At the completion the parties to occupy and enjoy a moiety [1/2]. Wit: BETTY VAUGHAN, DOLLEY EDGAR, LEVIN VAUGHAN. Ackn 10 Aug 1786.

300 Deed 8 Aug 1786. JOHN COLLINS, Broad Creek Hund, from WILLIAM HARDY, Suss. JAMES HARDY of Wor Co, seized in fee pt/o 2 tracts whereon he dwelt at time of his demise knowns as Cypress Swamp and Outlett, purch from DAY GIVANS for 230 ac and some more being seized in fee. In his will he devised the same to his sons ISAAC and said WILLIAM HARDY. To WILLIAM he devised 90 ac for which WILLIAM sells for 50 pounds. Attys GUNNING BEDFORD, WILLIAM DONE, WILLIAM PERRY. Ackn 12 Aug 1786.

301 Deed. WILLIAM BURROUGHS from PETER FRETWELL WRIGHT, Sheriff. Whereas at a Court of Common Pleas on 5 Aug 1783, NATHANIEL YOUNG, ROBERT YOUNG, WILLIAM POLK and WILLIAM BLACK recovered agnst JONATHAN BURROUGHS, late of Suss, debt of 189 pounds, 17 shillings, 9 pence plus 100 shillings for damages. On 6 May 1784 court ordered sale of property of JONATHAN BURROUGHS: tr in Cedar Creek Hund, 160 ac. That a tr was by order of the Orphans Court divided among the heirs of EDWARD BURROUGHS, decd, grandfather to said JONATHAN BURROUGHS whereby the quantity of 120 ac and 140 perches as his right for himself and assignee of WARREN BURROUGHS decd. On 4 May 1785 it was ordered by the Court of Common Pleas that this land of JONATHAN BURROUGHS be sold. Wit: D. HALL, W. HARRISON. Ackn 10 Aug 1786.

302 Deed. 8 Aug 1786. WM. BRITTINGHAM ENNES, Indian R Hund from LEVIN MILBEY, Indian R and Angola Hund and ANN his wife, for 180 pounds, moiety or half pt/o tr called Mill Lott in Indian R Hund beginning at Cowbridge Branch at the head of Indian R and a small distance above the westernmost end of Laceys Bridge, 4 ac. Also the moiety or one-half of 180 ac. Also one moiety of the mill on said mill lott and implements and utensils. Wit: EBENEZER PETTYJOHN, JOHN DOWNING, NAOMIE STOCKLEY. Ackn 8 Aug 1786.

302 Deed 11 Aug 1786. ISAAC COOPER from PETER FRETWELL WRIGHT,
Sheriff. Whereas a tr in Broad Creek Hund, 232 ac being pt/o 3
tracts called Cypress Swamp, Outlet and Addition. Out of Cypress
Swamp 157 ac, out of Outlet 53 ac and out of Addition 22 ac.
JAMES HANDY devised by his last will the same to his two sons
ISAAC HANDY and WILLIAM HANDY who by their deeds sold the same
unto GEORGE FARRINGTON who by his bond of conveyance sold the
same to STEPHEN HORSEY who assigned the said bond unto JOSHUA
HITCH who assigned said bond unto LEVIN FARRINGTON who by bond of
conveyance sold the said lands to JAMES TULLY. And whereas LEVIN
FARRINGTON lately in the Court of Common Pleas recovered a judgment agnst said JAMES TULLY for a debt of 120 pounds, 17 shillings, 2 pence. Land sold to ISAAC COOPER for 77 pounds and 6 p.
Wit: WILLIAM POLK, ELIJAH CANNON. Ackn 11 Aug 1786.

304 22 Mar 1762. Bond for conveyance of land, ISAAC FLEMING
from DANIEL NUNEZ. DANIEL NUNEZ of Suss, Innholder, bound to
ISAAC FLEMING, Suss, yeoman, in the sum of 95 pounds. DANIEL
NUNEZ to convey tr in Wor Co, MD, 15 ac, being pt/o larger tr of
200 ac, called Mill Land, formerly granted to JOHN CALDWELL and
afterward confirmed to JOHN SMITH which 15 ac was conveyed to
said DANIEL NUNEZ (and ROBERT GILL, decd) by THOMAS BRATTON as by
indenture bearing date 22 Jul 1746. Wit: --- RODNEY, RUTH RODNEY.
Ackn 11 Aug 1786.

304 Deed. 11 Aug 1796. WILLIAM POWELL, Suss, planter, from
GEORGE WALKER, Suss, planter. Parcel at head of the sound which
being pt/o a tr called Woodcrafts Venture, 50 ac, 50 pounds -
being the same land taken up by SOLOMON ROGERS, Senr, in 1750 and
conveyed from SOLOMON RODGERS to THOMAS WILDGOOSE and conveyed
from said WILDGOOSE to GAMAGE EVANS HODGESON and from HODGESON to
GEORGE WALKER. Wit: LITTLETON TOWNSEND, PETER WHITE. Ackn 11
Aug 1786.

305 23 Apr 1776. Deed of Partition between NATHL. BRADFORD,
Suss, wheelwright; COMFORT WRIGHT and SARAH TRUITT, widow of
MICAJAH TRUITT. Whereas by virtue of a purchase made by their
father (now decd), they have obtained a bill of sale from SAMUEL
HEAVERLOE (bearing date 8 May 1774) for 160 ac of land and 25 ac
of marsh in Suss in Broadkill Hund on n side of Broadkill Creek
in Broadkill Neck in two separate tracts near MARY COLLINGS land,
ANTHONY HEAVALOES, and JEHU CLAYPOOLES land, 160 ac. And the
second tr near land of SAMUEL HEAVERLOE and CORNELIUS WILTBANK,
25 ac of marsh. Ackn 10 Aug 1786.

306 Deed 12 Aug 1786. JOSEPH SCROGIN COLLINS from JOHN COLLINS
his father, of Broad Creek Hund, Gentleman - JOSEPH SCROGIN
COLLINS being the only surviving son of JOHN COLLINS and BETTY
his late wife. Whereas GEORGE COLLINS late of sd hund, decd, by
his will dated 30 Apr 1781 bequeathed to his brother JOHN COLLINS
a tr called Barron Field, 124 ac, and a tr called Mill Lott, 10
ac, with right to the saw mill built by him and ROBERT HOUSTON in
consideration of 230 pounds. And whereas said JOHN COLLINS the
grantor made and executed between him and BETTY SCROGIN a cove-
nant that "200 ac pt/o a tr called Running Mead to be laid off on
the n and nw of said tr to include my Mills too and for the use
of the males that may hereafter be born of the intended marriage
between said JOHN COLLINS and said BETTY SCROGIN (if any) to him

or them in fee." And whereas JOHN COLLINS is and stands seized of Coxes Performance, 100 ac; the whole of Mill Lott, 10 ac; Barrowfield, 199 ac; pt/o Running Meade, 111 ac, including the grantor's dwelling plantation whereon he has dwelt since 1780, grist mill, 2 saw mills. For "love and affection." Also 2 yoke of oxen, cart utensils, waggon, 10 head of sheep, 10 hogs, 1 cow, 2 desks, walnut table, cubbard, 2 beds, 2 negro slaves, JAMES and TOM, [and other goods and chattels described]. Wit: --- RUSSELL, PETER REA. Ackn 11 Aug 1786.

307 Deed. 11 Aug 1786. POLLY, JENNEY and PEGGY COLLINS from JOHN COLLINS, their father, Broad Creek Hund, Gentleman. In consideration of 401 pounds, 15 shillings, that is to say 133 pounds, 18 shillings, 4 pence current money of MD due each of the grantees from the grantors, exr of WILLIAM VENABLES decd, the receipt whereof the said JOHN COLLINS doth hereby acknowledge and thereof fully acquit, exonerate and discharge the said POLLY COLLINS, JENNEY COLLINS and PEGGEY COLLINS to whom he conveys the following tracts: Outlet of 100 ac, 287 ac of Cypress Swamp, tr called Partnership of 25 ac, 210 ac of tr called Industry, 75 ac of tr called Security inlarged, tr of 235 ac called Addition, Resurvey on Addition warrant originally granted to MARGARET BACON(?) descended to the grantor as her heir at law; also a resurvey on 16 ac pt/o COLLINS's Industry laid by the grantor - 1510 ac plus 3 negro slaves, CEASER, CIPP and MINGO, looking glasses, tables, desks, cows, etc. [listed]. Wit: JOSEPH GREENWAY, --- RUSSEL. Ackn 12 Aug 1786.

308 Petition of WILLIAM BURROUGHS for Leave of Court. WILLIAM BURROUGHS of Kent Co in reference to court order of 4 May 1785 by which lands of JONATHAN BURROUGHS were seized and sold to satisfy debt to NATHANIAL YOUNG, ROBERT YOUNG, WILLIAM POLK and GEORGE BLACK. Petitioner requests present sheriff who replaced then sheriff CORD HAZZARD, to execute deed. 15 Aug 1786.

308 Deed. 9 Aug 1786. EMANUEL RUSSEL, shipwright, from LEVI RUSSEL, Suss, yeoman, for 5 shillings, pt/o a larger tr being one moiety or half pt/o tr conveyed by deed of sale JOSEPH FEDDERMON to WILLIAM RUSSELL on 4 Nov 1760. Land on nw end of Broadkill Creek near the Drawbridge. 140 ac Wit: WILLIAM MARTIN, JAMES SNOWDEN. Ackn 6 Sep 1786.

309 9 Aug 1786. Deed. LEVI RUSSELL, Suss, yeoman from EMANUEL RUSSELL, Suss, shipwright. 5 shillings. pt/o a larger tr of land being one moiety or 1/2 of tr conveyed by deed of sale from JOSEPH FEDDEMAN to WILLIAM RUSSEL dated Nov 1760. 100 ac Wit: WILLIAM MARTIN, JAMES SNODEN. Ackn 6 Sep 1786.

309 6 Sep 1786. Deed. JOHN POSTLES from RICHARD SHOCKLEY, yeoman, Suss, for 241 pounds, 5 shillings, tr on Cedar Creek Hund whereon said RICHARD SHOCKLEY now dwells. 115 3/4 ac. Surveyed 11 Oct 1774 by CALEB CIRWITHIN. Wit: ELIAS SHOCKLEY, LYDIA SHOCKLEY. Ackn 6 Sep 1786.

310 7 Sep 1786. Deed. THOMAS EVANS, of Cedar Creek Hund, from THOMAS BOWMAN, Kent Co, Del, yeoman and ELISABETH his wife. DAVID THORNTON late of Cedar Creek Hund, Yeoman, was seized in his demesne as of fee in a tr in Cedar Creek Hund near land of

JOSHUA BARWICK and near St. Matthews Church - 122 ac 23 perches, being pt/o land said DAVID THORNTON purch from NEHEMIAH DRAPER conveyed by the exr of said NEHEMIAH DRAPER after his death. DAVID THORNTON by his bond was bound unto REYNEAR WILLIAMS late of Suss who died before any deed was made to him for the said tr. In his will, "I bequeath to my beloved wife ANN WILLIAMS the plantation whereon I now live during her natural life" and in a subsequent clause, "I give and bequeath unto my brother JAMES DRAPER the plantation whereon I now live after my wife's decease ..." The will was dated 1 Apr 1773 & duly proved. JAMES DRAPER afterwards died intestate and w/o issue leaving several sisters and legal representatives. And whereas in an indenture dated 3 Aug 1774 between DAVID THORNTON of the 1st part and ANN WILLIAMS widow relict of afsd REYNEAR WILLIAMS decd of the 2nd part and the heirs and legal representatives of afsd JAMES DRAPER, of the 3rd part; DAVID THORNTON conveyed above mentioned land of 122 ac and 23 perches to ANN WILLIAMS for her lifetime and to the heirs and legal representatives of afsd JAMES DRAPER decd, after her decease. ANN WILLIAMS afterwards married Dr. JOSEPH HALL of the town of Lewes and sometime after died. On 5 May in 1784 said THOMAS BOWMAN petitioned the Orphans Court setting forth that afsd JAMES DRAPER died intestate and under age leaving three sisters, ELIZABETH wife of petitioner, SARAH wife of NATHANIEL BOWMAN and PHEBE wife of CURTIS BESWICK, and one niece POLLY the d/o ALEXANDER DRAPER late of Suss, decd, to which the said lands descended. Now THOMAS BOWMAN and ELIZABETH his wife for 500 pounds sell their right to the land in behalf of themselves and the other heirs. Wit: JOHN LAWS, ISAAC BEAUCHAMP. Ackn 7 Sep 1786.

312 Petition of WILLIAM BRADLEY for Leave of Court for deed to property purch by him, being the property of MATTHIAS JONES and JOHN CHANCE, late of said co, yeoman, seized by the sheriff. Being tr of 130 ac whereon DANIEL CLIFTON then lived and 40 ac of marsh adj. 341 pounds. 7 Sep 1786. [See below]

312 Deed. WILLIAM BRADLEY, Kent Co, yeoman, from PETER FRETWELL WRIGHT Sheriff. JAMES THARP of Suss, yeoman, obtained a Judgment agnst MATHIAS JONES and JOHN CHANCE for 36 pounds and 100 shillings for damages, whereas the land of JOHN CHANCE in Cedar Creek Neck was seized, 130 ac whereon DANIEL CLIFTON then lived and also 40 ac of marsh adj the land was sold by the sheriff to WILLIAM BRADLEY, the highest bidder for 341 pounds. Wit: JOHN CLARK, W. HARRISON. Ackn 7 Sep 1786. [In the description of the land the acreage is given as 183 ac and 94 perches. Also a parcel adj the other, 14 ac and 106 perches with 40 ac of marsh.]

314 Deed. 8 Sep 1786. LITTLETON TOWNSEND, schoolmaster, Suss, from BRITTINGHAM HILL, farmer, Suss, for 15 pounds, pt/o tr called London Darry, containing 500 ac in the whole, on the s side of Indian R, taken up by WALTER LANE and sold unto LEONARD JOHNSON who by his will bequeathed pt/o said tr to his son JOHN JOHNSON and said JOHN JOHNSON died w/o will and the said JOHN JOHNSON's son JOHN fell heir to his father's land being pt/o said London Darry and said young JOHN JOHNSON sold same to WILLIAM HOLLAND and HOLLAND sold 3/4 ac to BRITTINGHAM HILL.

pt/o tr called London Darry, containing 500 ac in the whole, on
the s side of Indian R, taken up by WALTER LANE and sold to
LEONARD JOHNSON who by his will bequeathed pt/o said tr to his
son JOHN JOHNSON and the said JOHN JOHNSON died without will and
the said JOHN JOHNSON's son JOHN fell heir to his father's land
being pt/o said London Darry and the said young JOHN JOHNSON who
was heir of his father did sell same unto WILLIAM HOLLAND and
HOLLAND sold 9 3/4 ac to BRITTINGHAM HILL. Adj tr Friendship on
w side of London Darry, said part being in an Old Field and on sw
corner of BRITTINGHAM HILL's plantation. Wit: D. HALL, JOSEPH
MILLER. Ackn 8 Sep 1786.

314 Deed 6 Sep 1786. STEPHEN COSTON, Suss, yeoman, from JOSHUA
COSTON, Suss, yeoman, for 230 pounds, 17 shillings, 6 pence, 1/2
part and 1/8 pt/o the other half of a tr called Content, 460 ac
excepting 1 ac sold by JOSHUA COSTON to ROBERT PRETTYMAN and also
1/8 pt/o the land which was the property of EZEKIEL COSTON by the
afsd EZEKIEL dying without issue his lands descended to his
brothers and sisters and after distribution of the said land
COMFORT COSTON by her deed of sale conveyed her right to the land
to said JOSHUA COSTON. Also 56 ac pt/o a tr known as Liberty,
106 ac, 50 ac thereof being sold by said JOSHUA COSTON to said
ROBERT PRETTYMAN excepting 1/8 pt/o 150 ac sold to JOHN SCOTT of
the afsd EZEKIEL COSTON's lands. Also one other tr called Poplar
Ridge of 105 ac and one other parcel called Low Ground of 50 ac.
Also another piece containing 128 ac, being pt/o a larger tr
surveyed for JOHN MORRIS as per deed for the same from MITCHELL
SCOTT to said JOSHUA COSTON in Liber N.N. 13, folio 92 - which
several parcels is computed to contain in the whole 717 1/2 ac
Attys DAVID TRAIN, PHILLIPS KOLLOCK. Wit: JOHN W. DEAN, SOMERSET
DICKERSON. Ackn 8 Sep 1786.

315 7 Sep 1786. Petition of JOHN ORR, carpenter, Suss, for
leave of Court. [For conveyance of following deed.]

316 Deed. JOHN ORR of Lewes and Rehoboth Hund from PETER
FRETWELL WRIGHT. Whereas MARGARETT KOLLOCK exr of will of JACOB
KOLLOCK, Suss, decd, in the Court of Common Pleas Aug term 1784,
recovered agnst THOMAS WRIGHT and NAOMI (late NAOMI STOCKLEY) his
wife adminr of property of ALEXANDER STOCKLEY late of Suss, decd,
a debt of 208 pounds, 19 shillings, plus 4 pounds, 8 shillings, 9
pence for damages. Messuage and lot of ALEXANDER STOCKLEY on the
n side of the road leading from Lewes to a place called Quaker
Town in Lewes and Rehoboth Hund and adj lands of said PETER
FRETWELL WRIGHT was seized and sold, for 65 pounds. Wit: D. HALL,
WILLIAM DAVIS. Ackn 7 Sep 1786.

317 13 Aug 1785. Deed of Mortgage DANIEL RUNDLE, JACOB
SHOEMAKER and RICHARD FOOTMAN, all of the city of Philadelphia,
Gentlemen, from JOHN JONES, Suss, Esqr and MARY his wife. Whereas JOHN JONES stands bound for 1200 pounds, for the conveyance of
the 3 fourth parts of that land in Suss called Unity Grove beginning on w side of county road from Snow Hill to Lewes Town, on n
side of a Sandy Beach issuing out of the head of St. Martins R,
1768 ac. Also 3 undivided fourth parts called Lebanon beginning
near URIAH BROOKFIELD's Bridge, 2160 ac. Wit: JOHN FOSTER, DAVID
MILLER, MEIRS FISHER. Ackn 7 Feb 1786.

318 13 Aug 1785. Deed of Mortgage JOSEPH MIFFLIN, City of
Phila, merchant, from JOHN JONES, Suss, Esqr. and MARY his wife.
Whereas JOHN JONES stands bound for 250 pounds one undivided
fourth of tr in Suss called Unity Grove in Wor Co, MD, now Suss,
1768 ac. Also 1 undivided fourth part called Lebanon beginning
near URIAH BROOKFIELD's Bridge, 2160 ac. Wit: JOHN FOSTER, DAVID
MILLER, MEIRS FISHER. Ackn 11 Feb 1786. On 5 May 1791 DAGWORTHY
JONES (for the use of JOHN JONES) produced the mortgage and
receipt of JOHN ASHLEY assignee of the original mortgage.

320 12 Aug 1785. Deed. JOHN JONES from DANIEL RUNDLE and ANN
his wife, JACOB SHOEMAKER and REBECCA his wife and RICHARD
FOOTMAN and ELENOR his wife, all of the City of Phila, merchants;
and JOHN JONES, Suss, Esqr., for 3000 pounds the above described
trs, Unity Grove and Lebanon. Wit: DAVID MILLER, JOHN FOSTER,
MIERS FISHER. Ackn 11 Feb 1786.

321 12 Aug 1785. JOHN JONES, Esqr, from JOSEPH MIFFLIN, City of
Phila, merchant, and DEBORAH his wife, wife. 533 pounds One
equal fourth to Unity Grove and one fourth of Lebanon as
described above. Wit: JOHN FOSTER, DAVID MILLER, MIERS FISHER.
Ackn 11 Feb 1786.

322 1 Nov 1786. JAMES BRATTEN, Suss, from PETER F. WRIGHT,
Sheriff. Whereas there are 4 trs in in Broad Creek Hund one of
which is called Mill Landing Enlarged, 500 ac; another called
Liverpool containing 500 ac; another called Messicks Chance of 50
ac; another called Absoloms Lot containing 60 ac - late the
property of GEORGE FERRINGTON of Suss. Sd GEORGE FERRINGTON was
indebted to JOHN MITCHEL; the land was seized and sold, JAMES
BRATTEN being the highest bidder for 500 pounds. Wit: SARAH
LITTLE, WILLIAM PERRY. Ackn 8 Nov 1786.

323 13 Oct 1786. Deed. ELI McCALLEY, Suss, yeoman, from
WILLIAM OWENS, Suss, yeoman, and his wife TABBY, for 78 pounds,
tr called Double Purchase near Green Branch originally granted to
WILLIAM REYNOLDS, 66 ac. Wit: ABRAHAM ADAMS, ROBERT WATSON
McCALLEY. Attys PETER FRETWELL WRIGHT, WM. BRUINTON. Ackn 8 Nov
1786.

324 14 Oct 1786. Deed. WILLIAM JONES, Suss, farmer, from JOB
MASSEY, Suss, yeoman and his wife, EASTER, tr in Nanticoke Hund
called Masseys Folly, 52 1/2 ac which was left to said JOB MASSEY
by will of his father JOSEPH MASSEY. 51 pounds near Racoon
Savanah on n side of a county road leading from Fraims Saw mill
to Gravil Branch. Wit: JAMES LAWLESS, ISAAC HARDY JONES. Ackn 8
Nov 1786.

325 31 Dec 1774. Bond for conveyance of land WILLIAM VENEBLES,
Som Co, MD, is bound to GEORGE SMITH s/o ANDREW, and MARSHALL
SMITH of Wor Co in the sum of 1200 pounds WILLIAM VENABLES to
convey that parcel conveyed to him by CALEB BALDING, 145 ac, pt/o
tr called Turkey Trapp, in Wor Co, on Bald Cypress Branch, together with the saw mill and grist mill. Wit: ROBERT HOUSTON s/o
JOHN, JOHN COLLINS. GEORGE SMITH transfers easternmost side of
the run of sd SMITH's Mill Branch with half of the Mills unto
MARSHALL SMITH, only a priviledge of 5 ac excepted at the e end
of the Dam for the necessary use of the mills to be jointly

reserved for the use of both his two sons, MARSHALL and GEORGE and the above assignment is to my son MARSHALL. Wit: SAMUEL HEARN, SAMUEL ELLIOT. Ackn 8 Nov 1786.

326 8 Nov 1786. Deed. JOHN WINGATE, yeoman, from PETER F. WRIGHT. Whereas there is a tr in Broad Creek Hund, 58 ac, pt/o a larger tr called Crooked Lane, originally granted by patent from proprietary of MD to JOHN WILLEY (alias JOHN ALEXANDER WILLEY) who by indenture bearing date 4 Nov 1762 sold 58 ac to SOUTHY KING recorded in Wor Co, MD, Liber E, folio 381, 382. Also another parcel adj above 58 ac and pt/o a larger tr of 400 ac granted to SUTHEY KING by virtue of a warrant from proprietary of Pa., now in the possession of BETTY GUNBY, widow, 200 ac. And whereas JOHN WINGATE at the request of SUTHEY KING, together with SUTHEY KING by a certain obligation dated 7 Aug 1783 became bound unto WOODMAN STOCKLEY, FRANCIS STOCKLEY and CORNELIUS STOCKLEY, minors, and heirs of CORNELIUS STOCKLEY, decd, in the sum of 245 pounds, 12 shillings, 8 pence. Whereas JOHN WINGATE recovered a judgement agnst SUTHEY KING and the property was sold to WINGATE. Wit: D. TRAIN, SETH GRIFFITH. Ackn 8 Nov 1786.

328 Deed. 8 Nov 1786. JOHN BURTON of Angola Neck in Indian R Hund, from PETER F. WRIGHT, Sheriff. Wheras JAMES THOMPSON, Suss, yeoman, lately recovered a judgment agnst MOSES ALLEN, late of Suss, yeoman, for a debt of 39 pounds, 10 pence, also 44 shillings, 7 pence for damages. Hence, land of MOSES ALLEN was seized and sold, in Indian R Hund, 300 ac, to JOHN BURTON. Also for 555 pounds, the tr on n side of the road leading to St. George's Chappel and about 1 mile from thence on the e side thereof being pt/o a larger tr of 1200 ac originally granted by patent on 1 Mar 1684 to RICHARD BUNDICK called Arcadia which became the property of MOSES ALLEN, beginning at a corner of JOHNATHAN STEVENSON's land and adj the Indian R Road, 267 ac Wit: REECE WOOLF, JOHN CORNEL. Ackn 24 Nov 1786.

329 31 Jul 1786. Deed JOSEPH HARDY, son and heir of JOSEPH HARDY, decd, Suss, from JOHN GRUMBLE and TEMPERANCE his wife, Suss, for 5 pounds, pt/o tr called Orphans Lott which formerly belonged to JOHN WAINWRIGHT. Wit: WILLIAM MARTIN, WILLIAM WILSON. Attys JOHN RODNEY, PHILLIPS KOLLOCK. Ackn 8 Nov 1786.

330 6 May 1777. Deed. AARON McKIMMY, yeoman, from ELIZABETH and JANE McKIMMY, daus of JANE McKIMMY, decd, a tr in Broadkill forest adj land surveyed for JOHN JOHNSTON, THOMAS MACKLIN, and ELINOR DOBSON - for which a patent was granted to RICHARD DOBSON, 4th day, 8th month, 1718 - 200 ac And the said RICHARD DOBSON, at his death, left the property to his two daus, JANE and RACHEL; the said Jane never selling nor giving up her right, it therefore at the end of her life, fell to her children. 10 pounds paid to each. Wit: HENRY PARKER, WILLIAM ROBINS. Attys ZADOCK PINDAL. Ackn 8 Nov 1786.

331 14 Oct 1786. Deed. ISAAC HARDY JONES, planter, Suss, from JESTER CUNNINGHAM, Suss, planter, and SARAH his wife, for 45 pounds. Whereas a parcel of land in Nanticoke Hund, pt/o tr granted to JOHN FLEETWOOD by proprietors warrant dated Phila, 2 July 1761. NEHEMIAH FLEETWOOD the son and heir of JOHN FLEETWOOD

sold the warrant to JOHN CONWAY (70 ac). Wit: THOMAS WILLIN, ELI McCALLEY. Ackn 8 Nov 1786.

332 16 Oct 1786. Deed. ISAAC HARDY JONES, yeoman, Suss, from JESTER CUNNINGHAM, Suss, yeoman, and SARAH his wife. Whereas there is a tr in Nanticoke Hund called Severety(?) which was granted to ARTHUR CUNNINGHAM by patent on 14 Jun 1733, tr being in Som Co, MD, on se side of Nanticoke R and s side of main branch of Deep Creek to the se side of a tr formerly surveyed for said CUNNINGHAM called Second Choice, 100 ac, for 75 pounds. Wit: THOMAS WILLIN, ELI McCALLEY. Attys DAVID TRAIN, PETER FRETWELL WRIGHT. Ackn 8 Nov 1786.

333 25 Feb 1786. Deed. REECE WOOLF, Suss, yeoman, from ROBERT WHITE, Suss, yeoman. Whereas there is a parcel of marsh being pt/o a larger island of marsh in Lewes Creek known as White's Island whereof JACOB WHITE (father of above named ROBERT WHITE), devised to his two sons, ISAAC and ROBERT WHITE and his grandson JACOB WHITE, to be equally divided between them. ISAAC died intestate seized of his undivided right in said island of marsh, leaving ELIZABETH his widow who afterwards married WILLIAM HALL, and ISAAC's two children, to wit: JANE WILKINS WHITE and ISAAC WHITE to whom his undivided right in said island descended. And whereas ISAAC WHITE by WRIXAM WHITE his Guardian and the said JANE WILKINS WHITE and ISAAC WHITE by WILLIAM HALL and ELIZABETH his wife their guardians as plaintiffs of Nov Court 1779 caused a amiable suit of partition of the said island which was done. Wit: WM. DONE, JOS. MILLER. Ackn 8 Nov 1786.

333 6 Jul 1786. Deed. THOMAS WALLER (son of NATHL.), planter, Suss, from CUSTIS RODGERS, Accomack Co, VA, for 50 pounds, a tr called Callaways Intention near the road from Broad Creek to Salsbury. 100 ac Attys DAVID TRAIN, RHOADS SHANKLAND and ISAAC HENRY. Wit: JAMES BRATTON, JOHN SILLAVAN. Ackn 8 Nov 1786.

334 8 Nov 1786. Deed. ROBERT PRETTYMAN, Suss, yeoman, from STEPHEN COSTON, Suss, yeoman, parcel in the forrest of Broadkill Hund, being pt/o Costons Content and another tr called Liberty. 186 ac 130 pounds Wit: JACOB KOLLOCK, JOSHUA FISHER. Ackn 9 Nov 1786.

335 Bond for conveyance of land JOHN HOUSTON, Wor Co, planter, from JOHN COLLINS of Wor Co., planter. JOHN COLLINS bound to JOHN HOUSTON for 54 pounds, 9 Apr 1768, to convey to Houston 36 ac in Wor Co on Broad Creek a little above the bridge and adj the southernmost pt/o a tr formerly surveyed for JOHN WINDSOR called Coxes Performance. Wit: ROBT. HOUSTON, LUKE HUFFINGTON. Ackn 9 Nov 1786.

335 9 Nov 1786. Deed JOHN HASSEL WANGER, Suss, taylor, from EMANUEL RUSSEL, Suss, shipwright, for 8 pounds, pt/o a larger tr conveyed by deed of sale by JOSEPH FEDDEMON to WILLIAM RUSSELL as appears in deed dated 4 Nov 1760. Land in Broadkill Neck. Wit: ISAAC TURNER, NATHANIEL HICKMAN. Ackn 9 Nov 1786.

336 2 Sep 1786. Deed. JOHN HICKMAN, yeoman, from JNO. CRIPPEN, yeoman, and MARY his wife and NEHEMIAH BENNETT, cordwinder of Cedar Creek Hund. Whereas ROBERT HODGSON lately died seized of

lands in said hund on the s side of Cedar Creek bounded by lands of JAMES BEVINS, JOSHUA LOFFLAN, THOMAS HAYS and AARON OLIVER, 100 ac, leaving a widow and issue: JACOB, JESSE, the above named MARY, SARAH and MIRIAM HODGSON to whom the land descended except for the widow's 1/3 or dower right and the eldest son receiving 2 shares. And whereas the above JESSE died intestate and without issue his share became divideable between his surviving brothers and sisters equally and whereas JACOB as eldest s/o said intestate around May 1770 did allot and lay off to the said SARAH the widow of the said intestate 31 1/2 ac, 19 perches, as her dower right and whereas JOHN CRIPPEN and MARY his wife by their indenture dated 12 May 1775 sold to JACOB HODGSON their right to 69 1/4 ac, 4 perches, that being the 2/3 of the said tr after the widow's thirds or dower right and whereas MIRIAM HODGSON conveyed to JEREMIAH BENNETT her right to the land. Witnesseth that JOHN CRIPPEN and his wife MARY for 12 pounds and NEHEMIAH BENNETT for 15 pounds sell the reversion rights. Attys NEHEMIAH BENNETT. Wit: JOHN CLOWES, STEPHEN REDDEN. Ackn 2 Sep 1786.

337 Bond for conveyance of land WILLIAM PEARCE from WILLIAM POLK. WILLIAM POLK, Junr of Suss, yeoman, bound to WILLIAM PEARCE, Suss, cordwinder, in the sum of 300 pounds, to convey a lot in Cedar Creek Hund on the n and westernmost side of the town and road adj land said WILLIAM POLK sold to RICHARD MULNIX and JEHOSHAPHAT POLK, binding on land of BENNETT BRYAN. Wit: JOHN POLK, EDWARD POLK. Ackn 9 Nov 1786.

338 1786. Deed. LURANA CLIFTON, Suss, from WILLIAM DRAPER, yeoman, and ANNEhis wife, of Kent Co, Del, for 75 pounds, a parcel of land in Cedar Creek Hund, being pt/o larger tr granted by patent to JOHN HOLMES of Suss Co and by him conveyed to ELISHA KNOCKS by deed of sale and by ELISHA KNOCKS and MARGARET his wife conveyed to said WILLIAM DRAPER by deed of sale dated 6 May 1783. 128 1/2 ac running along Misspilion Creek. Wit: JOHN REVELL, ISAAC CLIFTON. Ackn 9 Nov 1786.

339 21 Oct 1786. Deed. PERCILLA MOONEY w/o CHARLES MOONEY, and heirs of CHARLES MOONEY, Suss, decd, from MOSES COX [Cocks] of Wor Co, MD, for 100 pounds, pt/o tr called Johnsons Venture, 66 2/3 ac in Grubby Neck on Green Branch, being pt/o land taken up by SIMON JOHNSON under Lord Baltimore for 150 ac. Conveyed by ELIAS JOHNSON to above named MOSES COCKS. Wit: ROBT. GRIFFITH, JOHN ODAY. Attys PETER WRIGHT. Ackn 21 Oct 1786.

339 JOHN COX's Deposition respecting a bond for conveyance of land from WM. WYATT. JOHN COX late of Wor Co, MD, but now of Gilford Co, N.C., aged 42 yrs, deposeth that on 9 Dec 1771, at the request of WILLIAM WYATT, Senr (now decd) drew a bond for conveyance of 200 ac from said WILLIAM WYATT to his two sons, JOHN and WILLIAM WYATT, 100 ac by the said bond was to be laid off convenient to the plantation or buildings whereon WILLIAM WYATT then lived - to be conveyed to said JOHN WYATT and the remaining to be conveyed by said bond to said WILLIAM WYATT. Sworn 29 Nov 1786.

340 26 Jul 1786. Deed JOSHUA COSTON, Broadkiln Hund, yeoman, from COMFORT COSTON, of Broadkiln Hund, Suss, Spinster. Whereas EZEKIEL COSTON (brother of the said JOSHUA and COMFORT), late of

Hund and co, yeoman, afsd, was seized of land 422 ac in said
Hund, and died intestate and without issue, leaving 8 brothers
and sisters, to wit, JOSHUA, COMFORT, DIRECTOR, BENTON, STEPHEN,
SOMERSET, MATHIAS and EUPHAMA, to whom the lands descended in
equal porportions; and whereas the afsd BENTON was seized of 250
ac, died intestate and without issue, leaving 6 brothers and
sisters living, to wit, JOSHUA, COMFORT, STEPHEN, SOMERSET,
MATHIAS and EUPHAMA, to whom the said lands descended. To
COMFORT 20 pounds. Wit: WILLIAM DICKERSON, EDMOND DICKERSON.
Attys PHILLIPS KOLLOCK, JOSEPH MILLER and AVID TRAIN of Lewes.
Ackn 10 Nov 1786.

341 Petition of HAP HAZZARD for order of Court to direct sheriff
to convey land. Whereas HUGH KING the elder, late of Suss, was
in his lifetime seized of a tr in Broadkiln Hund, Suss, 200 ac,
being the sw end of larger tr called Orphans Choice, and so being
seized died, first making his last will in which he devised said
200 ac to his two sons JAMES KING and HUGH KING, which said JAMES
KING (before division of the lands) died intestate leaving two
sons, WILLIAM KING and JAMES KING to whom his share in the land
descended, WILLIAM the eldest 2/3 thereof and JAMES 1/3. Whereas
HUGH KING the younger and the afsd WILLIAM and JAMES KING being
all of full age, made partition of the land and executed deed
accordingly. And whereas GEORGE CONWELL and EUNICE his wife,
late EUNICE WALLER, lately in the Court of Common Pleas recovered
judgment agnst said WILLIAM KING for a debt of 32 pounds, 73 ac
of said land of WILLIAM KING sold by sheriff to HAP HAZZARD for
95 pounds.

342 Deed recording above described land. HAP HAZZARD from PETER
F. WRIGHT, Sheriff. Wit: WILLIAM PERRY, DAV. TRAIN. Ackn 11 Nov
1786.

344 Bond PETER FRETWELL WRIGHT Sheriff for performance of the
Sheriff''s Office. Sureties: WOODMAN STOCKLEY and ARTHUR
HAZZARD, yeomen, Suss. 700 pounds. On 8 Nov 1786. Wit: PETER
ROBINSON, GEORGE ROBINSON.

345 1 Nov 1786. Deed of Gift ELIZABETH COLLINGS from ANN BELL,
Suss, midwife, for love and affection to her dau ELIZABETH
COLLINGS a bed and furniture and to dau SAFIAH MATTOX gives a
heifer 3 yrs old and dau ABAGAIL ANDERSON a bed and furniture and
cow and calf. Wit: SAMUEL LOCKWOOD, DAVID LONG. Ackn 20 Feb
1787.

345 Deed. WILLIAM PIERCE from WM. POLK, Esqr. adminr. NANCY
POLK adminr and EDWARD POLK, adminr, of WILLIAM POLK, Junr, late
of Cedar Creek Hund, Suss, decd, who died intestate, seized of a
lot of 3 1/3 ac on nw side of Townsend Road, binding land sold by
WILLIAM POLK to RICHARD MULLINIX and JEHOSHAPHAT POLK and adj
lands of BENNET BRYAN. 150 pounds paid by WM. PIERCE. Wit:
BETSY THOMPSON, ANNA POLK. Ackn 8 Feb 1787.

346 8 Feb 1787. Deed. GEORGE WALTON Senr, Cedar Creek Hund,
from WILLIAM PIERCE, Cedar Creek Hund, cordwainer, and ELIZABETH
his wife, for 50 pounds, parcel of land in Cedar Creek Hund, on a
line of Coverdale Cole's land which he bought of WILLIAM POLK and
on a line of RICHARD MULLINEX's, being pt/o a tr which WILLIAM

POLK, Junr, late of the hund, decd by his bond conveyed to said
WILLIAM PIERCE by NANCY POLK and EDWARD POLK, adminr of WILLIAM
POLK. 2 1/2 ac. Wit: EDWARD POLK, PEGGY POLK. Ackn 8 Feb 1787.

347 18 Jan 1787. Deed. JOHN HUBBART, Suss, planter, from JOHN
PRITCHETT, Kent Co, Del, farmer, and RHODA his wife, for 35
pounds, a parcel of land called Smiths Rainger and likewise
Addition to Smith's Range in Suss being whereon JOHN JONES now
lives and heretofore was sold by patented claim of JAMES SMITH to
PETER RUSS. Attys DAVID TRAIN, Esqr. and ABNOR DILL, of Sus and
Kent Co. Wit: JOHN LAWS, JOSEPH GODWIN. Ackn 8 Feb 1787.

348 8 Feb 1787. Deed. JAMES POLK, Suss, from JOHN POLK and
MARY his wife, Suss, for 5 shillings, pt/o tr called Polks
Conclusion on se corner of said tr containing the dwelling house
and pt/o dwelling plantation whereon said JAMES POLK now dwells
in Nanticoke Hund in Johns Neck. Wit: ZEPHANIAH POLK, EDWARD
POLK. Ackn 8 Feb 1787.

349 Deed. JOHN ORR from RICHARD HOWARD of Lewes, pilot, and
COMFORT his wife. Whereas EDWARD CRAIG of Suss, yeoman, and
SARAH his wife sold on 9 Feb 1782 for 50 pounds to RICHARD HOWARD
a parcel of land of 8 ac being 1/3 of a tr on s side of Lewes
Town which contained 23 3/4 ac being same land the one moiety
whereof JOHN SIMONTON by his last will devised to his three daus,
to wit, JANE, SARAH and MARY. The other moiety of the larger
parcel was conveyed to JOHN SIMONTON the younger by JOHN MEIRS
and the said JOHN SIMONTON the younger being seized thereof died
intestate and without issue leaving four sisters, to wit, JANE,
SARAH, MARY and ELIZABETH to whom the said moiety descended and
whereas said ELIZABETH married NOBLE LEWIS who by their deed
released to JANE, SARAH and MARY, all their right of said land;
and whereas said MARY by deed of release conveyed her part to
above EDWARD CRAIG. Wit: JNO. WILTBANK, W. HARRISON. Ackn 8 Feb
1787.

350 8 Jan 1787. Deed. ABNOR DILL, Kent Co, taylor, from THOMAS
DAWSON, Suss, planter and ANN his wife, for 50 pounds, 5 shillings that pt/o a tr sold by JOSEPH GODWIN being pt/o the
property of ZACHERY NICOLS, to THOMAS DAWSON by deed dated 7 May
1783, recorded in Liber M.N. 12, folio 508, being pt/o a tr taken
up by MARMADUKE STORY, Senr., surveyed in 1752, and bought by
afsd ZACHARY NICOLS as appears by a bond for conveyance of same
dated 11 Apr 1758, near Marshope Bridge, 33 ac Wit: JOHN LAWS,
JOSEPH GODWIN, JOHN HUBARTT. Ackn 8 Feb 1787.

351 12 Oct 17778. Bond for Conveyance of land WILLIAM ROSS,
Junr, Suss, from JOHN JESSOP, yeoman, and ELENOR his wife, Suss.
Bound for 600 pounds to convey tr called Hogg Range, 253 ac.
Wit: ISAAC BRADLEY, DANIEL MORRISS. Ackn 9 Feb 1787.

351 Deed of Mortgage, JOHN TENNENT, Suss, from LEVIN CANNON,
Suss, yeoman, who for 50 pounds confirms to JOHN TENNENT the
dwelling platation whereon LEVIN CANNON now lives, called Cannons
Conclusion, lying in Suss, Del, and Caroline and Dorchester
counties, MD, bequeathed to LEVIN CANNON by his father WILLIAM
CANNON, decd, for 140 ac. Also Negro man PLYMOUTH. Wit: HENRY
HOOPER, ALLY WARREN. Ackn 9 Feb 1787.

352 10 Jan 1787. Deed. BIBBINS MORRIS, Suss, yeoman, from JOHN
ADDISON, Suss, for 300 pounds, land and marsh that his father
JACOB ADDISON died seized thereof and by a certain award and
division made by arbitrators betweeen him the said JOHN ADDISON,
JACOB and JONATHAN ADDISON, in Broadkiln Hund on n side of
Beverdam Branch, 109 ac, and a pt/o a marsh on Prime Hook Creek,
14 ac; also another pt/o marsh which runs to a post in THOMAS
GROVE's line, 8 ac. Wit: CALEB CIRWITHIN, ZAIL HALL. Ackn 9 Feb
1787.

353 Deed of Release ROBERT BUTCHER from WILLIAM BUTCHER.
Whereas there is a tr in Indian R Hund granted to CHRISTOPHER
TOPHAM, by warrant dated 6th day of 6th month, who died intestate
and not having personal estate sufficient to discharge his debts,
the land was sold by his adminr WILLIAM GILL to NICHOLAS WILLIAMS
who conveyed the same on 4 Nov 1752 to ROBERT BUTCHER f/o the
above named WILLIAM BUTCHER and the said ROBERT BUTCHER by his
last will dated 4 Feb 1763 devised said tr to his two sons the
above named WILLIAM and ROBERT [the younger] BUTCHER. Said
WILLIAM BUTCHER in order to divide the land releases claim to a
certain pt/o the land. Wit: HUGH STEPHENSON, JAMES STEPHENSON.
Ackn 6 Mar 1787.

354 Deed of Release WILLIAM BUTCHER from ROBERT BUTCHER. [See
above] Wit: same. Ackn 6 Mar 1787.

354 7 Mar 1787. Deed. SAMUEL ROWLAND FISHER of City of Phila,
merchant, from PETER FRTT. WRIGHT, Sheriff. Whereas there is a
parcel of land on se side of Herring creek one of the arms or
branches of Mispillion Creek in Cedar Creek Neck and Hund adj
lands now or formerly belonging to BENJAMIN WYNKOOP of the city
of Phila, and lands late in the possession of JOHN CRAPPER, decd,
below the dam of a mill now in the possession of GEORGE BLACK,
agreeable to survey and platt made in 17th and 18th day of May
1765. 562 ac, being pt/o a larger tr called Timber Neck granted
5 Aug 1687 to WILLIAM SPENCER, junr, then of Suss Co for 600 ac,
which WILLIAM SPENCER sold by deed 13 Apr 1689 to HENRY BOWMAN
who died seized thereof intestate whereupon committed to WILLIAM
CLARK, Suss, who obtained an order from the Orphans Court to sell
the land to pay debts of WILLIAM SPENCER whereas the land was
sold to WILLIAM CLARK and whereof WILLIAM CLARK died seized
thereof and the land descended to EDWARD EVANS now or late of the
City of Phila, cordwainer and REBECCA his wife, late REBECCA
CLARK in her right the said REBECCA and ELIZABETH CLARK (the said
REBECCA and ELIZABETH being the daus and only surviving issue of
afsd WILLIAM CLARK the younger decd) which said EDWARD EVANS and
REBECCA his wife and said ELIZABETH CLARK for 30 pounds paid by
JAMES FISHER, late of Suss, did agree to grant a general warranty
to said JAMES FISHER to said FISHER who died before a deed was
executed. In his will dated 22 Feb 1757 he bequeathed to his dau
ESTHER all his lands but if she should died in her minority the
land to descend to his two cousins, MARY MEIRS and THOMAS WYN-
KOOP. EDWARD EVANS and REBECCA his wife and ELIZABETH CLARK
afterward by deed dated 7 Oct 1751 conveyed said land to ABRAHAM
WYNKOOP exr of estate of JAMES FISHER who before the estate was
settled died making his will and appointed his son BENJAMIN
WYNKOOP one of the exrs who obtained permission from Orphans
Court to sell pt/o estate. And thereupon sold to SIMEON LEWIS of

Suss afsd 200 ac thereof leaving remainder. The afsd ESTHER
FISHER having married the before named DANIEL DINGEE and having
attained the full age of 21 yrs, the said ESTHER became thereupon
seized of an absolute and indefeasable estate in fee simple and
the lands devised to her by her father, was by them by deed
indented dated 9 Apr1765 and conveyed to DANIEL NUNEZ, Junr, then
of Suss and said DANIEL NUNEZ, Junr, by indenture dated 2 May
same year conveyed same to afsd DANIEL DINGEE in fee simple. And
whereas JOSHUA FISHER, lately of Phila, merchant, recovered
judgment agnst afsd DANIEL DINGEE for a debt of 800 pounds, 44
shillings, 7 pence. And the land was sold to SAMUEL ROWLAND
FISHER on 8 Feb 1787, 300 ac, for 28 shillings per ac. The
remainder, 262 ac, was sold to SAMUEL ROWLAND FISHER at 30 shillings, 6 pence. per ac Wit: DAVID TRAIN, JOHN ROWLAND. Ackn 7
Mar 1787.

357 10 Mar 1786. Deed.   SIMON KOLLOCK, Suss, Esq. from MILBY
JOHNSON, Suss. Whereas there is a tr in Indian R Hund, 95 ac,
pt/o a larger tr of 265 ac granted to ALEXANDER REID by proprietary warrant dated at Phila 25 Dec 1747, lying on w side of
county road leading from St. George's chaple to the Doe Bridge
that is leading over the head of Indian R about 11 miles from
town of Lewes being the westernmost end of the tr that SAMUEL
LINGO lives on, being on the last now in posession of THOMAS
GRISE formerly taken up and secured by JOSEPH DAY and JOHN
PRETTYMAN and others and whereon the afsd MILBY JOHNSON now lives
and is called the Partridge tr which afsd described 95 ac was
sold to afsd MILBY JOHNSON by ALEXANDER REED Junr by deed dated 6
Nov 1782, recorded in Liber M.N. 12, folio 476. 15 pounds, 11
shillings, 6 pence, to be paid on or before 10 Mar 1788. Attys
NATHL. WAPLES, GEORGE FRAME, WILLIAM NEWBOLD. Wit: PETER HALL,
JOHN TINDALL. Ackn 8 Mar 1787.

358 6 Oct 1770. Bond for Conveyance of land, JOSEPH CARRELL,
Suss, yeoman, from LEVIN CRAPPER, merchant, Suss, for 200 pounds,
the tr on nw side of Herring branch, being pt/o tr bought of
WYNKOOPs exrs adj the ne side of said Carrells plantation, 86 ac
JOHN HAZZARD, PETER MILMAN. Ackn 8 Mar 1787.

359 Power of Attys JOHN WAINWRIGHT, yeoman, from WILLIAM OWENS,
senr, Suss, yeoman. Wit: EDWARD DINGLE, WILLIAM FREEMAN.

359 9 Mar 1786. Bond of Indemnity SAML. DODD exr of ALICE
SHELPMAN decd from JNO. DUTTON and JONA. CAHOON. JOHN DUTTON and
JONATHAN CAHOON both of Broadkiln Hund, yeomen, bound to SAMUEL
DODD of said hund, yeoman, exr (in right of his wife MAGDALINE
late MAGDALINE SHELPMAN) in the sum of 500 pounds, to be paid to
SAMUEL DODD regarding freedom of negro man JACK. Wit: JNO.
RUSSEL, ELIZABETH RUSSEL 30 Apr 1787.

359 11 Feb 1780. [second of two pages numbered 359] Bond for
Conveyance of land JOHN DAGWORTHY to WILLIAM BURTON, Junr, both
of Suss. DAGWORTHY's right to parcel of land called Barnnets
Choice, n of land in possession of BAKER WHARTON, 90 ac to be
conveyed to WILLIAM BURTON without further delay. Wit: JAS.
MITCHELL, Junr, GEORGE MITCHELL. Ackn 11 May 1787.

359 16 Mar 1779. Bond of Indemnity GEORGE MITCHELL from JOHN
DAGWORTHY. DAGWORTHY bound to MITCHELL in 1000 pounds to which
MITCHELL bound to REBECKA COX of Hunterdun Co, N.J., in sum of
1000 pounds on the loan of 500 pounds.

360 11 May 1786. Deed. EDWARD CREAGH from EPHRAIM KING and
MARGARET his wife, both of Little Creek Hund, for 9 pounds, pt/o
a tr known as Kings Venture, in Little Creek Hund, 3 ac. Wit:
SAMUEL HALL, CALEB BALDING, JAS. TRUSHAM. Attys DAVID HALL.
Ackn 9 May 1787.

360 11 May 1786. Deed. EDWARD CREAGH from from EPHRAIM KING,
for 9 pounds, a tr in Little Creek Hund called Creaghs Purchase.
Wit: JOHN GODDARD and ISAAC BENSON. Attys DAVID HALL. Ackn 9
May 1787.

361 9 May 1787. Deed. STEPHEN STYER, Suss, yeoman, and ELEANOR
his wife (late ELEANOR WYATT) adminrs of JNO. WYATT, late of
Suss, who died intestate, from WM. WYATT, Suss, yeoman, and MARY
his wife. WILLIAM WYATT the elder, late of Wor Co, MD, decd,
possessed 200 ac originally granted by patent dated 15 Nov 1736
to JOSEPH WYATT his father, then in Som Co, MD, called Desire
near the easternmost side of St. Martins R. WILLIAM WYATT the
elder being seized of the said land by his bond dated 9 Dec 1771,
recorded in Liber M.N. 12, folio 163, acknowledged himself by the
name of WILLIAM WYATT, Senr. of Wor Co, MD, planter, bound to
JOHN WYATT and WILLIAM WYATT, both of said co, his sons, in the
sum of 400 pounds. WILLIAM died intestate before any deed
of conveyance was executed. WILLIAM WYATT, Junr, sold his right
to said lands to his brother, JOHN WYATT on 3 Mar 1780 for 72
pounds and 15 shillings and further payment of 2 pounds 5 shillings by STEPHEN STYER. Wit: JOHN WOLF, JOHN BURTON. Ackn 9 May
1787.

363 9 May 1787. Deed. JACOB ROGERS, Suss, yeoman, from STEPHEN
STYER, Suss, yeoman, and ELEANOR his wife late ELEANOR WYATT,
wife, adminrs of JOHN WYATT. JOHN WYATT at the time of his death
was seized of a parcel of land in Baltimore Hund called Desire,
originally granted by patent by the proprietary of MD dated 15
Nov 1736 to JOSEPH WYATT, grandfather of said JOHN WYATT, beginning at a marked oak on easternmost side of St. Martins R, 200
ac, whereof said JOHN WYATT died intestate and whereas JOHN WYATT
did not have sufficient estate at the time of his death to pay
his debts, STEPHEN STYER and ELEANOR his wife adminrs of said
JOHN WYATT were authorized to sell the above mentioned land,
which was bought by said JACOB ROGERS. 13 pounds, 1 shillings
Wit: WOOLSEY BURTON, D. HALL. Ackn 9 May 1787.

364 9 May 1787. Deed. STEPHEN STYER from JACOB ROGERS. 13
pounds, 7 shillings [Described above]. Wit: WOOLSEY BURTON, D.
HALL. Ackn 9 May 1787.

364 4 May 1787. Deed. JAMES POLLOCK, Suss, merchant, from
ROBERT HART and ELIZABETH his wife, of Suss, pt/o a tr called Red
Oak Ridge adj lands of NATHANIEL HAYS and others, for 49 pounds,
4 shillings - 35 ac, 114 square perches. Wit: JOHN MARSH, JOHN
WILLIAMS, NATHANIEL HAYS. Ackn 9 May 1787.

365 27 Jul 1786. Deed. PAUL and PETER WAPLES, Suss, from WM.
WAPLES and ZADOC VEAZEY, Suss, yeoman, for 200 pounds paid by
PAUL and PETER WAPLES, as well in consequence of a bond given by
WM. WAPLES for the conveyance of pt/o a tr called Aydelotts
Meadow, the bond dated 23 Mar 1767, 3 trs, Aydelotts Meadow, Luck
and Narrow Chance, near Indian R on Piney Neck side, between two
landings, one called The Old and the other called The New R Land-
ings ... to a line of JOHN WAPLE's land. 117(?) ac Wit: WM.
TINGLE, EDWD. DINGLE. Ackn 9 May 1787.

366 27 Jul 1786. Deed. PETER WAPLES, Suss, yeoman, from
WILLIAM WAPLES, Suss, yeoman. BENJAMIN AYDELOTT was seized of a
tr called Aydelotts Ignorance which he devised to his dau RACHELL
GILLSTRAP w/o PETER GILLSTRAP which they sold to PAUL WAPLES,
father to said WILLIAM WAPLES. The said PAUL WAPLES died
intestate and the lands (then in MD) fell to above mentioned
WILLIAM WAPLES. PAUL WAPLES was also owned a tr called Aydelotts
Neglect of 7 ac which fell to WM. WAPLES. - In consequence of a
bond given by said WILLIAM WAPLES to PETER WAPLES for conveyance
of afsd trs dated 23 Mar 1767 - and a satisfactory sum of money.
Attys WOLSEY BURTON, RHOADS SHANKLIN, DAVID TRAIN, PHILLIPS
KOLLOCK. Wit: WM. TINGLE, EDWD. DINGLE. Ackn 9 May 1787.

367 3 May 1786. Deed. STEPHEN BAILY, Som Co, MD, yeoman, and
ELIZABETH his wife from RHOADS SHANKLAND, Lewes and Rehoboth
Hund, surveyor. There is a small tr in Lewes and Rehoboth Hund,
10 ac, on se side of Coldspring Branch, being that which was
lately sold by adminrs of JOHN McCULLAH, late of Suss, yeoman, by
order of Orphans Court, and was conveyed to WILLIAM HALL who with
MARY his wife on 11 Jun 1785 conveyed same to RHOADS SHANKLAND.
Also another parcel sold as real estate of afsd JOHN McCULLAH and
conveyed to ALEXANDER REED by adminrs of JOHN McCULLAH, and
ALEXANDER REED with ELIZABETH his wife conveyed same to RHOADS
SHANKLAND. The latter parcel adj the other one, below the dam of
the mill late of WILLIAM BURTON lately decd near the lands called
the Presbyterian Glebes. Containing in total 55 ac Wit: JOHN
BELL, DAV. TRAIN. Ackn 9 May 1787.

368 19 Mar 1787. Deed. JOHN PARKER, Kent Co, Del, sadler, from
ISAAC BRADLEY, Esqr, Suss, for 800 pounds, a tr called Rich
Bottom in Northwest Fork Hund, 200 ac. Also 100 ac of the s end
of a tr called Proprietarys Dispute in Northwest Fork Hund. Attys
DAVID TRAIN, THOMAS LAWS. Wit: THOMAS LAWS, JOSEPH BRADLEY. Ackn
9 May 1787.

369 11 Sep 1786. Deed. JOHN HANDY, joiner, from CLARKSON
CANNON, Suss, planter, for 100 pounds, pt/o tr called Addition to
Four Tracts near tr called Forrest Land, near where JAMES BROWN,
Junr., now lives. Wit: JOHN WILTBANK, PHILLIPS KOLLOCK. 82 1/2
ac Wit: FRANCIS WRIGHT, DANIEL POLK. Ackn 9 May 1787.

370 1 Jan 1787. Deed. FRANCIS WRIGHT, planter, from JAMES
HICKMAN, planter, and MARGARET his wife, Suss, for 40 pounds,
pt/o a tr called Saplin Ridge, also pt/o a tr called Conclusion
and pt/o a tr called Laytons Fancy starting in a lane between
LEVIN CLIFTON and WILLIAM LAYTON. 68 ac. Attys JOHN WILTBANK,
PHILLIPS KOLLOCK. Wit: SOLON. BREADY, DANIEL POLK. Ackn 9 May
1787.

371 10 Jun 1786. Deed. WILLIAM ROSS Junr., Suss, farmer, from
WILLIAM JESSOP, Suss, preacher and s/o JOHN JESSOP and ELINOR his
wife late of said co, decd. WM. JESSOP and ELINOR his wife on 12
Oct 1778 contracted to WILLIAM ROSS, Junr, to sell 253 ac, pt/o a
tr called Hog Range for 300 pounds Attys JOHN LAWS, JOHN
WILTBANK. Wit: EDWD. WHITE, DAVID RICHARDS. Ackn 9 May 1787.

371 9 May 1787. Deed. FOSTER DONAVAN from SARAH HEAVERLO and
DANIEL HEAVERLO exrs of will of ANDREW HEAVERLO, late of Broadkiln Hund, yeoman, decd, and FOSTER DONOVAN of said Hund, yeoman.
ANDREW HEAVERLO was conveyed from JOHN CLOWES, Esq. 19 ac, being
pt/o a larger tr on e side of se fork of Gravily Branch originally granted by MD patent to ABRAHAM INGRAM for 50 ac called Bare
Garden, taken away and included in elder surveys. ANDREW
HEAVERLO so possessed of this land in his will dated 29th day of
11th month 1783 directed that all his land in Broadkiln Forest,
consisting of 2 trs, be sold after his decease. For 19 pounds is
sold 19 ac not taken up in elder surveys. Wit: --- RODNEY, CALEB
RODNEY. Ackn 9 May 1787.

372 Bond for Conveyance of land WILLIAM SHARP, Wor Co, MD,
planter, that PETER SHARP, Wor Co, MD, planter, for 190 pounds
convey 130 ac being pt/o a tr of 150 ac called Elbo Rume which
130 ac became the right of PETER SHARP by the last will of his
father, WILLIAM SHARP. Wit: BENJAMIN PHILLIPS, WILLIAM SALMON,
junr. Ackn 9 May 1787.

373 2 Apr 1787. Deed. NUNEZ DEPUTY from ISAAC MESSICK and
RACHEL his wife and COMFORT MESSIX their mother [sic], widow of
OBEDIAH MESSICK decd, of Suss Co. Whereas a tr in Broadkill Hund
in Carr [?] Neck on s side and near the head of a Mill Pond of
ANDREW COLLINS about 1 mile distant for Captain JOHN COLLINS',
said tr granted by patent in MD, dated 25 Jan 1748 to OBEDIAH
MESSICK by his will devised afsd tr to his wife COMFORT and son
ISAAC MESSICK. Tr is called Long Delay, 100 ac 90 pounds ISAAC
and COMFORT MESSICK gave their bond of conveyance to JOB INGRAM
who conveyed his right to NUNEZ DEPUTY. Attys Col. HENRY NEILL,
Dr. JOSEPH HALL, RHOADS SHANKLAND, JOHN RODNEY, WILLIAM BRERETON.
Wit: SIMON KOLLOCK, N. WAPLES. Ackn 2 Apr 1787.

374 22 Mar 1787. Deed. JOSEPH CANNON Senr, Suss, from ISAAC
RIGGEN, Suss, planter, for 25 pounds tr called Venture in Som Co,
MD, now Suss, on branch of Broad Creek back in the woods on White
Oak Swamp in a neck called by the Indians Wimbosocom Neck. Wit:
JEREMIAH CANNON, EBENEZER CANNON. Attys SAMUEL HALL, SAMUEL
HEARN. Ackn 10 May 1787.

374 1 Mar 1787. Deed. JOSEPH CANNON, Senr, Suss, from JNO.
WHITTINGHAM ADAMS, Suss, planter, for 45 pounds, tr called
Eastwood in Wor Co, MD in s side of Nanticoke R on easternmost
side of one of the branches of Broad Creek being the uppermost
branch of the said R toward the Indian R, 30 ac. Attys ELIJAH
CANNON, Senr, SAMUEL HALL. Wit: JOSEPH CANNON, Junr., SAML.
HEARN. Ackn 10 May 1787.

375 22 Sep 1784. Deed. JONATHAN HEARN, Senr., Little Creek
Hund, from MOSES GORDY, Little Creek Hund, for 170 pounds a tr
called Forrest Grove, originally granted to ALEXANDER MITCHELL in

MD now in Suss, dated 29 Sep 1761. In Wicomoco Forrest on n side of Cypress Branch and w side of afsd MITCHELL's plantation. Also right of a resurvey, surveyed from said tr in 18 Jun 1776. Wit: ZEPHANIAH MADDUX, JONATHAN HEARN, Junr. Attys SAMUEL HEARN, SAMUEL HALL. Ackn 10 May 1787.

376 6 Jul 1787. Deed. JONATHAN HEARN, Senr., Suss, from JAMES and CLEMENT CALLAWAY, Suss, for 100 pounds, pt/o two trs called Iron Hill ... one of the lines runs to a division line between JONATHAN HEARN and NATHANIAL LECATT, 60 ac. And pt/o a tr called And What you Please, 25 ac. Attys SAMUEL HOLLAND, SAMUEL HEARN. Wit: JONATHAN HEARN, Junr, ISAAC LINCH. Ackn 10 May 1787.

377 9 May 1787. Deed. CLEMENT HEARN, Suss, from PLANNER SHORES, Suss, planter, for 50 pounds, a tr called Pleasant Grove, formerly lying in Worcester Co, MD, 50 ac, out of which SHORES has sold 1 ac for the building of a Methodist Preaching house. Attys ELIJAH CANNON, senr, JOSEPH CANNON, Senr. Wit: THOMAS HEARN, SAML. HEARN. Ackn 10 May 1787.

378 22 Sep 1784. Deed. SAMUEL HEARN, Suss, from ISAIAH CALLAWAY, Suss, for 47 pounds parcel of land called HEARNs Liberty formerly in Wor Co, MD, now Suss, granted to BENJAMIN HEARN, 34 ac. Attys JONATHAN HEARN, ELIJAH CANNON. Wit: ZEPHENIAH MADDUX, JONATHAN HEARN. Ackn 10 May 1787.

378 9 Aug 1786. Deed. JOHN WILLIS, Suss, from WILLIAM WALKER and SUKEY his wife, Suss, for 70 pounds, a parcel of land called Watsons Folly, granted and patented to JOHN HARVEY, decd, 12 Sep 1712, on e side of Gravally Branch, joining the afsd WILLIS's land, 50 ac. Wit: JOHN LAWS, Junr., NANCY BAYLEY. Ackn 10 May 1787.

379 16 Feb 1787. Deed. JAMES CANNON, Junr, yeoman, from JAMES CANNON, Senr, Suss, yeoman, for 50 pounds, a tr in Northwest Fork Hund called Cannons Meadows, 50 ac, as shown on the patent. Wit: JOHN TENNENT, JACOB CANNON, HOWARD HARRISON. Ackn 11 May 1787.

380 16 Feb 1787. Deed. HAYWARD CANNON, Suss, yeoman, from JAMES CANNON, senr, Suss, yeoman, for 40 pounds, all that pt/o a tr called Friendship in Northwest Fork Hund, on e side of Chepple Road, 40 ac. Attys WILLIAM PERRY, Esqr., PETER WRIGHT, Esqr. Wit: JOHN TENNENT, JACOB CANNON, JAMES CANNON, Junr. Ackn 11 May 1787.

381 Deed. WILLIAM ANDERSON PARKER from SARAH and THOMAS HART and wife, for 100 pounds, a parcel of land on s side of Lewes, Suss, containing 23 3/4 ac, one moiety whereof JOHN SIMONTON the Elder in his will of 29 May 1751 devised to his 3 daus, JENNETT, SARAH and MARY, and the other moiety thereof by deed conveyed by JOHN MEIRS to JOHN SIMONTON the younger who afterwards died intestate, and without issue, whereby his moiety descended to his four sisters, JENNETT, SARAH, MARY, and ELIZABETH, which said ELIZABETH afterward married NOBLE LEWIS who released their right therein to said JENNETT, SARAH and MARY - And by mutual agreement they divided the land. And SARAH afterwards married EDWARD CRAIG who on 21 May 1784 they conveyed 1 ac thereof to JOHN HART. And JOHN HART by his will dated 12 Oct 1784 appointed his wife SARAH

HART and his son THOMAS HART to be his exrs and they were authorized to sell said land to pay debts of decd. Wit: ISRAEL
BROWN [?], WILLIAM HARRISON. Ackn 12 May 1787.

382 12 May 1787. Petition, Genl. DAGWORTHYs' exrs for leave of
Court to convey land to WM. BURTON, joiner. Petition of MARTHA
DAGWORTHY, GEORGE MITCHEL, LAMBERT KIDWALLADAR, surviving exrs of
last will of JOHN DAGWORTHY, late of Dagsbury Hund, decd, that a
tr in Worc Co, now in Dagsbury Hund, Suss, originally granted by
patent in MD, on 11 Jun 1748, to JAMES BARNETT, 98 ac, called
Barnnets Choice, who conveyed 90 ac thereof to JAMES JONES who on
19 Jun 1764 conveyed same to HINMAN WHARTON who on 4 Apr 1768
conveyed said 90 ac to said JOHN DAGWORTHY who by his bond dated
11 Feb 1780 sold to WILLIAM BURTON, Joiner, for 10,000 pounds.
North of tr of BAKER WHARTON.

382 Deed. WILLIAM BURTON, Joiner, from Genl. DAGWORTHY's exrs.
[See above.] WILLIAM BURTON has paid the remainder of the
purchase money. Wit: JANE KOLLOCK, SAML. PAYNTER. Ackn 12 May
1787.

384 Deed of Mortgage. PAPTIS LAY, Shipwright, from HESTER MOORE
of Lewes, widow, ABRAHAM WILTBANK, late of afsd town, pilot, and
CATHARINE his wife. Whereas LEVIN DERICKSON, Esqr., Commissioner
for the sale of forfeited estates of the county by virtue of an
act of the assembly entitled, "An Act of free pardon and Oblivion
and for other purposes therein mentioned," did make public sale
of that land in Lewes, late the property of above named ABRAHAM
WILTBANK, he being one of the persons named in the above act of
assembly, which tr was sold to above named CATHARINE and she by
her deed dated 29 Jun 1780 conveyed to JACOB MOORE of Lewes and
whereas LEVIN DERICKSON by his deed dated 6 Nov 1780 conveyed the
above tr of 80 ac to JACOB MOORE. The land is bounded by Lewes
Creek, lands of JOHN WILTBANK, Esqr and JAMES THOMPSON. And
JACOB MOORE by his will dated 25 Apr 1784 devised unto above
named HESTER MOORE all his estate. And HESTER MOORE and ABRAHAM
WILTBANK by bond are held bound to BAPTIS LAY by 340 pounds. All
the land except the use of dwelling house wherein said ABRAHAM
WILTBANK now lives, the garden and burying ground. Attys
PHILLIPS KOLLOCK, JOHN RODNEY and DANIEL RODNEY. Wit: DAVID
TRAIN, PHILLIPS KOLLOCK. Ackn 5 Jun 1787.

386 10 Jan 1787. Deed. NORMOND LOFLAND, Junr., Suss, yeoman,
from HUGH BAKER, Suss. 100 pounds pt/o tr called RILEYs Forton
being the land that BENJAMIN RILEY sold to THOMAS WORTON of Suss
and said BENJAMIN RILEY, firmly bound by an obligation to convey
the 100 ac and THOMAS WORTON on 12 Apr 1763 assigned over his
rights to said obligation to Hugh Baker. And therefore THOMAS
and GEORGE RILEY, exrs of last will of BENJAMIN RILEY decd, by
order of Court of Common Pleas did make over said land according
to the said obligation. Attys ELIAS BAKER. Wit: WILLIAM LOFLAND,
WILLIAM RILEY. Ackn 8 Aug 1787.

386 8 Aug 1787. Deed. GEORGE MITCHELL, merchant, from GEORGE
ADAMS, Esqr., and ANN his wife, Suss. Whereas ALEXANDER ADAMS of
MD was in his lifetime seized of two trs in Som Co, MD, then Wor
but now Suss, one parcel called Narrow Ridge, 25 ac, and another
tr called Long Ridge of 50 ac. ALEXANDER ADAMS devised above

land to GEORGE ADAMS, making valid certain instruments of sale
he the said ALEXANDER ADAMS in his lifetime had made to GEORGE
ADAMS including the above described land, saving elder surveys
of the 50-ac tr. Said GEORGE ADAMS for 83 pounds conveys same
to GEORGE MITCHELL. Attys PHILIPS KOLLOCK, WOOLSEY BURTON,
RHOADS SHANKLAND, ISRAEL HOLLAND. THOMAS EVANS, JOHN FLEMING.
Ackn 8 Aug 1787.

388 2 Jan 1786. Deed. GEORGE MITCHELL, Esqr., Suss, from
JOHN NICHOLSON, Suss, taylor, and SIPPORAH CRAPPER now w/o
WILLIAM HALL of said co. GEORGE DIRICKSON of this state, was
seized of a tr by virtue of MD patent dated 26 Aug 1760 called
Georges Good Luck formerly lying in Wor Co, MD, but now Suss, 45
ac, which on 27 Aug 1768 he conveyed to SOLOMON CRAPPER. When
SOLOMON CRAPPER died the land fell to his three daus, that is,
SIPPORAH CRAPPER, now w/o WILLIAM HALL, PUELLA CRAPPER now w/o
said JOHN NICKELSON and RHODA CRAPPER now w/o WILLIAM DIRICKSON.
JOHN NICKELSON by his marriage to PUELLA became seized of her
portion of the land, and SIPPORAH by her bond dated 10 Nov 1781
did bind herself in the sum of 50 pounds. Now for the sum of 75
pounds 28 ac, the above sale is made. Land begins on s side of
small branch called Herring branch on n side of county road
leading from Cedar Neck to head of Indian R, being a bounder of
a tr formerly surveyed for JOHN COLLINS, Senr, now belonging to
SAMUEL LOCKWOOD. Includes dwelling house wherein JOHN NICHOLSON
lives. Attys PHILLIPS KOLLOCK, RHOADS SHANKLIN, ISRAEL HOLLAND.
Wit: EDWD. DINGLE, JOHN EVANS, JOHN CLOWES. Signed JNO.
NICHOLSON, PAULINE NICHOLSON [w/o JOHN NICHOLSON], ZIPPORAH
HALL. Ackn 8 Aug 1787.

389 7 Aug 1787. Deed TRUSTEN LAWS POLK of Northwest Fork Hund,
yeoman, from PETER WRIGHT, Sheriff. There is a tr in said Hund
of 300 ac adj lands of THOMAS LAWS, THOMAS MILLICAN, ROBERT
LAYTON and CALEB NUTTER, consisting of parts of lesser trs, to
wit, 38 ac, pt/o tr called Long Ridge, 54 ac of pt/o Laytons
Fancy, 19 ac of Williams Purchase, about 120 ac of Conclusion,
35 ac of Resurvey made by THOMAS LAYTON, about 13 ac being a
small survey called Little North, about 9 ac, pt/o tr called
Clearance [described], of about 300 ac, whereas THOMAS HICKMAN
late of this co afsd was seized. Whereas JAMES POLLOCK lately
in the County court of Common Pleas recovered judgment agnst
afsd THOMAS HICKMAN whose land was seized and sold to TRUSTEN
LAWS POLK for 240 pounds, 2 sh, 5 p. Wit: JACOB KOLLOCK, DAVID
TRAIN. Ackn 8 Aug 1787.

391 2 Dec 1786. Deed. DANIEL POLK, Esqr., Suss, farmer, from
JOHN ECCLESTON, Dor Co, MD, Doctor, for 500 pounds, parcel in
Suss that HUGH ECCLESTON bought from PATRICK BROUGHAWN and JAMES
KIRKMAN, it being sold to them by JOHN JESSOP and wife, called
Attawattocoquin. 400 ac. Wit: WM. POLK, JOHN SMITH. Ackn 8
Aug 1787.

392 8 Aug 1787. Deed. WOOLSEY BURTON of Dagsberry Hund, yeoman, from SARAH BURTON of Angola and Indian R Hund, spinster.
Whereas a parcel of land in Angola and Indian Hund containing 90
ac, being pt/o larger tr called Bottle and Cake, whereof WILLIAM
BURTON (commonly called LONG BURTON), late of Suss by his will
devised same to his son JOSEPH, f/o afsd SARAH, subject to the

thirds or dower of ELIZABETH the widow of said WILLIAM which being alloted to her by virtue of an Order of the Orphans Court and whereas JOSEPH died intestate, siezed of the remaining 2/3, leaving a widow and 6 children, afsd SARAH, and MARY, THOMAS, ELISABETH, WILLIAM BAGWELL and PATIENCE to whom the lands descended. The widow's third was laid off but the remaining 2/3 would not admit to partition among the heirs. In consideration of 97 pounds, 10 shillings for the 52 ac, SARAH BURTON conveyed [the entire 2/3 which belongs to her and the other children?]. Tr adjoins land devised by BENJAMIN BURTON to his son the afsd WOOLSEY BURTON and runs along Herring Creek.

394 1 Oct 1785. Deed. DAVID RICHARDS, of Indian R Hund, farmer, from STOCKLEY HOSMAN of Lewes and Rehoboth Hund, Suss, carpenter, and HANNAH his wife. ISAAC RICHARDS was seized of a messuage plantation and tr in Indian R Hund and in his will dated 22 Nov 1779, "I bequeath to my living friend STOCKLEY HOSMAN of the City of Philadelphia, house carpenter, all the rest of my estate ..." 100 pounds near a tr laid by JOHN PRICE. 159 ac. Attys DAVID HALL. Wit: JOHN STOCKLEY, CORNELIUS PAYNTER. Ackn 9 Aug 1787.

396 Deed of mortgage STOCKLEY HOSMAN from DAVID RICHARDS, 159 ac called Providence, 75 pounds. Wit: JOHN STOCKLEY, CORNELIUS PAYNTER. Ackn 9 Aug 1787.

397 28 Jul 1787. Deed. JOSEPH BRADLEY, Suss, planter, from ISAAC BRADLEY, Esqr., Suss, and ELIZABETH his wife, for 170 pounds, their right to tr called Providence, their pt/o which contains 170 ac, being the land willed to said ISAAC BRADLEY by his father. Wit: WM. POLK, HENRY HOOPER. Ackn 8 Aug 1787.

397 2 Jul 1787. Deed. THOMAS WALLER s/o NATHL., from WM. BEVINS, Suss. 60 pounds, 1/3 pt/o a sawmill standing on a tr called Addition to Folly with 1/3 of the utensils that belong to said mill, also 1/3 of half of the mill dam adj said mill, and 1/3 of stock yard. Attys DAVID TRAIN, Suss and ISAAC HENRY of Som Co. Wit: BENJAMIN ELLIS, JOHN SILLAVAN. Ackn 8 Aug 1787.

398 --- Mar 1787. Deed. CHARLES MOORE s/o JOHN MOORE, planter, Suss, from WILLIAM WROE [ROW] and MARY ANN WROE [ROW] his wife, Suss, for 50 pounds pt/o tr called Manloves Grove. 50 ac. Attys JOHN WILTBANK and PHILLIPS KOLLOCK of Lewes. Wit: CLEMENT SAFFORD, MATTHIAS MOORE. Ackn 8 Aug 1787.

399 8 Aug 1787. Deed. WILLIAM WALKER, Cedar Creek Hund, yeoman, from JAMES HALL of Cedar Creek Hund, Yeoman, and NANCY his wife, for 200 pounds, 149 ac, being pt/o a larger tr containing by a survey made 20 Jan 1756 by virtue of a warrant granted to JOHN COVERDALE Junr. and assigned to PHILLIP HUGGEN, 255 ac in Great Neck in Cedar Creek Hund, called Silver Plains, being the same 149 ac PHILLIP HUGGENS conveyed by deed to said JAMES HALL and which JAMES HALL sold or swopt with WILLIAM COLLINS who sold same to above WILLIAM WALKER. The said JAMES HALL's bond for conveyance thereof to said WALKER. Wit: THOS. GRAY, ZADOK LINDALL. Ackn 8 Aug 1787.

400 Deed. GEORGE RICKARDS from LITTLETON TOWNSEND. Whereas a
tr in Cedar Creek Hund known by name of the Brook Tract, 280 ac,
being the moiety of a larger tr on n side of Prime Hook, begin-
ning on the w side of branch which proceeds out of Prime Hook
Creek on s side of the road near CALEB CIRWITHIN's [decd] land.
And whereas WILLIAM CRAMER on 4 Feb 1721 conveyed same to JOHN
WATTSON of Suss, who by his will dated 3 Jan 1729 devised as
follows, "I bequeath unto my three sons, JAMES, HEZEKIAH and
LUKE WATTSON ... all my plantation ... containing 300 ac... in
Prime Hook Neck on the n side of the road that goes up the Neck
to the Kings Road, and on the west of the branch called the
Brook which proceeds out Prime Hook Creek, ..." And whereas
said JAMES WATTSON died intestate and without issue, and the
land vested in afsd HEZEKIAH and LUKE WATTSON, and said Luke's
moiety of said lands were sold by sheriff for discharge of his
debts and the other moiety descended unto THOMAS WATTSON by the
death of his father the above named HEZEKIAH WATTSON as next of
kin and heir at law, which said THOMAS died intestate and without issue whereby the said moiety descended to the heirs of
ELIZABETH the w/o STEPHEN TOWNSEND, decd, (one of the daus of
afsd JOHN WATTSON the testator) namely one-half thereof to
STEPHEN TOWNSEND, ABIGAIL the w/o AARON OLIVER, COSTON TOWNSEND
since decd leaving issue three children (to wit) LITTLETON
TOWNSEND, ELIZABETH the w/o WILLIAM WALTON, and STEPHEN TOWN-
SEND, BETTY SPENCER since decd leaving issue (SAMUEL, EBENEZER,
SARAH and BETTY SPENCER and MARY MITCALF), LITTLETON, NOAH and
JEHU TOWNSEND and the other half thereof to the heirs and rep of
MARY late w/o COSTON TOWNSEND the Elder, decd, one of the daus
of afsd JOHN WATTSON, the Testator, namely ISAAC TOWNSEND, JOHN
TOWNSEND and JAMES TOWNSEND. And whereas the above named
LITTLETON TOWNSEND purchased the undivided rights of the above
named JEHU TOWNSEND, LITTLETON TOWNSEND, JR., ISAAC TOWNSEND and
JOHN TOWNSEND which rights with the said LITTLETON TOWNSEND's
own undivided right to the quantity of 75 ac, for 105 pounds
Attys JOHN RODNEY, PHILLIPS KOLLOCK and DAVID TRAIN of Lewes.
Wit: RICKETTS MILLS, W. HARRISON. Ackn 9 Aug 1787.

401 28 Jul 1785. Deed. WILLIAM PASSWATERS, farmer, from LEVIN
WILLEY, Suss, farmer, for 50 pounds all that messuage or tene-
ments called [blank] in Nanticoke Hund beginning at a corner
post of WILLIAM PASSWATERS and his brother RICHARD PASSWATERS
land, 67 ac, also another messuage being pt/o the same tr adj
said WILLIAM PASSWATERS Tusekah Branch place or parcel of land,
91 ac. Wit: THOMAS TRUITT, THOS. GRAY. Ackn 8 Aug 1787.

403 20 Oct 1786. Deed LEVI KING, planter, from ROBERT KING,
Suss. Whereas ROBERT KING is seized of a tr in a Resurvey made
by him from a tr where he now lives containing 50 ac and was
conveyed to said LEVI KING in 1783 in Little Creek Hund, pt/o tr
patented to sd. ROBERT KING 27 Jul 1750 called Kings Venture.
20 pounds. Wit: JOHN HALL, OBADIAH MORRIS, JOHN WILLIAMS. Ackn
8 Aug 1787.

403 --- Mar 1787. Deed. MATTHIAS MOOR s/o JOHN MOOR, planter,
Suss, from WILLIAM ROE and MARY ANN his wife, Suss, planter, for
50 pounds, pt/o tr called Manloves Grove. 70 ac. Attys JOHN
WILTBANK, PHILLIPS KOLLOCK. Wit: CLEMENT SAFFORD, CHARLES MOOR.
Ackn 8 Aug 1787.

404 28 Jul 1787. Deed. ISRAEL COVERDALE from LEVIN WILLEY,
for 100 pounds in Nanticoke Hund in Hines Neck adj land of JOHN
OWENS and ALEXANDER LAWS, 57 1/2 ac. Attys RHOADS SHANKLAND.
Wit: THOMAS TRUITT, THOS. GRAY. Ackn 8 Aug 1787.

405 9 Jul 1787. Deed. WILLIAM PERRY, Suss, from WILLIAM
MATTHEWS, Suss, and ANN his wife. Whereas there is a tr in
Broadkiln Hund, 200 ac, being pt/o a larger tr granted to
WILLIAM CLARK by patent dated 2d day, 2d month, 1686 for 1000
ac, which 200 ac became the property of RICHARD DOBSON of Suss,
and said DOBSON dying intestate leaving issue, 3 daus: ISABELLA,
ANN and SARAH and by order of Orphans Court, 130 ac, was laid
off to ISABELLA and ANN which came to be the property of JESSE
DEAN and said JESSE DEAN and JEMIMA his wife on 11 May 1781
conveyed same 130 ac to above named WILLIAM MATTHEWS, and the
remaining pt/o the said 200 ac being laid off unto SARAH DOBSON,
she by the name of SARAH ANDERSON in her will devised same to
WOODMAN STOCKLEY and ELIZABETH his wife who on 25 Nov 1783
conveyed same to above WILLIAM MATTHEWS. Tr begins at a tree
bounding mill pond formerly belonging to WILLIAM STEPHENSON, it
being a corner tree of land of heirs of WILLIAM STEWART... to a
corner post in the line of land formerly belonging to GEORGE
WEST ... to a corner post of the land of heirs of JONATHAN
SCUDDER, 193 ac for 54 pounds Wit: ELIZABETH MATTHEWS, SALLY
MATTHEWS. Ackn 8 Aug 1787.

407 9 Dec 1785. Deed. WILLIAM MATHEWS, Suss, from JAMES
STEPHENSON, Suss, ship carpenter, a tr in Broadkiln Hund late
property of SAMUEL STEPHENSON late of Suss, who died intestate,
and the land descended to his heirs and representatives, the
afsd JAMES STEPHENSON being his eldest son who preferred a
petition to value and sell the land. Wit: JAMES VENT, JAMES
MARTIN. Ackn 8 Aug 1787.

408 30 Jul 1787. Deed. JOSEPH GRIFFITH, Junr., from JOHN
MITCHELL, merchant at Broad Creek, Suss. By a bond of conveyance from JOHN MITCHELL to JOSEPH GRIFFITH, Junr, dated 15 Apr
1773. JOHN MITCHELL for 50 pounds, 52 3/4 ac and 18 perches, it
being a grant from LEVIN GALE, Esqr., and surveyed for JOHN
WELCH in 10 Apr 1740, called Welches Delight, beginning at an
oak between Hog Pen Swamp and the Great Swamp in Hindses Neck on
e side of the ne fork of Nanticoke R. Wit: MITCHEL KERSHAW,
ROBT. JONES. Ackn 8 Aug 1787.

408 1 Jan 1787. Deed. JAMES BROWN, Junr, planter, Suss, from
CLARKSON CANNON. Suss, planter, for 100 pounds, pt/o a tr called
Addition to Four Tracts, beginning at first course of another tr
called Forrest Land ... to a line of a tr called Clarkson
Forrest, 100 ac. Attys JOHN WILTBANK and PHILLIPS KOLLOCK,
Lewes. Wit: DANIEL POLK, FRANCIS WRIGHT. Ackn 8 Aug 1787.

409 8 May 1786. Deed. JOHN HALL, Wor Co, MD, planter, from
PETER HALL, Suss, 25 ac, pt/o a tr called Halls Addition, in
Little Creek Hund near Pond Branch on n side of said Hall's
planttion where he now lives. 10 pounds Attys DAVID HALL,
WILLIAM PERRY. Wit: SAMUEL HALL, OBADIAH MORRIS. Ackn 8 Aug
1787.

410 15 May 1787. JOB GOSLEE, Suss, bond for conveyance of land
from WM. GOSLEE, Suss, farmer. WILLIAM GOSLEE bound to JOB
GOSLEE in the sum of 40 pounds, for 20 ac on n side of tr called
Hobs Choice where said JOB GOSLEE has formerly lived. Wit: JOHN
MORRIS, JESSE TOWNSEND. Ackn 8 Aug 1787.

410 18 May 1786. Deed. JOHN GORDY, Suss, planter, from PETER
HALL, Suss. 25 ac, for 10 pounds, pt/o tr called Halls Addition
in Little Creek Hund. Attys Col. DAVID HALL, WILLIAM PERRY,
Suss. Wit: SAMUEL HALL, OBADIAH MORRIS. Ackn 8 Aug 1787.

411 9 Oct 1786. Deed. JOHN GORDY, Suss, from ROBERT KING,
Junr and his wife TABITHA, ROBERT KING, Senr, and his wife
ELIZABETH KING, all of Suss, for 100 pounds, tr called Pore
Chance originally granted to JAMES KING by patent, formerly in
Som Co, lying to the east of main road that leads from Broad
Creek to the head of Wacom. 50 ac. Attys ISAAC HENRY, RHOADS
SHANKLAND. Wit: SAML. HEARN, OBADIAH MORRIS. Ackn 8 Aug 1787.

412 Bond of Convenance WILLIAM TINGLE, Suss, planter, to GEORGE
SPENCE, of Wor Co, planter. GEORGE SPENCE bound to WM. TINGLE
to the sum of 1200 pounds, for 250 ac in Indian R called Thomp-
sons Purchass, being the whole of the tr that formerly belonged
to Capt. THOMAS ROBINS before his decease. Wit: BENJAMIN
PURNALL, JOHN EVANS. Ackn 8 Aug 1787.

413 26 Jul 1787. Deed. CURTIS JACOBS, Suss, planter, from
HEZEKIAH SMITH, LOVEY his wife, and ISAAC RIGGEN and ELIZABETH
his w/o Suss, yeoman, for 200 pounds their title to tr called
White Levil with the Resurvey as it now stands, dated 8 May
1776, made for HEZEKIAH SMITH, on e side of Wolf Swamp in
SMITH's dwelling plantation, 110 3/4 ac. Attys JOHN RODNEY and
PHILLIPS KOLLOCK, Lewes. Wit: WM. POLK, MARY POLK, OBEDIAH
SNOW. Ackn 8 Aug 1787.

414 28 Dec 1786. Deed. JOSHUA ROBINSON, Suss, blacksmith,
from JOHN LEGOTT, Suss, yeoman. BEVINS MORRIS possessed a tr by
a MD patent called Batchellors Lott, now in Suss, s side of
Indian R in Dagsbury Hund, which by the death of BEVINS MORRIS
fell to his son BEVINS MORRISS who when he died the said lands
were divided amongst the last mentioned BEVINS's children,
amongst which was LEAH MORRIS (afterwards LEAH THARP by marriage
to JOHN THARP) to whom was allotted 30 ac of said tr which they
sold to JOHN LEGOTT on 21 Nov last. Also whereas the above last
mentioned BEVINS MORRIS by a resurvey on a tr called Security in
Suss on s side of Indian R in Dagsberry Hund and off of which a
resurvey was alloted to said LEAH MORRIS (afterwards LEAH THARP)
as well 50 ac thereof which she and her husband sold to said
JOHN LEGOTT. 35 pounds. Attys WILLIAM LOCKWOOD, ISRAEL
HOLLAND, WOLSEY BURTON. Wit: ARMWELL LOCKWOOD, BENJN. HOLLAND.
Ackn 8 Aug 1787.

415 9 Aug 1787. Deed. STEPHEN BAILEY, Suss, from RHOADS
SHANKLAND, Suss, yeoman, for 9 pounds, parcel of land in Rehoboth Hund, being pt/o patent called Grays Inn of which is bounded by tree on Coolspring Road, a corner of STEPHEN BALEY's other
land bought of sd. RHOADS SHANKLAND. 2 ac. Wit: DAVID TRAIN,
CHARLES ROBINS. Ackn 9 Aug 1787.

415 26 May 1787. Deed. JOSEPH CANNON, Senr., Suss, from
REBECCA PARKER and BETTY PARKER, widow, both of them of Suss,
for 15 pounds, pt/o a tr called Winter Meadow, 3 ac. Attys
DAVID TRAIN, WILLIAM PERRY, PETER FRETWELL WRIGHT. Wit: JESSE
SAUNDERS, JAMES CANNON. Ackn 9 Aug 1787.

416 4 Sep 1786. Deed. JOHN MITCHELL from ROBERT HOUSTON,
Suss, and LEVIN WAILES and MARY his wife, late MARY HOUSTON,
which said ROBERT and MARY are exrs of JOHN HOUSTON, yeoman,
decd. Whereas there is a tr called Piney Grove in Little Creek
Hund, beginning on s of Broad Creek on n side of Main Road that
leads from head of Wicomoco R to Broad Creek Bridge, 100 ac,
originally granted by MD patent dated 3 Jul 1760 to JOHN
HOUSTON, late of Suss Co, who devised same to his son the afsd
JOHN HOUSTON, decd, who devised same to his sons JOHN and JAMES
which said JAMES afterwards died under the age of 21 yrs intestate, wnd without issue and whereas afterward to wit 6 Aug 1783
afsd ROBERT HOUSTON, exr above named. Since the personal estate
of afsd JOHN HOUSTON decd was insufficient to satisfy his debts,
the exrs were authorized to sell 100 ac of tr called Piney Grove
and 50 ac belonging to decd JOHN HOUSTON called Whitefield. The
land was sold on 17 Sep 1783 to JOHN MITCHELL for 230 pounds.
Attys HENRY NEILL, JOHN RODNEY, PHILLIPS KOLLOCK. Wit: ISAAC
COOPER, LEONARD HOUSTON, STEPHEN ANDERSON. Ackn 9 Aug 1787.

418 5 Sep 1786. Deed JOHN GOBY ANDERSON Suss, yeoman, from
JOHN MITCHELL, Broad Creek Hund, for 150 pounds, tr called Piney
Grove in Little Creek Hund, 100 ac originally granted by propri-
etary of MD on 3 July 1760 [See above]. Sold to JOHN MITCHELL
by exrs of estate of JOHN HOUSTON. Attys JOHN RODNEY, HENRY
NEILL, PHILLIPS KOLLOCK. Wit: ISAAC COOPER, LEONARD HOUSTON,
STEPHEN ANDERSON. Ackn 9 Aug 1787.

419 20 Mar 1787. Deed. STEPHEN WRIGHT, Suss, from THOMAS
MOORE, Suss, for 25 pounds, pt/o two trs, Jobs Lott, 50 ac; and
Addition, 19 1/2 ac - being lands devised to THOMAS MOORE by his
father JOHN MOORE. Attys PHILLIPS KOLLOCK, PETER WHITE and
JONATHAN WOOLF. Wit: THOMAS JONES, HENRY SAFFORD. Ackn 9 Aug
1787.

419 29 Mar 1787. Deed. HENRY SAFFORD, Suss, from STEPHEN
WRIGHT, Suss, for 100 pounds, 50 ac and 19 1/2 ac, Addition sold
by THOMAS MOORE to afsd STEPHEN WRIGHT. Attys PHILLIPS KOLLOCK,
PETER WHITE and JONATHAN WOOLF. Wit: MATTHIAS MOORE, CLEMENT
SAFFORD. Ackn 9 May 1787.

420 6 Aug 1787. Deed. JAMES SAFFORD, Suss, from WILLIAM WROE,
Suss, for 50 pounds, pt/o tr called Manloves Grove, beginning at
the w nw point of tr called Jobs Lott, 50 ac. Attys ROBERT
HOUSTON, CHARLES MOORE, JONATHAN WOOLF. Wit: CHARLES MOORE,
HENRY SAFFORD. Ackn 9 Aug 1787.

421 6 Aug 87. Deed. JAMES SAFFORD, Suss, from HENRY SAFFORD
and ANNA STATIA his wife, Suss, for 200 pounds, pt/o a tr called
Jobs Lott and another called Addition, 50 ac and 19 1/2 ac.
Addition sold by THOMAS MOORE to STEPHEN WRIGHT 20 Mar 1787.
Wit: CHAS. MOORE, CLEMENT SAFFORD. Ackn 9 Aug 1787.

421 24 Mar 1787. Deed. RISDON MOORE, Suss, from WILLIAM
BEVINS, Suss, and ABIGAIL his wife, for 140 pounds, tr in Little
Creek Hund whereon said WILLIAM BEVINS now lives, pt/o which
WILLIAM BEVINS, Senr. conveyed to the afsd WILLIAM BEVINS Junr
by deed dated 9 Apr 1776 and all the land devised to said
WILLIAM BEVINS, Junr by his father WILLIAM BEVINS, Senr, will
dated 5 Jul 1781. Tr on a course of the tr of Callaways
Neglect. 100 ac. Attys PETER WHITE, JONATHAN WOOLF and
PHILLIPS KOLLOCK. Wit: CHAS. MOORE, ISAAC COOPER, JOHN G.
ANDERSON. Ackn 9 Aug 1787.

422 7 Apr 1787. Deed JOSEPH WARD, Suss, from WILLIAM BURNS,
Suss, planter, for 5 pounds, pt/o a tr called Callaways Neglect
which was granted to WILLIAM BEVINS 19 Dec 1759 by proprietary
of MD, being in Wor Co, but now Suss. 8 ac. Attys ELIJAH
CANNON, SAMUEL HALL. Wit: CHAS. MOORE, MITCHEL KERSHAW. Ackn 9
Aug 1787.

423 30 Jul 1787. Deed. WILLIAM PERRY, Suss, from JOSEPH DODD,
Suss, and SARAH his wife, parcel of land in Broadkiln Hund, 40
ac, which was granted to JACOB SHELPMAN by warrant dated 8 Jun
1737 called Come by Chance, surveyed on 12 Mar 1760 for 250 ac
and the said JACOB SHELPMAN by his last will dated 26 Apr 1773
devised said larger tr to his son ISAAC SHELPMAN and the said
ISAAC SHELPMAN by his will dated 22 Feb 1777 devised the same to
his two sisters, above named SARAH DODD and ALICE SHELPMAN to be
equally divided and the said ALICE SHELPMAN by her last will
dated 11 Sep 1770 devised her pt/o said tr to her two nephews
WILLIAM SHELPMAN and JACOB LAWS and said WILLIAM SHELPMAN and
JACOB LAWS, and the above named JOSEPH DODD and SARAH his wife
by their mutual consent appointed JOHN CLOWES, MARNIX VIRDEN and
JOHN WILSON DEAN to make petition of said lands, in which partition 40 ac was laid off for the said JOSEPH DODD and SARAH his
wife. 100 pounds. Wit: JAMES VENT, CHARLES OLIVER. Ackn 9 Aug
1787.

424 1 Aug 1787. Deed JOSEPH DODD, Suss, from WILLIAM PERRY,
Esqr, Suss, a parcel of land in Broadkiln Hund containing about
40 ac, [see above] 100 pounds Wit: JAMES VENT, CHARLES OLIVER.
Ackn 9 Aug 1787.

425 10 Sep 1787. Deed of Mortgage WILLIAM WHAYLEY, Broad Creek
Hund, from SMITH LINGO, same hund. SMITH LINGO for 29 pounds, a
crop of corn of 87 bushels on the plantation whereon LINGO now
dwells, three feather beds and furniture, 2 cows and calfs, 1
heifer and 7 head of sheep, 1 sow and 12 shoats, maple desk,
looking glass, old mare and horse worth about 3 pounds each,
linen wheel and old woman's saddle, 3 beehives and some pieces
of pewter. Wit: THOMAS HARPER, SIMON KOLLOCK. Ackn 10 Sep
1787.

426 22 Jan 1787. Deed of Mortgage WILLIAM NEWBOLD, Dagsbury
Hund, yeoman, from JNO. DARBY of Dagsbury Hund. Whereas there
is a tr in Dagsbury Hund of 76 ac being pt/o a tr called Good
Hope, originally granted by patent to SIMON KOLLOCK, Esqr.
Senr., from the proprietary of MD who conveyed said land to
EBENEZER JONES the elder and said EBENEZER JONES dying intestate
it became property of his son THOMAS JONES and the said THOMAS

JONES conveyed said 76 ac to his son EBENEZER JONES Junr. and
said EBENEZER JONES conveyed said parcel to above named JOHN
DARBY. And whereas there is another parcel adj the above parcel, which is called First Choice, containing 100 ac granted by
the proprietary of PA to said EBENEZER JONES Junr. who conveyed
same to above named JOHN DARBY. And also adj the two trs whereon a new saw mill is erected and stream running through the same
originally belonging to ROBERT INGRAM and conveyed by him to
said EBENEZER Junr. who conveyed same to JOHN DARBY. And whereas there is 300 ac of land on s side of aforementioned trs 100
of which is called Dispute and was originally granted to WILLIAM
PHILLIPS and the said WILLIAM PHILLIPS conveyed same to HENRY
WALLER who conveyed same to ZACHARIAH JONES the Elder and said
ZACHARIAH JONES by his last will bequeathed same to his son
ZACHARIAH JONES, Junr with addition of 200 ac of Resurvey called
Dispute Disputed and said ZACHARIAH JONES the younger conveyed
said 300 ac to afsd JOHN DARBY. Conditioned on the payment of
62 pounds. Wit: JOHN WINGATE, SIMON KOLLOCK. Ackn 9 Aug 1787.

428 9 Aug 1787. Deed. WINEFRED BAILY, Lewes, Spinster, from
SARAH LUNDY, Lewes, Spinster. Whereas WINEFRED BAILY by deed
dated 13 Apr 1786 confirmed to SARAH a lot on Pilot Town Bank
containing in front on Lewes Creek 60 feet and running back 200
feet next adj line of JOHN MACELLS land where (h)is dwelling
house stands being pt/o the lands whereof JOSEPH BAILY late of
Lewes afsd died seized. For love and affection. Wit: JOHN
STAFFORD, W. HARRISON. Ackn 9 Aug 1787.

429 Deed THOMAS FISHER Junr from JABEZ FISHER, Suss, yeoman.
JABEZ FISHER gives to his son THOMAS FISHER for 5 shillings a
parcel of land in Lewes and Rehoboth Hund being a tr afsd JABEZ
FISHER bought of OBEDIAH and JACOB DINGEE, reserving the use for
his lifetime - along the w side of Rehoboth Road ... to a corner
stake in the Old line by SAMUEL ROWLAND's fence ... to a corner
of land let unto THOMAS MOORE and OBEDIAH ELDRIDGE. 150 3/4 ac.
Wit: FRANCIS WOOLF, STEPHEN WOOD, JOSHUA FISHER. Ackn 10 Aug
1787.

430 Deed PHILLIPS KOLLOCK, Esqr. from MARGARET KOLLOCK. Comes
MARGARET KOLLOCK exr of last will of JACOB KOLLOCK late of Suss,
Esqr., decd. Whereas JAMES FINWICK late of Suss, yeoman, decd,
and SIDNEY his wife by a deed of conveyance, dated 7 Aug 1722
granted to JOSEPH ROYAL of Suss, Gent. and JACOB KOLLOCK a tr in
Suss on sw side of Lewes adj Pagan Creek Branch, ... intersecting with the line of 30 ac formerly purchased of PETER LEWES,
69 1/2 ac, said land being pt/o a tr formerly granted by patent
to JOHN KIPSHAVEN who sold it to WILLIAM CLARK which said
WILLIAM CLARK sold to NATHANIEL WALKER, who bequeathed same to
Major WILLIAM DYER whose exr WILLIAM DYER confirmed his interest
therein with warrantee to THOMAS FINWICK, decd, and also pt/o
another tr called Middleborough granted by patent to ALEXANDER
MOLLESTON, decd, who sold same to PETER LEWIS above named and
said PETER LEWIS conveyed thereof 30 ac to afsd THOMAS FINWICK
who by his last will dated 22 Mar 1708 devised same to his son
the above mentioned JAMES FINWICK, and whereas above named
JOSEPH ROYAL by his deed of release dated 3 Nov 1724 and
released unto JACOB PHILLIPS thereof Suss afsd Gent. all his the
said JOSEPH ROYAL's right to the land. And whereas PHILLIPS

RUSSEL late of the co, afsd decd, by his deed bearing date 3 Feb 1729 sell to above named JACOB KOLLOCK and JACOB PHILLIPS which formerly belonged to SIMON KOLLOCK, 20 ac and at the death of JACOB PHILLIPS the land became the property of said JACOB KOLLOCK. Whereas HERCULAS KOLLOCK of Lewes, yeoman, by his deed with warrantee dated 7 Mar 1769 did grant JACOB KOLLOCK a tr in Lewes and Rehoboth Hund, adj lands of said JACOB KOLLOCK and the lands of JOHN RUSSEL, the lands then of GILBERT MARRINER and said HERCULAS KOLLOCK, 40 ac, said 40 ac is pt/o a tr whereof SHEPHERD KOLLOCK late of Lewes afsd and MARY his wife died intestate. And whereas said JACOB KOLLOCK afterwards made hs last will on 17 Feb 1767 and appointed his wife MARGARET KOLLOCK, party to the presents, his exr. 388 pounds, 10 shillings. Attys JOHN LAWS, JOHN RODNEY. Wit: WILLIAM BRERETON, W. HARRISON. Ackn 10 Aug 1787.

432   10 Aug 1787. Deed. LITTLETON TOWNSEND, schoolmaster, Suss, from JOHN AYDELOTT, bricklayer, Suss, for 16 pounds, 12 1/2 ac, pt/o a tr called Londondary containing 500 ac taken up by WALTER LANE and sold to LEONARD JOHNSON who by his will bequeathed same to his son JOHN JOHNSON and said JOHN JOHNSON sold same 12 1/2 ac with 12 1/2 ac more to above JOHN AYDELOTT. Wit: HERCULAS KOLLOCK, WM. DAVIS. Ackn 10 Aug 1787.

433   30 Aug 1777. Deed. PETER F: WRIGHT, Lewes, yeoman, from PURNAL JOHNSON, Broadkiln Hund, yeoman, and SARAH his wife. 30 pounds for a parcel in Broadkiln Hund being pt/o a larger tr called Haskolds Fortune. Beginning in Hills Branch (alias Hills Run), along dividing line of this tr and SAMUEL HOPKIN's land, 200 ac. Wit: LUKE SHIELD Junr, D: TRAIN. Ackn 10 Aug 1787.

434   9 Aug 1787. Deed. THOMAS FISHER Junr, Lewes and Rehoboth Hund, yeoman, from PETER F. WRIGHT, Sheriff. Whereas there is a tr called Abrahams Lott on nw side of Coldspring Branch in Broadkiln Hund originally granted by patent of PA to ABRAHAM POTTER for 300 ac which after sundry descents and conveyances became the property of ROBERT CRAIG who died intestate, leaving brothers and sisters: HAMILTON CRAIG, JOHN CRAIG, MARY WHITE (then w/o JACOB WHITE) and RUTH then w/o PARKER ROBINSON (late of co afsd) and a nephew, ROBERT CRAIG, a minor s/o ALEXANDER CRAIG decd - to whom the land descended. [In the text it reads that ROBERT is the father but is corrected in the record as shown here.] And whereas the said HAMILTON CRAIG, JOHN CRAIG, JACOB WHITE and MARY his wife, on 5 Aug 1763 conveyed their rights to afsd PARKER ROBINSON who preferred a petition for sale of the land, which was sold 6 Dec 1774 to WILLIAM MATTHEWS for 379 ac, exclusive of 2 ac condemned for use of a mill now owned by JOHN ROWLAND. WILLIAM MATTHEWS and his wife, ANNE, on 24 Feb 1776 conveyed same to WILLIAM BURTON of Broadkiln Hund, yeoman. WILLIAM BURTON and his wife MARY on 20 Dec 1779 conveyed 62 ac of said land to HAP HAZZARD and afterwards the said WILLIAM BURTON died intestate seized of the residue of said tr without sufficient personal estate to pay his debts. Whereupon MARY BURTON his widow and adminr, on 17 Dec 1785 sold 148 ac for 170 pounds, 4 shillings and conveyed same on 6 Jun 1786 to JOSEPH STOCKLEY, blacksmith, recorded in Book N.N. 13, folio 277. And whereas JEHU HILL recovered a judgment agnst MARY BURTON adminr of WILLIAM BURTON, for a debt of 140 pounds the sheriff, PETER

F. WRIGHT seized the tr containing 160 ac which was sold for 105 pounds, 5 shillings, to THOMAS FISHER, Junr. Ackn 10 Aug 1787.

437 10 Aug 1787. Deed. PETER F. WRIGHT from THOMAS FISHER, Junr. [The same 160 ac as purchased by THOMAS FISHER above.] Wit: D: HALL, WILLIAM POLK. Ackn 10 Aug 1787.

438 9 Aug 1787. Deed. JOHN WOOLF, Lewes and Rehoboth Hund, cordwainer, from PETER FRETWELL WRIGHT, Sheriff. REECE WOOLF lately recovered a judgment agnst EVAN W. HAMM late of Suss, blacksmith, for 27 pounds. As a result the sheriff seized a parcel of land in town of Lewes between 3d and 4th sts adj southeastward, South St, to the southwestward Fourth afsd to a parcel of ground owned by GEORGE PARKER, in right of his wife, to a parcel in the possession of ISAAC TURNER which with the above described was conveyed by HENRY NEALL, Esqr. and MARY his wife to said ISAAC TURNER who conveyed the part above to afsd EVANS M. HAMM, together with a blacksmith shop thereon erected. JOHN WOOLF for 18 pounds, 12 shillings, 6 pence, bought the above. Wit: ROBT. JONES, THOMAS FISHER, junr. Ackn 9 Aug 1787.

440 11 Aug 1787. Deed. JOHN RODNEY, Esqr., merchant, Suss, from PETER F. WRIGHT, Esqr., adminr of JOHN LEWIS Junr. of Suss, bricklayer, decd. Piece of land near Lewes of 4 ac, 39 square perches, being pt/o a tr of 476 ac called Middleborough first sold by ALEXANDER MOLISTON, Senr, decd, and afterwards conveyed by PETER LEWIS and GRACE his wife to JACOB KOLLOCK, decd, cooper, f/o Simon KOLLOCK who sold and conveyed same 4 ac and 39 square perches to THOMAS JENKINS on 6 Feb 1738 who mortgaged same to JOHN LEWIS Senr who became the purchaser when it was conveyed to him by JACOB KOLLOCK, Junr, High Sheriff, in 1753. Said JOHN LEWIS, Senr conveyed same to his son JOHN LEWIS Junr above mentioned who died intestate indebted to sundry persons. It was sold for 42 pounds - adj land of PETER F. WRIGHT (former-ly DANIEL PALMER's) near dwelling house where JOHN LEWIS Senr lately dwelt, adj land of PHILLIPS KOLLOCK. Wit: SAMUEL THOMPSON, GEORGE WILTON, Junr. Ackn 10 Aug 1787. Sold to DANIEL RODNEY in behalf of JOHN RODNEY.

441 5 Sep 1787. Deed. HENRY NEILL, Esqr., merchant, Lewes, from PETER F. WRIGHT, Sheriff. HENRY NEILL lately recovered a judgment agnst NICHOLAS LITTLE, exr of last will of JOHN LITTLE of Suss decd for 487 pounds, 19 shillings, 1/2 pence on the occasion of non performance of a certain promise and assumption to afsd HENRY. Sheriff was ordered to seize and sell tr of 800 ac whereon NICHOLAS LITTLE now dwells in Lewes and Rehoboth Hund and Angola and Indian R Hund and one other tr called Irish tr, 513 ac in Angola and Indian R Hund and one other tr in Broadkiln Hund called MOSES WILSON's Land containing 200 ac whereon JAMES RICKARD then dwelt, also parcel called Holmes's Place (and whereon THOMAS FISHER then dwelt) in Angola and Indian R Hund containing 150 ac. Also tr whereon MAGDALINE COURSEY then dwelt, in hund last afsd, containing 95 ac. Also tr whereon MICAJAH PAYNTER then dwelt in hund last afsd, containing 90 ac. Also parcel then and now in possession of JOHN FIELD in Hund last afsd containing 60 ac. Also tr whereon RICHARD PUCKHAM then dwelt containing 135 ac in Broadkiln Hund. Also tr whereon THOMAS CLARK then dwelt containing 50 ac in hund last afsd, also

tr said to be purchased by afsd JOHN LITTLE containing 88 ac.
Also tr in Broadkiln Hund, 100 ac, for 620 pounds; also 500 of
550 ac of portion on nw side of branch called Bundoks Branch in
Lewes and Rehoboth Hund as HENRY NEILL should choose. The
entire tr contains 800 ac whereon said NICHOLAS LITTLE dwells.
Residue of 50 ac from the 550 ac sold by NICHOLAS LITTLE to
WALTER HUDSON, whereon WALTER HUDSON and others dwell. The
remainder of the tr remains in the hands of NICHOLAS LITTLE in
accordance with Articles of Agreement between HENRY NEILL,
NICHOLAS LITTLE   THOMAS and SAMUEL ROWLAND FISHER and heirs of
JEREMIAH WARDER, decd. Wit: JOSEPH MILLER, WILLIAM PERRY. Ackn
5 Sep 1787.

444 11 Sep 1777. Bond of Conveyance JOSHUA SPENCER from
WILLIAM BAGWELL, Suss. For 700 pounds WILLIAM BAGWELL to convey
a tr and marsh adj the land of WILLIAM C... on sw side and the
land of said JOSHUA SPENCER on the ne side, containing 176 ac
and 53 perches, being pt/o an ancient tr called Hills Content on
s side of Mispillion Creek. Wit: JOHN CHANCE, JOHN NUTTER.
Ackn 5 Sep 1787.

444 15 Aug 1787. Deed. JOHN CLOWES Esqr., from WILLIAM TULL,
Suss, yeoman, for 32 pounds 10 shillings, 40 ac being pt/o a tr
called Rolfs Delight and Walkers Folly which tr was Resurveyed
by WILLIAM SHANKLAND for JOSIAH ROLFE on 5 Mar 1742/3. Said
ROLFE died intestate and ABRAHAM WYNCOPE with JOHN NILE by their
deed of sale dated 8 Feb 1748 conveyed the tr as adminrs of
JOSIAH ROLFE to JOSEPH PHITTEMAN who by his deed dated 1 May
1758 conveyed tr to afsd WILLIAM TULL. Wit: JOHN W. DEAN, RHODS
SHANKLAND. Ackn 5 Sep 1787.

445 30 Aug 1787. Deed. JOHN CLOWES, Esqr. from JANE McNEILL,
adminr, of estate of JAMES McNEILL decd. Sale of land on 31 Jul
1786 [in order to pay decd debts] to JOHN CLOWES for 230 pounds,
land in Broadkill Hund, adj lands of JOHN CLOWES, WILLIAM TULL,
heirs of WILLIAM CLARK, EBENEZER WARRING and others. Wit: HUGH
PATTERSON, WILLIAM TULL. Ackn 5 Sep 1787.

446 30 Aug 1787. Deed. JOHN CLOWES, Esqr., from SARAH MASON,
adminr of ELIAS MASON, Suss, decd. ELIAS MASON on 15 May 1781
entered into a written Article of Agreement with afsd JOHN
CLOWES for the building of a fulling mill on the land between
the said MASON's line and the Branch which land said CLOWES was
to have surveyed by virtue of warrant dated at Phila, 1 Dec
1760, called Two Strings to a Bon and was in part laid by
WILLIAM SHANKLAND on 30 Mar 1762 and by virtue of afsd agreement
the lines of said warrant was opened by CALEB CORWITHIN and
adjoyned to the said MASONs land thereby including the land
whereon the fulling mill, press house and tenter barrs was built
and also the branch to the river containing 5 1/2 ac which by
agreement was the joint property of MASON and CLOWES. - And the
said ELIAS MASON afterwards died intestate and before said
CLOWES had made a deed and said MASON's personal estate being
insufficient to pay his debts, and to raise and educate his
small chldren. Land and utensils sold on 23 Jul for 45 pounds
to JOHN CLOWES. Wit: HUGH PATTERSON, WILLIAM TULL. Ackn 5 Sep
1787.

447 28 Sep 1787. JOHN HILL's Manumission of Negro woman
HESTER. JOHN HILL of Lewes, taylor.

447 27 Sep 1787. WILLIAM ARGO's Manumission of Negro MARGARET
about 20 yrs of age. To be free when she arrives at the age of
24 yrs. Wit: WILLIAM PERRY, DEBORAH McKNIT.

448 17 May 1787. Deed of Gift. COMFORT MESSEX of Suss, for
love and affection, and other, to my mother COMFORT MESSEX for
her lifetime or widowhood whichever is first, my negro boy named
PETER on the condition that she pay the several doctor's bill
which may come agnst my estate at or after my decease. And at
her death or marriage the negro be the sole property of niece
MILLY SHORT. I give to my sister SARAH TRUIT my bedstead,
quilt, a sheet and bolster belonging to the same. And to my
mother 1/4 pt/o negro woman named ROSE as left me by my father's
will, 1/4 part to my niece PEGGY SHORT, and to niece LITTICY
MESSEX I give the first cow calf that the cow has that I now own
and a gold ring. [Mentions sisters, JESESIA SHORT, SARAH TRUIT
and RACHEL SHORT.] Wit: SIMON KOLLOCK, ISAIAH JOHNSON.

448 8 Jan 1787. Deed of Mortgage SMITH FASSETT, Kent Co, Del.,
from LUKE TOWNSEND, Wor Co, and MARGRET his wife. Whereas LUKE
TOWNSEND is bound to sd SMITH in the sum of 496 pounds, 19 shillings, conditioned for the payment of 248 pounds 9 shillings 6
pence on 1 Sep next, for tr or pt/o two trs called Calf Paster
and Cow Quarter, 1/2 mile to the southward of Inlet Creek by
Assommon Bay. 150 ac. Wit: THOS. BATSON, ANN MITCALF.

449 8 Nov 1786. Deed of Mortgage RUTH RUSSEL, Lewes, widow and
adminr of PHILLIPS RUSSEL late of town, afsd, house carpenter
and joyner, decd, from JOHN BURTON s/o ROBT. of Angola Neck in
Indian R Hund, yeoman, for 63 pounds, 1 shilling, 5 pence, parcel of land in Angola Neck, Indian R Hund, 217a., being pt/o a
larger tr originally granted by patent to RICHARD BUNDICK called
Arcada, bought from M--- ALLEN and ELIZABETH his wife by JOHN
BURTON, dated 3 Nov 1784, recorded in Liber N.N. 13, folio 66.
217 ac. Wit: JNO. RUSSEL, ELIZABETH RUSSEL. Ackn 7 Nov 1787.

450 22 Sep 1786. Bond. MARY YOUNG of Suss, to her grandchildren, 500 pounds Wit: JACOB COVINGTON, ESTHER COVINGTON.
N.B. See depostion of JACOB and ESTHER COVINGTON respecting
this bond recorded in Liber B. folio 296.

451 12 Apr 1760. Bond of Conveyance LYDIA POLLOCK, widow, Dor
Co, from ISAAC DAWSON, Dor Co, planter. ISAAC DAWSON bound to
LYDIA POLLOCK for 100 pounds for 100 ac called Hogg Quarter
lying at the head of a branch called Double Fork Branch that
issueth out of e side of Northwest Fork of Nanticoke R in Dor
Co, excepting two trs which they may take from sd. land called
Quarter. The names of the two excepted trs are the Folly taken
up by WILLM. ADAMS s/o ROGER ADAMS and the other called Wilsons
Swamp taken up by JAMES SMITH, to be made over at the request of
LYDIA POLLOCK or her heirs, etc. Wit: ROBERT POLLOCK, JOHN
DAWSON. Ackn 7 Nov 1787.

451 1 Oct 1787. Deed. HENRY LINGO, Indian R Hund, yeoman,
from WILLIAM FASSETT of Indian R Hund, bricklayer, and

TEMPERANCE his wife (late TEMPERANCE RICHARDS), DAVID RICHARDS
of Suss, yeoman, and COMFORT his wife, and JACOB RICHARDS of
Suss, blacksmith. Whereas ISAAC RICHARDS, decd, was seized of a
messuage, plantation and tr in Indian R Hund and in his will
dated 22 Nov 1779 states, "I give and bequeath unto my loving
Friend STOCKLEY HOSMAN of the City of Philadelphia house carpenter, all the rest of my estate. STOCKLEY HOSMAN and his wife
HANNAH sold by their deed dated 1 Oct 1785 to DAVID RICHARDS, tr
called Providence at the head of Longneck Branch, which proceeds
out of Rehoboth Bay, beginning at a sapling in the line of a tr
laid out for JOHN PRICE. 159 ac. Wit: -- WILTBANK, THOS.
COULTER. Ackn 9 Nov 1787.

453 10 Jul 1787. Deed of Mortgage. JOB DIRICKSON, Suss, from
WM. DIRICKSON and RODY his wife, Suss. JOB DIRICKSON stands
bound with the above WILLIAM DIRICKSON in a judgment bond to
GEORGE MITCHELL, Esqr., dated 10 Jul 1787 in the sum of 150
pounds conditioned for the payment of 60 pounds, 17 shillings, 7
pence. That WILLIAM and his wife RODY as well as the security
of the above sd JOB DIRICKSON for payment of above mentioned sum
to GEORGE MITCHELL do grant to said JOB DIRICKSON all that tr
called Georges Goodluck which was granted to GEORGE DIRICKSON by
patent dated 26 Aug 1750. Attys RHODS SHANKLAND, PETER WHITE,
PETER FRETWELL RIGHT. Wit: --- DIRICKSON, WILLIAM FREEMAN.
Ackn 7 Nov 1787.

454 5 Jun 1787. Deed. WILLIAM WALLS Junr. from WILLIAM WALLS,
Senr., 10 pounds paid to WILLIAM WALLS by his son WILLIAM WALLS
Junr. for land willed to WILLIAM WALLS, Senr by his father and
conveyed by deed of sale by ---UEL WALLS and JOSHUA WALLS. 40
ac. Wit: WILLIAM JOHNSON, JONATHAN JOSEPH. Ackn 7 Nov 1787.

454 27 Feb 1784. Bond of Conveyance BARKLEY TOWNSEND from
CALEB BALDING. CALEB BALDING of Suss bound to BARKLEY TOWNSEND,
Suss, for the sum of 500 pounds, for tr called Batchulers
Delight part of which is n of a division line between CALEB
BALDING and BARKLEY TOWNSEND. Wit: ISAAC HORSEY, LEVIN WAILES.
Ackn 7 Nov 1787.

455 7 Feb 1787. Deed. JONATHAN JOSEPH from ELISHA JOSEPH. At
a Orphans Court on 6 Aug 1783 NATHAN JOSEPH, Suss, preferred a
petition that JEREMIAH JOSEPH late of said co possessed two trs
in Indian R Hund, containing 600 ac, and died intestate leaving
issue, 8 [sic] children, to wit, ELISHA, WILLIAM, LAVINA,
JEREMIAH, NATHAN (the petitioner), JOSEPH, JONATHAN, HEZEKIAH
and ZACHARIAH; and two grandchildren, to wit: (1) ELIZABETH HALL
dau of WILLIAM HALL and ESTHER late ESTHER JOSEPH his wife, and
(2) SAMUEL JOHNSON s/o SAMUEL JOHNSON and ELIZABETH late
ELIZABETH JOSEPH his wife - to whom the lands descended. And
the said petitioner seeking partitioning of the land. To above
party ELISHA JOSEPH, eldest s/o decd, 130 ac. His parcel begins
at a gum standing by Sockarockets or Peterkins Branch. 15
pounds Wit: THOMAS SMITH, W. HARRISON. Ackn 8 Nov 1787.

455 12 Oct 1787. Deed. ROBERT WILLIAMS from LYDIA POLLOCK,
ZEPHENIAH POLLOCK, LUCRESEY POLLOCK his wife, Suss, 413 ac, laid
out in one body of land but in four surveys, the eldest survey
originally granted by Lord Baltimore by patent dated 1 Jul 17-3,

containing 50 ac, a 2nd tr called Wilsons Swamp containing 87
ac, patent dated 10 Dec 1740, a third tr called Adams Delight
containing 94 1/2 ac, granted by patent dated 10 Dec 1740, a 4th
tr called Hog Quarter containing 100 ac - to which Adams Delight
and Hog Quarter was added by a warrant of a Resurvey granted to
above mentioned LYDIA POLLOCK 9 Aug 1776. 83 ac of vacant land
with Adams Delight reduced into one tr called the Ramble which
became the property of LYDIA POLLOCK and ZEPHANIAH, containing
413 ac. Wit: JOHN LAWS, THOMAS EVANS, JOHN JONES. Ackn 12 Oct
1787.

456 6 Feb 1787. Deed JOHN FREENEY Junr, Suss, from ELISHA
PARKER, Senr, Wor Co, MD, for 100 pounds, tr called Piney Ridge
formerly in Som Co, MD, now Suss, granted to GEORGE PARKER in MD
on 29 May 1750, beginning on e side of road leading from
Salsbury to Broad Creek and on sw side of tr surveyed for
JEREMIAH MORRIS. Attys JONATHAN HEARN, Senr, JOSHUA HASTING.
Wit: ELIJAH HASTING, JOHN FREENEY, Senr.   Ackn 8 Nov 1787.

457 5 Nov 1787. Deed. SHADRIC LACATT, planter, from JAMES and
MOSES CALLAWAY, Suss, planters, one tr called Iron Hill, -45
ac[?], another tr called --- You Please, ---5 ac, also tr called
--- Chance, 10 ac. Attys JOSHUA HASTING and Col. DAVID HALL.
Wit: JOHN FREENEY, ELIJAH HASTING, EDWD. CREAGH. Ackn 8 Nov
1787.

458 21 Sep 1785. ELIJAH HASTING, Little Creek Hund, from JOHN
PARKER, of Little Creek Hund, for 150 pounds, parcel called
Kings Lott, originally granted to MITCHEL KING in MD but now in
Suss. Beginning on w side of main road that leads to Broad
Creek and at the west end of a plantation of the widow KING, 22
ac. Attys JONATHAN HEARN Senr, JOSHUA HASTING. Wit: ROBERT
KING, SHADRACH LECATT. Ackn 8 Nov 1787.

459 9 Nov 1787. Deed. JAMES POLK, planter, Suss, from JOHN
POLK, Suss, planter, for 300 pounds, moiety or 1/2 of tr called
Polks Conclusion on se side of tr where the houses and manor
plantation lie. Wit: JNO. CLARK, WM. NEWBOLD. Ackn 8 Nov 1787.

460 26 Sep 1785. JOSHUA HASTING, Little Creek Hund, from JOHN
FREENEY, Senr, Little Creek Hund, a tr called Water Million,
originally granted to SAMUEL HEARN under seal of MD, but now in
Suss, beginning at head of Wicomico R and nw side of tr belong-
ing to JAMES BRADLEY, 39 ac. Wit: SOLOMON HASTING, SAMUEL
HEARN. Ackn 8 Nov 1787.

460 7 Nov 1787. Deed. LITTLETON TOWNSEND, school master, Suss,
from BRITTINGHAM HILL, Suss, planter, for 100 pounds, 86 1/4 ac,
pt/o a tr called Londondary, 500 ac of WALTER LANE who conveyed
same 500 ac to LEONARD JOHNSON who by his last will bequeathed
same 86 1/4 ac to his son JOHN JOHNSON, the third son, the land
then being in Wor Co, MD, but now Suss, on s side of Indian R
and said JOHN JOHNSON died intestate and his land fell to his
eldest son JOHN JOHNSON who by deed of sale conveyed the land
called Londondary to WILLIAM HOLLAND who conveyed same to above
said BRITTINGHAM HILL. Land is where BRITTINGHAM now lives and
RACHAEL JOHNSON formerly lived. Atty JOHN STEPHEN HILL, JOHN

WISE [?] BATSON, HERCULAS KOLLOCK. Wit: JOHN AYDELOTT, LUKE AYDELOTT, HANNAH AYDELOTT. Ackn 8 Nov 1787.

461 25 Jul 1786. Mortgage deed THOMAS CARY, Suss, from WILLIAM CARY, Suss. Whereas a parcel of land in Indian R Hd, containing 175 ac being pt/o a tr called the Vinyard which said WILLIAM CARY lives on and being the western most end of .... ing his natural life and then to descend unto the afsd THOMAS CARY Junr ... CARY Senr, dated 24 May 176-. 50 pounds Atty GEORGE FRAME, WILLIAM NEWBOLD and ROBERT LACEY. Wit: SIMON KOLLOCK, EDWARD R. HALL. Ackn 8 Nov 1787.

462 3 Dec 1787. Deposition of JOSEPH NEAL respecting the s/o CHARLES NEAL. JOSEPH NEAL saith that on 8 Feb 1783 a child called CHARLES NEAL s/o JOHN NEAL did lose his left ear by the bite of a horse belonging to afsd JOHN NEAL. The afsd child being in the 8th year of his age.

462 4 Dec 1787. Deed WILLIAM and DANIEL POLK Esq. from PETER F. WRIGHT, Sheriff. Whereas JOHN JACOBS of Suss, lately at court Feb term 1786 recovered for the use of DAVID RICHARDS agnst ISAAC BROWN and LEVIN BROWN a certain debt of 190 pounds, plus damages; the court directed the sale of two trs in Northwest Hund, known as Poplar Ridge and Addition to Poplar Ridge, containing 100 ac which were purchased by WILLIAM POLK and DANIEL POLK on 16 Jun last for 245 pounds.

464. 4 Dec 1787. Deed. JOHN RODNEY, merchant, from PETER F. WRIGHT, Sheriff, a lot in Lewes Town beginning at a lot which NEHEMIAH FIELD purchased of CORNELIUS WILTBANK, on ne side of Second St. ... [runs] to bank of Lewes Creek. Lot was conveyed by CORNELIUS WILTBANK and RACHEL his wife to MOSES ALLEN on 4 Aug 1772. Whereas JOHN MAULL obtained a judgment agnst afsd MOSES ALLEN the lot was sold by the sheriff on 26 Oct to DANIEL RODNEY for 120 pounds who bought the lot in behalf of JOHN RODNEY.

465. 4 Dec 1787. Deed. CLAYPOOLE DAVIDSON from PETER F. WRIGHT, Sheriff. CLAYPOOL DAVIDSON Suss, yeoman, in Nov Term Court 1785 recorded a Judgment agnst WILLIAM SIMPLER of Suss, yeoman, for 18 pounds. Land in Indian R Hund of 84 1/2 ac of WILLIAM SIMPLER was sold to said CLAYPOOLE DAVIDSON the highest bidder for 18 pounds, 15 shillings, the 84 1/2 ac being pt/o a larger tr of 400 ac originally granted to BENJAMIN STOOKLEY by warrant dated 24 Aug 1740 and assigned by BENJAMIN STOOKLEY 8 Aug 1751 unto the several heirs of DANIEL COOPES as appears by the said warrant which lands are situate in Indian R Hund on the ne side of Sockrackets Branch.

466. 5 Dec 1787. Deed. THOMAS SIMPLER from CLAYPOOLE DAVISON s/o WILLIAM DAVISON Suss, and MARY his wife, for 19 pounds, 84 1/2 ac being pt/o a warrant granted to BENJAMIN STOOKLEY for 400 ac on 24 Sep 1740 [see above]. Wit: D. HALL, PETER F. WRIGHT.

466. 4 Dec 1787. Deed. JOHN RODNEY, merchant, from PETER F. WRIGHT, Sheriff, a piece of land near Lewes Town which SARAH HART and THOMAS HART executors of JOHN HART decd, conveyed to WILLIAM ANDERSON PARKER late of Suss on 12 May 1787 beginning on

the division line SARAH and MARY's pt/o said land (two of the
heirs of JOHN SIMONTON, decd) containing 1 ac. And whereas
MARGARET KOLLOCK executrix of JACOB KOLLOCK decd and others
obtained judgments agnst afsd WILLIAM ANDERSON PARKER a parcel
of land in Lewes and Rehoboth Hund of 1 ac with improvements was
sold to DANIEL RODNEY for 57 pounds in behalf of JOHN RODNEY.
Wit: ROBERT SHANKLAND, SAMUEL THOMPSON.

467. 24 Sep 1787. Deed. JOSEPH WILDGOOSE, Suss, from ELIZABETH
ROBINSON, executrix of JOSEPH ROBINSON. Whereas JOSEPH ROBINSON
in his last will on 26 Dec 1773 left his wife ELIZABETH ROBINSON
and JOHN ROBINSON authority to convey a tr on head of Assawoman
Creek called Somerfields, being pt/o the tr beginning at run by
SAMUEL WALLIS' house which said run forks out of the run of the
deep Branch below Wallises House ... 165 ac. Wit: ISAAC DUNCAN,
CADA ROBINSON, SAMUEL MEGEE. Ackn 4 Dec 1787.

468. 1 Dec 1787. Deed. WILLIAM JACOBS, Sussex Co, planter,
from JOHN JACOBS and SARAH his wife, Sussex Co, planter. For
300 pounds, pt/o a tr called Williams Beginning, 16 ac, also
pt/o a tr called Poplar Ridge whereon said JOHN JACOBS lately
lived, containing 55 ac in Northwest Fork Hund. Atty JOHN
WILLIAMS and PHILIP KOLLOCK. Wit: WM. POLK, DANIEL POLK.

469. 4 Dec 1787. Deed. JOHN RODNEY, Sussex Co, merchant, from
JANE CORD, Sussex Co, widow of JOSEPH CORD, a tr near Lewes
Town, 20 ac being pt/o a larger tr belonging to ALEXANDER
MOLESTON the elder who sold the same to SAMUEL DICKINSON who on
4 May 1708 conveyed same to JOHN MEIRS the elder who on March
26th 1721 devised afsd 21 ac equally to his sons JOHN and JAMES
MEIRS and the son JAMES on 8 Feb 1723 released his part to his
brother JOHN MEIRS the younger who by his will of 31st, 11th
month --- devised all his land to dau and only child, the afsd
JANE CORD, which was sold to DANIEL RODNEY in behalf of JOHN
RODNEY. The land lies about 200-300 yards from WILLIAM HALL's
house formerly built by JOHN NEILL decd and ... SAMUEL PAYNTER's
house which he purchased of the heirs of STEPHEN GREEN, decd.
For 35 pounds. Wit: ANDREW McILVAIN, ROBERT SHANKLAND. Ackn 5
Dec 1787.

470. 10 Feb 1775. Deed. JOSHUA FISHER from MARY WYNKOOP of
New Castle Co, widow; PHEBE VINING of Philadelphia, widow,
heretofore PHEBE WYNKOOP; and BENJAMIN WYNKOOP of Philadelphia,
merchant - executors of last will of ABRAHAM WYNKOOP, late of
Sussex Co, decd. ABRAHAM WYNKOOP owned a tr in Cedar Creek Hund
called Farmers Delight on which is a late survey ... on se side
of Herring Branch of Mispillion Creek being a corner of JOHN
CRAPPER's land ... to a corner of DANIEL DINGEE's and JOHN
DRAPER's land .. to a corner of THOMAS CAREY Junior's land ...,
657 ac. For 300 pounds. ABRAHAM WYNKOOP made his will dated 15
Nov 1753; appointed MARY WYNKOOP, PHEBE VINING and BENJAMIN
WYNKOOP and a certain THOMAS WYNKOOP who is since dead as exrs.
Wit: P. VINING and B. WYNKOOP, P.(?) RODNEY, JOHN WOODS, MEIRS
FISHER, JOHN RIDGELY. Ackn 6 Feb 1788.

472. 6 Feb 1788. Return and Plott on Division of JOHN
HARMONSON's Lands. Whereas JOHN HARMONSON late of Sussex Co,
decd, by his last will dated 17 Apr 1784 devised to his son,

84

PETER HARMONSON all that tr of which JOHN HARMONSON purch as the estate of his brother WILLIAM HARMONSON and by his will his remaining land JOHN HARMONSON left to his four children, WALLACE HARMONSON, LYDIA HARMONSON, ELIZABETH HARMONSON and MARY HARMONSON to be equally divided among them, and appointed DAVID HAZZARD, PETER MARSH and THOMAS MARSH to make partitions of the said lands. First the partition for WALTER HARMONSON begins at small ditch cut out of Love's Creek that proceedeth out of Rehoboth Bay which ditch divides lands of JOHN HARMONSON decd from lands of JOSEPH DARBY, 110 ac Secondly, is laid off the land to ELIZABETH HARMONSON [metes and bounds given], 120 ac. Thirdly is laid off the land to MARY HARMONSON, 88 ac Lastly is laid off the land to HEBERN DODD and LYDIA his wife late LYDIA HARMONSON, 88 ac [The plats are shown.]

473. 6 Feb 1788. Deed. ROBERT HOUSTON Junr from PETER F. WRIGHT, Sheriff. Whereas there is a parcel of land (late situate in Wor Co, MD, but now Dagsbury Hund, Sussex Co, originally granted by the Proprietary of MD by patent dated 27 Aug 1762 to EDWARD HITCHINS for 215 ac called Hitchen's Choice who conveyed 50 ac thereof to ELISHA COLLINGHAM, lying on the easternmost side of said tr being pt/o the lands added by the Resurvey to the original grant and afterwards on 1 Jan 1773 conveyed the residue of the said 215 ac to JONATHAN NOTTINGHAM. And whereas JOHN CLOWES of Sussex Co, Gentleman, in the Nov term 1774, recovered a judgment agnst said JONATHAN NOTTINGHAM for sum of 40 pounds plus costs, in Snow Hill and filed same with court of Common Pleas at Lewes, Del., and the land was sold to ROBERT HOLSTON [HOUSTON] of Dagsbury Hund for 46 pounds, 12 shillings, 165 ac Wit: ISAAC HENRY, D: HALL.

474. 6 Feb 1788. Deed JOHN MITCALF, Sussex Co, yeoman, from THOMAS DAVIS, Sussex Co, for 38 pounds, pt/o a tr called Bowmans Farms, joining 50 ac of land that said THOMAS DAVIS formerly sold unto said JOHN MITCALF lying in Slaughter Neck, Cedar Creek Hund, containing 16 ac and 54 perches. Wit: SETH GRIFFITH, THOMAS FISHER Jr. Ackn 6 Feb 1788.

475. 6 Feb 1788. THOMAS DAVIS, Sussex Co, yeoman, from JOHN MITCALF, Sussex Co, yeoman, for 24 pounds, pt/o a tr called Bowmans Farm and pt/o 40 ac that LUKE DAVIS sold to HENRY DRAPER joining said THOMAS DAVIS's other land lying in Slaughter Neck, Cedar Creek Hund, 8 ac, 12 perches. Wit: SETH GRIFFITH, THOMAS FISHER, Jr. Ackn 6 Feb 1788.

476. 9 Aug 1781. Bond of Conveyance. ESTHER HALL from JESSE HALL assigned to ZAIL and CASA HALL. JESSE HALL of Sussex Co, yeoman, bound to ESTHER HALL of Sussex Co, spinster, for 100 pounds. If JESSE HALL shall convey 24 ac of land in Broadkiln Neck, joining on the west SHADA VIRDIN's line, on the south by JOHN BENSON's line, on the e by the Addison's line and on the n by Primehook Creek, at the payment of 30 pounds. Wit: CALEB CIRWITHIN, JOHN CADE. LOT CLARK and ESTHER CLARK his wife, for 50 pounds paid by ZAIL HALL and CASA HALL assigned to them title and right to within bond, signed 29 Jan 1785 and wit: STRINGER TILNEY and BETTY TILNEY.

476. 26 Oct 1784. Bond of Conveyance. PLANNER WINGATE and
TRANEY his wife to LOTT CLARK assigned to ZAIL and CASA HALL.
PLANNER WINGATE and TRANEY WINGATE his wife, Sussex Co, are
bound to LOTT CLARK, Sussex Co, yeoman, in the sum of 50 pounds,
to be paid to LOTT CLARK. If above bound PLANNER WINGATE or
TRANEY WINGATE at the expiration of three year from 20 Nov next
convey by deed a tr in Broadkiln Neck adj land of STRINGER
TILNEY on s side of Primehook Creek, being the same tr that
MOSES HALL late of this co died seized of. Wit: JOHN CADE,
JAMES COULTER. LOT CLARK in consideration of 11 pounds paid by
ZAEL HALL and CASA HALL assigned to them rights of within bond
(29 Jan 1785). Wit: STRINGER TILNEY, BETTY TILNEY. Ackn 6 Feb
1788.

477. 4 Feb 1788. Deed. ZAEL HALL, Sussex Co, yeoman, from
LOTT CLARK and ESTHER his wife; CASA HALL and EASTER his wife,
all of Sussex Co HERMANUS WILTBANK, had surveyed by CORNELIUS
VAHOOF in 1681, 560a. in Broadkill Hund adj on s side of Primehook Creek, a pt/o which said tr, 240 ac, was laid off to ISAAC
WILTBANK by order of Orphans Court and said ISAAC WILTBANK on 18
Nov 1755 conveyed the 240 ac to JOHN HALL and JOHN HALL on 3 Feb
1768 conveyed 120 ac of the said 240 ac, along with about 11 ac
of marsh taken up by him, to MOSES HALL, and MOSES HALL died
intestate leaving a widow afsd EASTER CLARK and issue, 6 children, to wit: JESSE, ZAEL, SHADA, CASA, TRANEY and MOSES to whom
the said land and marsh descended. The widow received the 1/3
dower right and the children received 2/3 of the property.
EASTER CLARK when a widow, purchased of JESSE eldest s/o decedent, 24 ac, being his division of said land and marsh; and LOTT
CLARK purchased of PLANNER WINGATE and TRANEY his wife (d/o
decedent) their right to said land, recourse being had to their
several bonds of conveyance. In consideration of 110 pounds for
130 ac of land and marsh. Wit: JAMES McNAIRYTH [?], THOMAS
McKAM [?]. Ackn 6 Feb 1788.

478. 6 Feb 1788. Deed. WILLIAM BARTON, Sussex Co, farmer,
from JOSEPH GODWIN, Kent Co, Del., farmer, for 200 pounds, a
parcel of land in Sussex Co, pt/o which formerly called Sarahs
Delight and Taylors Interest but now resurveyed by the said
JOSEPH GODWIN and called Godwins Choice. Wit: WILLIAM BRERETON,
W. HARRISON. Ackn 6 Feb 1788.

479. 2nd day, 2nd mo, 1788. Deed. JAMES HARRIS, Caroline Co,
farmer, from THOMAS ALCOCK FOWLER of Caroline Co, MD, farmer and
his wife MARY, for 41 pounds, 5 shillings, parcel of land in
Sussex Co originally resurveyed by WILLIAM ADAMS by a warrant
granted to resurvey a parcel called Taylors Desire and when
resurveyed then called Addams Venture but now resurveyed by
DANIEL GODWIN and now called Godwins Venture. Beginning for the
pt/o said Godwins Venture belonging to said THOMAS ALLCOCK
FOWLER by virtue of a purchase or purchases from MARK MARRET and
from WILLIAM ADAMS s/o WILLIAM the original claimant of said
land now called Godwins Venture. Wit: JOHN DAWSON, WILLIAM
BARTON. Ackn 6 Feb 1788.

480. 4 Nov 1787. Deed. JACOB MORAIN, Suss Co, from JOHN
WILLIAMS and BARBARY his wife, Suss Co, for 76 pounds, parcel of
land called Hogg Island which land was conveyed to JOHN WILLIAMS

by WILLIAM OWENS (see records of Som Co, Md, dated 4 Jun 1757), lying in Suss Co on the e side of Nanticoke R near northernmost of Baron Creek beginning about 1/2 mile to the nw of WILLIAM RALPH's house ..., laid for 50 ac. Atty PHILLIPS KOLLOCK and PETER WHITE. Wit: CHAS. MOORE, SAML. J. BAILY, HUFFINGTON NICHOLSON. Ackn 6 Feb 1788.

481. 20 Dec 1787. Deed. CYRUS MITCHELL, Suss, from JNO. MITCHELL, Suss, for 1000 pounds, parcels of land in Nanticoke Hund, one known as Knoxes Hazzard and the other called Good Neighbourhood, 10 ac, and a parcel called pt/o Rich Land, 1 1/2 ac, and parcel called Long Swamp, and pt/o a tr which WILLIAM LAWS is to convey and a survey that was taken up by the said JOHN MITCHELL and WILLIAM OWENS in Company and Not Yet Divided. Wit: JOHN MITCHELL, Jr., JAMS. POLLOCK, JAMES BRATTAN. Atty JAMES BRATTAN. Ackn 7 Feb 1788.

481. 23 Jan 1788. Deed. EDWARD WRIGHT, Caroline Co., yeoman, from BAREZELAI CLARKSON, Suss, yeoman, for 3 pounds, parcel of land called Store House Landing, on Nanticoke R, adj tr called Luck, 5 ac. Wit: JOHN TENNENT, JOSHUA O. BEIR, GEORGE CANNON. Atty WILLIAM PERRY, PETER WRIGHT. Ackn 7 Feb 1788.

482. 12 Mar 1787. Deed. JOSHUA O. BEAR, Suss, yeoman, from CHARLES CANNON and EASTER his wife, Suss, yeoman, for 99 pounds and 15 shillings, two trs called Salamander and Noble Quarter, lying in the Northwest Fork Hund ... 66 1/2 ac. Atty WILLIAM PERRY, PETER WRIGHT. Wit: WM. POLK, JAMES BUCHANAN. Ackn 7 Feb 1788.

483. 8 Feb 1888. Deed. JOHN RUSSEL from PETER FRETTWELL WRIGHT, Sheriff. SHEPHARD KOLLOCK, late of Suss, Gentleman, possessed a tr of 397 ac, pt/o a larger tr near Lewes Town on s side thereof called Middlebourough, originally granted to ABRAHAM MOLESTON, decd. Shephard devised on 24 Jun 1756 his whole estate to his wife MARY for her widowhood and should she marry she would enjoy only an equal portion with her children: ELIZABETH KOLLOCK, COMFORT PRETTYMAN, GEORGE KOLLOCK, SIMON KOLLOCK, ALICE KOLLOCK, HERCULUS KOLLOCK and SHEPARD KOLLOCK. MARY made an indenture dated 1 Sep 1761 with JACOB KOLLOCK and RYERS HOLT, for 59 pounds and 10 shillings, 100 ac, pt/o tr Middleborough, bounded as may appear in a deed of sale from FENWICK STRETCHER and HESTER his wife to SHEPART KOLLOCK, late decd, dated 29 Mar 1749, recorded in Book HN 7, folio 218. Condition made that if MARY or her successors paid the 59 pounds, 10 shillings with interest then the indenture to be void. And MARY died intestate before she paid any interest or principal. By order of Orphans Court was sold by GEORGE KOLLOCK to WILLIAM GILL 71 ac, pt/o the first above mentioned lands. And by the 2nd order of the Orphans court GEORGE KOLLOCK sold the mansion house and 41 ac of which he became the purchaser himself. The residue of the land was divided by a commission as set forth in their return and platt dated 25 Mar 1767 in which division was alloted to WILLIAM PRETTYMAN in right of his wife 41 ac, 25 ac lying on the nw side of the county and 16 ac lying on the se side of the road. The partition and platt recorded in Book K, No. 10, folio 269. And whereas WILLIAM PRETTYMAN sold the 41 ac for 99 pounds, 10 shillings, to JOHN RUSSEL but died

before he had acknowledged a deed whereupon COMFORT his widow by her deed dated 5 May 1770 conveyed said land to JOHN RUSSELL as recorded in Book L. No. 11, folio 84. Whereas JOSEPH HALL, trustee of the General Loan Office of Suss, Aug Term 1787, obtained a judgment agnst JOHN RUSSEL, PHILLIPS KOLLOCK and ELIZABETH DRAIN late ELIZABETH KOLLOCK, tenants of the land in the indenture of mortgage mentioned. The sheriff was directed to sell 100 ac of tr called Middlebourugh 12 Jan 1788 to JOHN RUSSEL 41 ac alloted to WILLIAM PRETTYMAN, for 4 pounds, 10 shillings. Wit: PETER ROBINSON, SETH GRIFFITH. Ackn 8 Feb 1788.

485. 15 Feb 1785. Deed. REECE WOOLF Jr., and SARAH his wife from HANNAH NUNEZ of town of Lewes. Whereas DANIEL NUNEZ late of town of Lewes owned a dwelling house and parcel of land between Mulberry and Shipcarpenters Streets at w end of town, containing 1 ac it being the same ELIZABETH MAXWELL and WILLIAM HENRY on 25 Apr 1768 conveyed to said DANIEL NUNEZ who devised same to wife HANNAH NUNEZ for her lifetime and remainder over in fee simple to SARAH PRETTYMAN. Now HANNAH NUNEZ conveys same for and in consideration of natural love and affection which she bears REECE WOOLF Jr and SARAH his wife (late SARAH PRETTYMAN) and also 5 shillings. Wit: J. RUSSEL, JOHN PARKER. Ackn 8 Feb 1788.

486. 22 Feb 1788. Deed. JOHN ROWLAND from JAMES PONDER and others. Whereas THOMAS HAND, WILLIAM HAND, JOHN HAND and THOMAS SKIDMORE on 22 Nov 1782 conveyed unto JOHN PONDER a parcel of land in Broadkiln Hund on w side of Round Pole Branch near road leading from upper Road to town of Lewes to lower Road leading to said town... 17 1/4 ac Whereas JOHN PONDER in his will dated 15 Aug 1786 devised to his son JAMES PONDER above described parcel of land, reserving to his dau KEZIAH ALLEE 1 ac contiquous to the dwelling house, shop and well. Now this indenture made between JAMES PONDER and ELENOR his wife, ISAAC ALLEE and KEZIAH his wife on the one part and JOHN ROWLAND of Sussex Co, tanner, of the other part, for 60 pounds paid by JOHN ROWLAND. Wit: JOHN CLOWES, JOHN W. DEAN [McDEAN?]. Ackn 8 Feb 1788.

487. 7 Feb 1788. Deed. JOHN RODNEY, Suss, from PETER F. WRIGHT, Sheriff. Whereas a lot of land in Lewes Town bounded on the front by Second St., and on the nw by a lot formerly belonging to JAMES SIMPSON and on the se by a lot lately belonging to FRANCIS CAHOON containing 60 feet in front and 200 feet in length back to Third St., the title of which is handed down as by indenture from JOHN LEWIS to MOSES ALLEN recorded in Liber L. No. 11, page 200 and the said MOSES ALLEN and wife conveyed same to DANIEL MURPHY on 2 May 1778. In consequence of a judgment obtained by LEVIN MILBEY agnst DANIEL MURPHEY and SAMUEL THOMPSON for the sum of 163 pounds with costs the house and lot were sold on 20 Oct 1787 to DANIEL RODNEY on behalf of JOHN RODNEY, for 150 pounds. Wit: ISAAC TURNER, JOHN ORR. Ackn 9 Feb 1788.

488. 9 Feb 1788. Deed. JOHN WOOLF, cordwainer, from REECE WOOLF Jr, Suss, bricklayer, and SARAH his wife. 4 lots or 1 ac being one fourth pt/o a four acre lott lying in the town of Lewes, bounded on the nw by Ship Carpenters St., on se by

Mulberry St., originally granted by the court on 6 Sep 1693 to
Capt. THOMAS PEMBERTON who died intestate, leaving issue two
daus, to wit: ELIZABETH and MARY, to whom said four acre lott
descended which said ELIZABETH afterwards married DANIEL BROWN
and said MARY married THOMAS CARLILE. They conveyed the lot to
JONATHAN HENRY who died seized thereof intestate leaving issue
WILLIAM his only son and two daus: SARAH and ELIZABETH to whom
the one four acre lott descended. Said SARAH afterwards married
BENJAMIN STOCKLEY and they conveyed their right to said WILLIAM
HENRY (being 1/4 pt/o the lott). WILLIAM and ELIZABETH now
owned the lott (his 3/4 part and her 1/4 part). ELIZABETH
married JOHN MAXWELL of Suss, barber, whom she survived, and
afterwards WILLIAM and ELIZABETH on 25 Apr 1768 conveyed and
released their right to DANIEL NUNEZ, Jr. of the town of Lewes,
described as bounding on nw side of Mulberry St., on the ne side
of land then the property DANIEL HOSEMAN, on se side of Ship
Carpenters St. and on sw side of WILLIAM HENRY's part or dividend of the four lots. And DANIEL NUNEZ Jr being so seized of
the lot made his will dated 9 May 1772 in which he devised to
SARAH PRETTYMAN dau of WILLIAM and COMFORT PRETTYMAN "after the
death of my wife the house and lots of land whereon CHARLES
ELBERT now lives." And whereas said SARAH PRETTYMAN afterwards
married REECE WOOLF Jr, HANNAH NUNEZ late w/o said DANIEL NUNEZ
by her deed of release dated 15 Feb 1785 released all right to
said house and lots to said REECE WOOLF Jr and SARAH his wife in
right of said SARAH. REECE WOOLF Jr and SARAH his wife for the
sum of 70 pounds paid by JOHN WOOLF. Wit: -- WILTBANK, ---
RUSSEL. Ackn 9 Feb 1788.

489. 15 Jan 1777. Bond of Conveyance. WOOLSEY BURTON from
THOMAS ROBINSON, Suss, merchant, bound to WOOLSEY BURTON,
blacksmith, in the sum of 200 pounds to be paid to WOOLSEY
BURTON on condition that THOMAS ROBINSON convey a tr at a place
called Burtons Landing, granted by a proprietary warrant to said
THOMAS ROBINSON. Wit: ARCADA ROBINSON, ELIZABETH TULL.

490. 8 Feb 1788. Deed. ELIZABETH DRAIN, widow, of Suss, from
PETER F. WRIGHT, sheriff. Whereas a tr in Lewes and Rehoboth
Hund, 100 ac, being pt/o a larger tr called Middleborough
orginally granted by patent to ALEXANDER MOLESTON late of Suss
decd which after several conveyances became the right and
property of of SHEPHARD KOLLOCK, decd, who by his will dated 24
Jun 1756 directed his whole estate to be at the disposal and
direction of his wife MARY KOLLOCK who by indenture dated 1 Sep
1761 between MARY KOLLOCK and the Trustees of the General Loan
Office for Suss a tr of 100 ac called Middleborough as afsd
bounded as appearing by a deed from FENWICK STRETCHER and HESTER
his wife to SHEPARD KOLLOCK late decd, dated 29 Mar 1749,
recorded in Book H., No. 7, folio 218. If said MARY pay to said
Trustees the consideration in the said indenture with interest,
it shall be void. And whereas after the death of said MARY
KOLLOCK and before the principal monies and interest in the said
indenture were paid, admin of all the goods and chattels and
credits of said MARY KOLLOCK and likewise of the said SHEPARD
unadministered by said MARY were committed unto GEORGE KOLLOCK
eldest s/o said SHEPARD and MARY KOLLOCK, who having admini-
stered the personal estate of the decd, made application to the
Orphans Court to sell pt/o the land of which said SHEPARD and

MARY KOLLOCK died seized, to discharge the debts of the decd which was granted, and on 4 Mar 1767. On 12 Jan 1788 40 ac was sold for 4 pounds, 10 shillings, to ELIZABETH DRAIN. Wit: HAP HAZZARD, JOSEPH MILLER. Ackn 9 Feb 1788.

492. 1 Mar 1788. Deed. NEHEMIAH DAVIS Senr. from THOMAS DAVIS and his wife MARY and ELIAS TOWNSEND and wife MARY, for 110 pounds, a tr and marsh known as Good Look, it being pt/o a patent granted by Sir EDMON ANDROSS Governor of New York to THOMAS DAVIS dated 29 Sep 1677 for 300 ac and marsh lying in Slaughter Neck on se side of flatt inlett that is included by afsd patent called Good Look containing 110 ac of land and marsh which was laid off to said NEHEMIAH DAVIS - which was laid off by NATHANIEL YOUNG, RHOADS SHANKLIN, ROBERT YOUNG, BURTON ROBINSON and ISAAC BEACHAMP. Beginning at a corner post of EDWARD FURLONG standing in the marsh on the sw side of Black Walnut Island and running e n e ... to a corner post stainding by Hog Island Gutt. Atty JOHN RODNEY and PHILLIPS KOLLOCK. Ackn 6 Mar 1788 in open court.

493. 29 Feb 1788. Deed. STEPHEN STYER, merchant, from SOLOMON PERKINS, Wor Co, taylor, for 51 pounds, 2 shillings, a tr in Baltimore Hund called Adventure and Linches Addition, originally granted by the Proprietary of MD by patent: Adventure 12 Sep 1712; Linches Addition 15 Dec 1738 unto ABRAHAM LINCH late of Wor Co, decd, containing 116 ac being pt/o two trs lying on n side of Indian Town Branch near the head of sound according to the original patent and grant from the Proprietary unto ABRAHAM LINCH late of Wor Co, decd, containing 116 ac, being all that pt/o two tr on the n side of Indian Town Branch near the head of the sound. Wit: ROBT. SCHOOLFIELD, MATTHIAS AYDELOTT. Ackn 6 Mar 1788.

493. 19 Feb 1788. Deed. WILLIAM NEAL, planter, from EDWARD ROSS and CURTIS BROWN and RACHEL his wife, planters, for 16 pounds, tr called Second Addition to Canaan in Northwest Fork Hund, 16 ac Atty JOHN RODNEY, PHILLIPS KOLLOCK. Wit: JOHN LAWS, HUMPHRESS BROWN. Ackn 20 Feb 1788.

494. 27 Dec 1787. Deed. NICHOLAS HICKMAN of Kent Co., Del., farmer, from JONATHAN MORGAN of Suss, Gentleman, and NICEY his wife, for 133 pounds, tr called Morgan's Delight, in Suss on west side of Marshihope Branch then runs across same with JOHN MASTON's [Martin?] land ... to a corner of JOHN GULLET's land, 100 ac and 116 square perches. Also that parcel of land called Purchase ... from MASTONS to THOMAS CLIFTON's it being a corner of JOHN MASTON's land called Maston's Lott, 77 ac 30 square perches. Wit: JOHN LAWS, ZACHARIAH JONES. Ackn 6 Mar 1788.

495. 20 Feb 1788. Deed. JOHN LANGRELL, carpenter, from EDWARD ROSS, CURTIS BROWN and RACHEL his wife, Suss, planters, for 112 pounds, 10 shillings, parcel of land called Second Addition to Cananan... to a red oak sappling on the e side of JOSEPH DAWSON's plantation..., 100 ac Atty JOHN RODNEY, PHILLIPS KOLLOCK. Wit: JOHN LAWS, HUMPRESS BROWN. Ackn 6 Mar 1788.

496. 1788. Deed. MOLLY MORRIS, Widow of GEO: MORRIS, and JEREMIAH, RACHEL, JACOB, NOAH and POLLY MORRIS, minors and heirs

of GEO: MORRIS, decd, from DENNIS MORRIS, Suss, Gentleman, for
30 pounds, pt/o a larger tr which DENNIS MORRIS purch of ELIAS
TOWNSEND and EZEKIEL COLLINS and his wife ESTHER taken up by her
father CHARLES TOWNSEND, on e side of a fresh marsh and adj the
land of JOB SMITH, 149 1/2 ac; also a parcel in the southeas-
ternmost corner of said tr afsd, 15 1/2 ac Wit: DENNIS MORRIS,
Jr., SUSANNA MORRIS. Atty JOHN CLOWES. Ackn 6 Mar 1788.

498. 8 May 1788. Deed of mortgage. GEORGE READ, Esqr. of the
town and co of Newcastle, Esqr., from JOHN ROBINSON, Primehook
Neck, husbandman. JOHN ROBINSON stands bound to GEORGE READ in
the sum of 800 pounds conditioned for the payment of the sum of
50 pounds on 1 Jan 1789, 50 pounds on 1 Jan 1890, ...etc. to 1
Jan 1796 plus interest. Granting GEORGE READ, tr in Primehook
Neck near the head thereof, the upper or southwesterly corner of
a tr of 100 ac conveyed by GEORGE READ and GERTRUDE his wife to
JOHN RECORDS, decd .. stake by Slaughter Branch ... 545 1/2 ac
as per a draught and survey thereof among others by MARK McCALL
in 1772 and also two undivided fifth pt/o and in a tr of Marsh
containing 50 ac lying in the marsh commonly called Watson's
Marsh on the n side of a ditch adj the marsh late of CALEB
CIRWITHIN decd. Atty JOHN RODNEY, PETER FRETWELL WRIGHT. Wit:
CHARLES DRAPER, JOSHUA FISHER. Ackn 8 May 1788.

499. 14 Apr 1788. Deed of mortgage. GEORGE READ of town of
Newcastle, Gent., from JESSE DEPUTY of Primehook Neck, husbandman. Whereas JESSE DEPUTY is bound to GEORGE READ in the sum of
441 pounds, 12 shillings conditioned for the payment of 50
pounds on 1 Apr 1789, 50 pounds in 1790, 50 pounds in 1791, 50
pounds in 1792, 20 pounds, 16 shillings in 1793, together with
the lawful interest annually. Whereas JESSE DEPUTY in consideration of the sum in the whole of 220 pounds and 16 shillings
--- JESSE DEPUTY to convey plantation in the Forrest known as
TOWNSEND's Forrest about 7 miles from the head of Cedar Creek in
Suss being pt/o a tr know as the Goosepond tr. Boundary extends
to corner of JOSHUA DEPUTY's land and to corner gum of ALEXANDER
LAYTON's land and to a corner post of CHARLES DEPUTY's land -
150 ac Also a moiety or half pt/o all that parcel in Primehook
Neck beginning at a stake on Slaughters Creek being the upper
corner of MARK DAVIS's land ... to a stake being a corner of
land sold to JOHN RICKETS - 200 ac Also one undivided fifth
pt/o parcel of marsh of 50 ac being a pt/o Watson's Marsh, adj
CALEB CIRWITHIN's Marsh, late of said co. decd. Atty JOHN
RODNEY, PETER FRETWELL WRIGHT. Wit: W. ROBINSON, JNO. ROBINSON.
Ackn 9 May 1788.

500. 7 May 1788. Deed. SARAH and SELAH POSTLES daus of said
JOHN POSTLES, from JOHN POSTLES, Suss, yeoman, for 30 pounds,
reserving the use for his lifetime, the parcel in Forrest of
Slaughters Neck in Cedar Creek Hund, binding on lands of WILLIAM
WILSON, JOHN SMITH and WILLIAM SHOCKLEY, Sr. whereon they now
dwell, which said land was granted to JAMES JONES who by his
devised the upper pt/o said tr to his son JACOB JONES whose
heirs sold same to RICHARD SHOCKLEY who conveyed same to afsd
JOHN POSTLES - 115 ac. Wit: J. RUSSEL, JAMES HUDSON. Ackn 7 May
1788.

501. 7 May 1788. Deed. SHADRACH POSTLES from JOHN POSTLES, Suss, yeoman. Whereas there is a tr called Taylors Plot in the forest of Cedar Creek Hund which said tr was surveyed by virtue of a warrant granted to THOMAS POSTLES, decd, dated 1 Mar 1742 and conveyed to afsd JOHN POSTLES - 190 ac, 105 square perches, a pt/o said tr - in consideration of 50 pounds. Wit: J. RUSSEL, JAMES HUDSON. Ackn 7 May 1788.

502. 7 May 1788. Deed. THOMAS POSTLES, Suss, from JOHN POSTLES, Suss, yeoman, pt/o a tr called Taylors Plot in the Forest of Cedar Creek Hund ...etc. [see above] ..245 ac, 60 square perches, for 60 pounds. Wit: J. RUSSEL, JAMES HUDSON. Ackn 7 May 1788.

503. 28 Apr 1788. Power of Attorney. LITTLETON TOWNSEND and JACOB RODGERS from ROBERT DENNIS. ROBERT DENNIS of Suss who has executed a deed to JAMES FASSETT of Suss for 266 ac of land, appoints LITTLETON TOWNSEND and JACOB RODGERS of Suss to acknowledge said deed in court. Wit: ELIJAH FASSETT, JOHN POSTLES. Proved 7 May 1788.

503. 23 Apr 1788. Deed. JAMES FASSETT from ROBERT DENNIS, Wor Co, MD, ROBERT DENNIS in 1773 possessed 266 ac, pt/o a tr called Friends Desire formerly in Wor Co, now Suss, adj Assawamon Creek, which ROBERT DENNIS in 1773 sold to JOSHUA HILL and gave bond to said HILL for the conveyance thereof, but said HILL never paid the whole of the purchase money and said HILL in the late war went off to the English and his property was confiscated by Act of Assembly of Delaware and the aforementioned 266 ac with some other lands adj were sold under the confiscation laws to said FASSITT in 1780 and conveyed by LEVIN DIRRICKSON so empowered by said act. Now ROBERT DENNIS in consideration of further sum of 200 pounds grants to said FASSETT his right to the land. Wit: ELIJAH FASSITT, JOHN POSTLES. Ackn 7 May 1788.

504. 29 Apr 1788. Deed. JOHN HOLLAND, Suss, from WILLIAM MATTHEWS of Suss and ANN his wife. Whereas a tr in Broadkiln Hund containing 330 ac being pt/o a larger tr which was granted by patent May 1686 to JOHN STREET who conveyed same containing 400 ac to WILLIAM CLARK who conveyed same to THOMAS FISHER who devised to his son JOSHUA FISHER and said JOSHUA FISHER conveyed same to GERSHAM MOTT who conveyed 100 ac to SOLOMON KNOX and the remaining part by deed of sale dated 8 Jan 1752 conveyed to ABSOLAM LITTLE which said ABSOLAM LITTLE conveyed on 2 Aug 1765 to WILLIAM BURTON who conveyed same remaining portion on 24 Feb 1775 to WILLIAM MATTHEWS - which remaining pt/o tr is described as beginning at a gutt called Wolf Pitt Gutt and running along a line of land of the heirs of JOSEPH CORD... to a corner post of the heirs of LEVI ROBINSON - 330 ac, the whole of the tr granted by patent as 400 ac commonly called Swan Hill. In consideration of 500 pounds. Wit: JAS. WILEY, JOHN S. DORMON. Ackn 7 May 1788.

505. 1 May 1788. Deed. JESSE GRAY from JOHN DENNIS of Wor Co, MD, for 200 pounds, tr called Smallwoods Security, formerly in Wor Co, granted to JOHN DENNISS f/o aforementioned JOHN DENNISS for 100 ac, now in Suss, beginning at a white oak on nw side of a county road from Snow Hill to Blackfoot Town in the forrest.

Atty WILLIAM PERRY, JOHN WISE BATSON. Wit: JOHN POSTLES, GEORGE
COOKE, ELIJAH FASSITT. Ackn 7 May 1788.

506. 24 Aug 1777. Deed. JOSHUA OBEIR, Suss, planter, from
NATHANL. HORSEY, ISAAC HORSEY and WILLIAM HORSEY s/o ISAAC, all
of Suss, planters, for 180 pounds, pt/o a tr called Salamander
in Northwest Fork Hund, 100 ac. Also pt/o tr called Conclusion
surveyed for JOHN CANNON which part contains 41 1/4 ac. Atty
DANIEL POLK and ANDERSON PARKER. Wit: NEWTON CANNON, LEVIN
TULL. Ackn 7 May 1788.

506. 7 Mar 1788. Deed. JOHN METCALF, yeoman, of Cedar Creek,
Suss from BETHUEL WATTSON Jr, Suss, adminr de Bonis Non of DAVID
WATTSON, lately decd. Whereas DAVID WATSON decd possessed a
piece of land in Cedar Creek and Slaughter Neck on the e side of
Cedar Creek, being pt/o a larger tr formerly known by the name
of Little Button being pt/o the same land which belonged to
COSTON TOWNSEND decd containing 2 ac and 5 perches. And whereas
the said DAVID WATSON decd sold the same to afsd JOHN MIDCALF
for which said MIDCALF did pay said WATSON a very good and
valuable consideration which appears on the records of chancery
of March 1788 in which BETHUEL WATTSON was compelled to convey
same to MITCALF. Parcel beginning at a post at the edge of
Cedar Creek one perch below ISAAC TOWNSEND's worff [wharf?] ...
to a line of the land that formerly belonged to THOMAS LAY decd
- 2 ac, 5 perches. Wit: D. DAVIS, JOHN W. BATSON. Ackn 7 Mary
1788.

507. 7 May 1788. Deed. EBENEZER SPENCER, Cedar Creek Hund,
yeoman, from JOHN METCALF, Cedar Creek Hund, yeoman, pt/o a
larger tr called Little Button, being pt/o the same land which
formerly belonged to COSTON TOWNSEND, decd, containing 2 ac, 5
perches. [See above] Wit: ELI SHOCKLEY, JOHN W. BATSON. Ackn
7 May 1788.

508. 6 Apr 1785. Power of Attorney. RICHD: and CURTIS
SHOCKLEY from JONATHAN HILL. JONATHAN HILL appoints RICHARD
SHOCKLEY, yeoman, and CURTIS SHOCKLEY as attorneys for the
recovery of 200 pounds with interest from JOHN GRACE and the
recovery of 50 pounds with interest from WILLIAM CONAWAY. On
recovery the 200 pounds plus interest to be delivered to ELSEY
HILL s/o JONATHAN HILL when he reaches 21 yrs. The 50 pounds
plus interest to be delivered to d/o JONATHAN HILL, ELENOR HILL
on 5 Apr 1789. That the young mare and bed in the possession of
CURTIS SHOCKLEY be given to son ELSEY HILL at age of 21. Wit:
ELIAS SHOCKLEY, NATHANIEL SHOCKLEY. Ackn 7 May 1788.

508. 7 May 1788. Deed. JESSE READ, cordwainer, Cedar Creek
and Slaughter Neck Hund, from THOMAS WILSON, Cedar Creek and
Slaughter Neck Hund, farmer, for 155 pounds, the plantation and
tr on s side of the main branch of Cedar Creek being pt/o a tr
which formerly belonged to WILLIAM BURTON and ELIZABETH his
wife, conveyed by them to WILLIAM FISHER, which said lands
became the property of JAMES READ as shown on deed from JOHN
SHANKLAND, sheriff dated 7 Feb 1737 it being pt/o that tr whereon said JESSE READ now lives on n side of the lands which belong
to BETHUEL WATTSON Sr whereon his son JESSE WATTSON now lives,
containing 123 1/2 ac being the sw division of said JAMES READ's

land which was divided after his death between his two sons JOHN
READ and JESSE READ. JOHN READ sold his part agreeable to divi-
sion above to said THOMAS WILSON. Wit: JOHN METCALF, BETHUEL
WATTSON, Jr. Ackn 7 May 1788.

509. 29 Apr 1788. Deed. JONES RICKARDS, Suss, from WILLIAM
RICKARDS and MARY RICKARDS of Suss; and LUKE TOWNSEND and
MARGARETT TOWNSEND of Wor Co, MD, planters and seamsters. There
is a small remnant of land in Suss on the s side of Indian R and
on the n side of Assawamon Creek and near said Creek called Fair
Haven which said land was formerly surveyed by WILLIAM KNOCK of
Som Co and deeded by said KNOCK to AMBROS WHITE. WRIXAM WHITE
s/o afsd AMBROS WHITE by his deed of conveyance sold to WILLIAM
RICKARDS 2/3 of said tr called Fair Haven containing 450 ac.
After several conveyances and grants to several people there are
a small number of acres yet unconveyed which said number of
acres was in controversy between said heirs to this land and
DAVID TUBS until they left the decision to a commission of
STEPHEN HILL, ISRAIL HOLLAND, JOSEPH DIRICKSON and LITTLETON
TOWNSEND who determined the parcel to be 45 ac and for which
JONES RICKARDS now pays 75 pounds. The parcel borders on the
division line between JONES RICKARDS and the heirs of JOSHUA
ROBINSON and intersects the division line that was laid off to
said JONES RICKARDS by JOHN RICKARDS. Atty JOHN BATSON, WILLIAM
LOCKWOOD, and LITTLETON TOWNSEND. Wit: BETSEY .OILES, JOHN
EVANS. Ackn 7 May 1788.

510. 11 May 1786. Deed LITTLETON TOWNSEND, schoolmaster,
Suss, from HENRY SMITH, Senr, Suss, planter, for 8 pounds, pt/o
a tr called Stockley's Adventure, on s side of Indian R and s
side of a main road from Cedar Neck to Blackwater Meeting House,
lying between a road that leads from Baltimore Town to WILLIAM
PONDER's and a road that leads from JACOB BANKS to a plantation
of Mr. SPARINS, on a division line between JOHN MASSEY Junr. and
others - 4 ac. HENRY SMITH purch said land of SACKER MUMFORD
who purch it from JOHN HOPKINS who purch it from WILLIAM HOLLAND
(decd) who purch it from HAMPTON HOPKINS. Wit: ISAAC WEST,
PETER JOHNSON, CORNELIUS POSSEY. Atty JOHN EVANS, schoolmaster,
DAVID TRAIN and ISRAIL HOLLAND. Ackn 7 May 1788.

511. 14 Apr 1788. Deed. JOHN NORMAN Junr, from his father
JOHN NORMAN Senr both of Suss, for love and affection and 5
shillings, tr called Folly in Suss, 108 ac, warrant dated 10 Sep
1740, beginning s side of a branch called Guby Neck Branch that
leads out of the ne fork branch at the head of Nanticoke R and
on the w side thereof near a water hole. Wit: FRANCIS WRIGHT,
THOMAS PEACHEY COATES. Atty JOHN RODNEY, PHILIPS KOLLOCK. Ackn
7 May 1788.

512. 7 May 1788. Deed. BENJAMIN McELVAIN, Suss, taylor, from
JOHN LITTLE, Sussex Co, yeoman, and SARAH his wife, for 228
pounds, a parcel of land on s side of Bracey's Branch, pt/o a tr
conveyed by a deed of release from JAMES THOMPSON and MARGARET
his wife to sd JOHN LITTLE, 128 ac Wit: ROBERT MARRINER, JOHN
HAZZARD. Ackn 7 May 1788.

512. 5 May 1788. Deed. PETER WHITE, Suss, merchant, from
SARAH MIFFLIN, Suss, relict of BENJAMIN MIFFLIN. Whereas

ANTHONEY WOODWARD, f/o afsd SARAH MIFFLIN, had surveyed on 25
Jul 1728 by ROBERT SHANKLAND 74 square perches near the town of
Lewes beginning at a post where the County Road and the line of
SIMON KOLLOCK (now the line of afsd PETER WHITE) intersect, with
a line parallel with the land of said ANTHONY WOODWARD now the
Rev. MATTHEW WILLSON's land - which was conveyed to ANTHONY
WOODWARD from JOHN CHAMBERS recorded in Liber F, folio 325, and
when the said ANTHONY WOODWARD died intestate seized of the 74
perches, the same descended to his dau and only surviving heir,
SARAH MIFFLIN. Atty JOHN CLOWES. Wit: JAS. WILEY, WILLIAM
TULL. Ackn 7 May 1788.

513. 10 Mar 1788. Deed. JOSEPH WYATT s/o afsd JEHU WYATT,
yeoman, from JEHU WYATT, yeoman. Whereas a tr in Indian R Hund
on which JEHU WYATT now dwelleth and was assigned over by
WILLIAM BUTCHER to said JEHU WYATT, on w side or most part
thereof of the road leading from Doe Bridge to Saint Georges
Chapel and adj the land taken up by HUGH MACINTUSH and on which
LITTLETON ABDELL decd called Red Oak Ridge, 106 ac, for 32
pounds, 10 shillings. Wit: ISAIAH BURTON, LYDIA BURTON, J. F.
BAYLIS. Ackn 7 May 1788.

514. 7 May 1788. Deed. JOHN ROWLAND, Suss, tanner, from
JOSEPH STOCKLEY, Suss, blacksmith, and ELIZABETH his wife.
Whereas there is a tr on the nw side of the Coldspring Branch in
Broadkiln Hund called Abraham's Lott, originally granted by
WILLIAM PENN to ABRAHAM POTTER for 300 ac which became the
property of ROBERT CRAIG (the younger) late of Suss, who died
seized thereof intestate and without issue, leaving HAMILTON
CRAIG, JOHN CRAIG, MARY WHITE (then the wife of JACOB WHITE) and
RUTH, then the wife of PARKER ROBINSON, his brothers and
sisters, and a nephew, ROBERT CRAIG, a minor, s/o ALEXANDER
CRAIG decd, to whom the land descended. And whereas the said
HAMILTON CRAIG, JOHN CRAIG, JACOB WHITE and MARY his wife on 5
Aug 1763 conveyed the right to said lands to afsd PARKER
ROBINSON who with his wife RUTH conveyed on 6 Dec 1774, to
WILLIAM MATTHEWS for 379 ac exclusive of 2 ac which had been
condemned for a mill, recorded in Book L. No. 11, folio 460
which said WILLIAM MATTHEWS and ANN his wife on 24 Feb 1776,
recorded in Book M No. 12, folio 76, sold same to WILLIAM BURTON
of Broadkiln Hund afsd who died intestate, and not having sufficient estate to pay his debts, MARY BURTON adminr of his estate,
sold 148 ac to JOSEPH STOCKLEY on 17 Dec 1785 for 170 pounds, 4
shillings - recorded in Book N No. 13, folio 277. In consideration of 190 pounds [sic]. Wit: JESSE BOUNDS, EDWARD CRAIGE.
Ackn 7 May 1788.

516. 3 May 1788. Deed. JOHN ROWLAND, tanner, from WILLIAM
LUKER and CATHARINE his wife, Suss Whereas WILLIAM FISHER, late
of this co. decd, by his indenture dated 6 Aug 1747, sold to
JOHN CLOWES late of the co. afsd, a parcel of marsh or meadow
ground of 10 ac, pt/o an undivided tr of marsh belonging to said
WILLIAM FISHER and others, the heirs of JOHN FISHER, decd, which
undivided tr was bounded s by the marsh of JAMES KING, on e by
Broadkiln Creek and whereas JOHN CLOWES afterwards on 8 Apr 1761
devised all his lands to his seven children, namely: WILLIAM
CLOWES, JOHN CLOWES, DAVID CLOWES, GERARDUS CLOWES, CATHARINE
CLOWES, MARY CLOWES and LYDIA CLOWES, to be equally divided.

The afsd 10 ac was alloted to the afsd WILLIAM CLOWES who died
intestate before his father leaving issue 4 children: CATHARINE
CLOWES, MARY CLOWES, LYDIA CLOWES and JOHN CLOWES to whom the
land descended.   And CATHARINE CLOWES afsd afterwards married
PETER DICKINSON. Based on the valuation made by an appointed
commission PETER DICKINSON paid to the other heirs of said
WILLIAM CLOWES their respective shares. CATHARINE DICKINSON now
the w/o WILLIAM LUKER. Land sold for 3 pounds, 15 shillings.
Wit: JAS. WILEY, JOHN CLOWES, JOHN WILTBANK. Ackn 7 May 1788.

517. 8 Apr 1788. Deed. JOHN WOOLF, cordwainer, of Lewes and
Rehoboth Hund, from THOMAS FISHER Junr of same place, yeoman, tr
of 151 1/2 ac being pt/o a tr in hund afsd, 2 miles from Lewes,
called Flatt Lands, originally granted by the Court of Deal (now
Sussex) on 2nd day of 2nd month 1682 to JOHN VINES who being
seized thereof afterwards by WILLIAM CLARK his atty, on 5th day
of 12th month 1688 sold same to HENRY STRETCHER who on 7th of
12th month in same year conveyed same for the quantity of 350 ac
to GRIFFITH JONES of Phildelphia, merchant, who on 6 Mar 1693/4
by JOHN HILL his atty sold to HENRY STRETCHER, having first
obtained a patent for same dated 9 Dec 1690. HENRY STRETCHER
sold on 13 Oct 1702 to SAMUEL ROWLAND of Lewes, marriner, who on
22 Jan 1725 made his last will in which "I give and bequeath
unto my son in law JOSEPH ELDRIDGE and my daughter MARY his wife
and to their heirs and assignes forever, all that my tract of
land at the Flatt Lands where they now dwell ... provided they
discharge the mortgage thereof in the Loan Office in this
County..." and afterwards died. The said MARY survived her
husband JOSEPH ELDRIDGE and by her will dated 8 Jul 1766,
devised the land, 151 1/2 ac to her two grandsons OBEDIAH and
JACOB DINGEE in fee tail who sold on 6 Nov 1767 151 1/2 ac to
JABEZ FISHER who on 10 Dec 1783 sold same to his son THOMAS
FISHER Junr. (party to these presents). Now for 227 pounds, 5
shillings THOMAS FISHER Junr sells to JOHN WOOLF. [...runs to a
post in JOHN CADDY's line ... to post in WILLIAM COLEMAN's
land.] Wit: JNO. RUSSEL, ELIZABETH RUSSEL. Ackn 7 May 1788.

518. 16 Apr 1788. Deed. JOHN FLEMING from PETER F. WRIGHT,
sheriff. Whereas THOMAS FISHER and SAMEUL ROWLAND FISHER,
surviving partners of JOSHUA FISHER and Sons, lately in the
Supreme Court for the county afsd, as of April Term 1786
recovered agnst NICHOLAS LITTLE late of the co afsd, executor of
the last will of JOHN LITTLE late of the co, merchant, decd, a
debt of 2000 pounds, 14 shillings, 6 pence. The following 11
trs were seized by the sheriff in Lewes and Rehoboth and Indian
R Hund, 2281 ac which was sold of which 76 1/2 ac being pt/o a
Manor Plantation known as Gray's Inn whereon said JOHN LITTLE
lived and died which was purch by RHODS SHANKLAND for the use of
JOHN FLEMING for 131 pounds, 19 shillings, 3 pence which begins
on Coolspring Road being a corner of the Meeting House land ...
with the line of the land of the heirs of ALEXANDER BRUCE ... to
the land of the heirs of JOHN MUSTARD, decd ... to a dividing
line of this land and that land conveyed to HENRY NEILL. Wit:
HESTER MOORE, WM. HARRISON. Ackn 7 May 1788.

520. 2 Apr 1788. Deed. JOHN ROBINSON of Primehook Neck, Suss,
from GEORGE READ Esqr. of the town and co of Newcastle, Del, and
GERTRUDE his wife, for 500 pounds, parcel of land in Primehook

Neck near the head thereof ... to a stake being a corner of 12
3/4 ac heretofore contracted on the pt/o the said GEROGE READ to
be conveyed to JOSHUA JONES since decd ... to a stake on Slaughter Branch being another corner of said Recard's Hundred acre tr
... containing 545 ac as per a draught and survey by MARK McCALL
in 1772. And also two undivided fifth parts of a tr of marsh
containing 50 ac being in the marsh called Watson's Marsh on the
n side of a ditch where next the marsh late of CALEB CIRWITHIN
decd (being pt/o the neck of land known as Primehook) on 21 Jun
1671 granted by patent from Coll. FRANCIS LOVELACE the Governor
of New York and its dependancies unto RICHARD PERROT who on 4
Jan 1672 conveyed same neck of land to RICHARD PERROTT his son
upon whose death same descended to his son also named RICHARD
PERROTT who on 29 Oct 1718 conveyed same neck of land to BERKLEY
CODD Esqr. who having first granted and confirmed divers trs on
the s side of the said neck by his last will dated 29 Sep 1723
devised the residue of same neck to his wife MARY CODD in fee
who by her last will dated 26 Sep 1733 devised same residue to
her great grandson THOMAS TILL in fee who on Oct 1760 died
intestate leaving said GERTRUDE his widow and an only child
named WILLIAM who attained the age of 5 yrs and 3 months and
died without brothers or sisters ca. 11 Dec 1762 leaving his
mother next of kin. GERTRUDE afterwards married said GEORGE
READ. Excludes any possible claims by JOHN BELLAMY, WILLIAM
BELLAMY or GABRIEL THOMAS all late of Suss decd, or by Capt.
NATHANIEL PUCKLE of City of Philadelphia or WILLIAM TILL the
elder of the town of Newcastle, Esqr, both decd. Wit: JOSHUA
FISHER, ISAAC CARTY. Ackn 8 May 1788.

521. 5 Sep 1787. Deed. JOB GOSLE, Dagsbury Hund, planter,
from SARAH GOSLE widow, executrix of Wm. GOSLE, late of Suss,
decd. Whereas there is a parcel of land in Dagsbury Hund of 20
ac being pt/o the tr called Hobs Choice and the northern most
end of the same and now in possession of the heirs of WILLIAM
GOZLEE. The said WILLIAM GOZLEE in his lifetime on May last by
his bond did bind himself in the penalty of 40 pounds, to convey
said 20 ac which runs from COLLINS Mill Pond ... For 20 pounds.
Ackn 8 May 1788.

522. 2 Apr 1788. Deed. JESSE DEBUTY, Primehook Neck, husbandman, from GEO: READ, Esqr. of the town of Newcastle, Del. and
GERTRUDD his wife, for 135 pounds, one moiety or half pt/o tr in
Primehook Neck beginning on Slaughter Creek being the upper
corner of MARK DAVIS's land ... to a corner of the land sold to
JOHN RICKETS (otherwise RICARDS), 200 ac, and also one undivided
fifth pt/o a tr of marsh of 50 ac lying in Watsons Marsh and
adj CALEB CIRWITHIN's Marsh late of Sussex Co, decd [see above
original page 520 for further details]. Wit: JOSHUA FISHER,
ISAAC CARTY. Ackn 9 May 1788.

524. 4 Jan 1787. Deed. JOHN WILLIS, Suss, blacksmith, from
THOMAS LEVERTY, Suss, yeoman, and MARY his wife, for 35 pounds,
parcel of land of 50 ac being pt/o a larger tr of 530 ac called
Bashan laid out for WARREN BURROUGHS by virtue of a proprietary
warrant granted to him in 1756, a pt/o which was conveyed by
WARREN BURROUGHS to JOHN WHITE who conveyed 100 ac thereof to
said THOMAS LAVERTY of which the above 50 ac is a part, to wit,
the w side thereof. Beginning at an oak standing in a line of

GEORGE WHITE's land. Wit: DAV: TRAIN, JOS. MILLER. Ackn 9 May
1788.

525. Deed. RICD. BASSETT and SAML. ROWLAND FISHER, as
tenants in common, from PETER F. WRIGHT, Sheriff. Whereas
GEORGE DAVIS of the city of Philadelphia, merchant, Nov Term,
1785, recovered agnst THOMAS BATTSON late of Suss, Esqr., a debt
of 640 pounds, and 3 pounds, 12 shillings, 8 pence, for damages,
whereas two trs were seized and sold in Baltimore Hund, containing 1000 ac, one tr being the dwelling or Manor Plantation
whereon the said THOMAS BATTSON then dwelt, containing 303 ac;
also one other tr of 607 ac called Poplar Swamp. Wit: NICHOLAS
RIDGELY, WM. HARRISON. Ackn 10 May 1788.

526. 16 May 1788. Deed. WILLIAM PERRY, Suss, from JNO.
STOCKLEY, Washington Co, Pa., atty of JEHU CONWELLL of Fayette
Co., PA., tr in Broadkill Hund on the nw side of Broadkill Creek
and on the head thereof formerly property of THOMAS CONWELL,
decd, which descended to his two sons WILLIAM CONWELL and the
above name JEHU CONWELL. Beginning at a bounder of another tr
formerly the property of BRYAN ROLLS ... to land now possessed
by the heirs of ISAAC JONES ... to line of JAMES PONDER's land
... to Cypress Branch - 235 ac, for 100 pounds to be paid by
ISAAC DRAPER in behalf of WILLIAM PERRY. Atty Doctor JOSEPH
HALL and PETER FRETWELL WRIGHT. Wit: ARCHIBALD HOPKINS, ROBERT
HOPKINS. Ackn 3 Jun 1788.

527. 4 Jun 1788. AARON BURTON, joiner, from ROBERT MARRINER,
Suss, yeoman, and MARY his wife, for 35 pounds, 5 ac in Indian R
Hund whereon JOHN GOSLEE now lives and whereon BOWMAN MARRINER
lately dwelt, 3 ac beginning at Prettyman Branch on the line of
JOHN PRETTYMAN's land now belonging to the heirs of MICAJAH
HOUSTON decd, the 3 ac being the same which MARGARET BRYAN decd
purch of JOHN FLETCHER also 2 ac binding on MICAJAH HOUSTON
heirs' land on the w. Wit: ADAM HALL, NICHOLAS LITTLE, THOMAS
COULTER. Ackn 4 Jun 1788.

528. 7 Nov 1775. Bond of Conveyance WM. CLIFTON from LEVIN
and LILLISTON LATON assigned to SAML. IRELAND. LEVIN and
LILLISTON LATON are bound to WILLIAM CLIFTON in the sum of 120
pounds, for the conveyance of a tr of 150 ac at the fork of two
branches tuck up by ELIZABETH PORE unto WILLIAM CLIFTON. Wit:
JEHUE CLIFTON, MARY CLIFTON. WILLIAM CLIFTON transfers his
right of said bond to SAMUEL IRELAND 8 Apr 1777. Wit: WILLM.
YEATES, ELIZABETH CLIFTON. WM. CLIFTON transfers over bond to
PETER JOHNSON on 3 Jun 1788. Wit: WILLIAM PERRY, JEHU CLIFTON.
Proved 10 Jun 1788.

528. 30 May 1788. Deed. PETER JOHNSON, yeoman, Suss, from
SAMUEL IRELAND and SARAH his wife, of Sussex Co, shallapman. A
tr in Cedar Creek Hund on the n and w side of Turks Branch,
surveyed for 410 ac at the request of ELIZABETH POOR and by
virtue of the Proprietor's warrant unto ELIZABETH POOR and of
which 150 ac being all that was not before lawful made over
became the right and property of afsd SAMUEL IRELAND and SARAH
his wife by virtue of a deed of sale from LILLISTON LATON dated
19 Apr 1777. 100 ac of the 150 ac now conveyed to PETER
JOHNSON in consideration of 125 pounds. Beginning at the

westermost side of Turks Branch ... to a small branch by JESSE
WATTSONs. Wit: JAMES JOHNSON, JEHU CLIFTON. Atty SARAH
IRELAND, JEHUE CLIFTON. Ackn 3 Jun 1788.

529. 1 Jul 1788. Prothonotary Commission directed to NATHANIEL
MITCHELL.

530. 28 Jul 1788. Deed. DAVID RICHARDS, Suss, planter, from
ISAAC BRADLEY, Esqr. and ELIZABETH his w/o Suss and JOHN PARKER,
sadler and LEAH his wife, Kent Co., Del. for 700 pounds, trs
called Rich Bottom together with a resurvey made thereon still
called Rich Bottom as before, containing 285 ac as also one
other tr called Proprietary's Dispute together with a resurvey
made thereon still called Proprietary's Dispute containing 344
ac lying in the Northwest Fork Hund being the land whereon said
ISAAC BRADLEY's dwelling plantation lyeth. Atty JOHN WILTBANK,
PHILLIPS KOLLOCK. Wit: THOS. LAWS, WM. POLK. Ackn 6 Aug 1788.

531. 17 Jun 1787. Deed. GEORGE MITCHELL, merchant of Suss,
from JOHN WINGATE, Suss and his wife. Whereas PHILIP PARKER was
seized of a tr called Cabbin Ridge, surveyed to 100 ac which
land was patented PHILIP PARKER the younger and by him on 23 Mar
1786 conveyed to JOHN WINGATE . For 33 pounds. 27 1/2 ac Wit:
ISAAC TUNNELL [?], WILLIAM FREEMAN [?]. Ackn 6 Aug 1788.

532. 18 Sep 1788. Deed. SACKAR WYATT, Suss, from WILLIAM
HALL, Suss, and ELIZABETH his wife. Whereas there is a parcel
of land in Lewes Hund of 57 ac being pt/o a larger tr which
formerly belonged to JOSIAH MARTIN late of same co, decd, which
said JOSIAH MARTIN by his will of 9 Sep 1775 devised said larger
tr to his son JOSIAH MARTIN and when said JOSIAH the younger
died intestate and without issue the said tr of land descended
to his brothers and sisters. ELIZABETH HALL being the only
child and heir of JANE MARTIN, sister of the before mentioned
JOSIAH MARTIN the younger, the quantity of 57 ac descended to
her as a full share. For 85 pounds, 10 shillings. Wit: WILLIAM
PERRY, JOSEPH DAWSON. Ackn 5 Nov 1788.

533. 2 Aug 1788. Deed. JOHN NEAL, Suss, farmer, from PETER
RUST, Suss, farmer, and SALLEY his wife for 110 pounds, parcel
of land called Courtesy, 100 ac beginning at the eastern most
end of a tr formerly laid out for JAMES CANNON in a neck between
the two branches of Turtle Creek which said creek falls into the
N.E. fork of Nanticoke R. Atty JOHN RODNEY, PHILIPS COLLOCK.
Wit: WILLIAM NEAL, THOMAS LEDINGHAM, SARAH HORSEY, JOSHUA OBEAN
[?], ALEXR. LAWS. Ackn 5 Nov 1788.

534. 4 Nov 1788. JOHN CLOWES, Esqr. Commission Second Justice
of the Court of Common Pleas and Orphans Court.

534. 4 Nov 1788. ALEXANDER LAWS, Esqr. Commission Third
Justice of the Court of Common Pleas and Orphans Court.

534. 4 Nov 1788. PETER FRETWELL WRIGHT, Esqr. Commission
Fourth Justice of the Court of Common Pleas and Orphans Court.

535. Deed. FRANCES MOUNTFORD, widow, and executrix of SAMUEL
MOUNTFORD, decd, of Broadkiln Hund, from WILLIAM FENWICK,

Broadkiln Hund, and AGNES his wife, for 50 pounds. CORNELIOUS
WILTBANK late of Suss decd was seized of a large tr in fee
simple to him patented and known as Luck by Chance in Broadkiln
Hund and whereas CORNELIUS WILTBANK by his testament dated 10
Mar 1723 appointed Revd. WILLIAM BECKET and JACOB KOLLOCK, Esqr.
his executors who were directed to convey 275 ac out of said
large tr to ABRAHAM PARSLEY which was done 7 May 1724. And
ABRAHAM PARSLEY and FRANCES PARSLEY his wife on 4 May 1725
conveyed said 275 ac to JAMES FENWICK who by his will dated 21
Dec 1732 devised same as all his estate both real and personal
(excepting his wife's thirds) to his five children to be equally
divided; the youngest died first without issue and the land
became the right of the surviving four: THOMAS, WILLIAM, JAMES
and MARY. THOMAS mortgaged his share and then died without
issue and his part was sold to discharge said mortgage and was
purch by WILLIAM for himself and his sister MARY. Afterwards
JAMES died without issue whereas WILLIAM and MARY became entitled to the whole 275 ac. After this MARY married ELIJAH
SKIDMORE who conveyed their part on 15 Dec 1770 to JOHN RODNEY,
Esqr. And whereas WILLIAM FENWICK stands bound in a bond dated
1 Feb 1773 to SAMUEL MOUNTFORD in the sum of 84 pounds, 16 [sic]
and 6 pence for his conveying by deed of General Warrantee to
said SAMUEL MOUNTFORD 29 1/4 ac which was laid off to said
SAMUEL MOUNTFORD adj the tr whereon he then lived [described]
... to a stake of BAPTIST LAY's marsh - which has been in the
peaceable possession of said SAMUEL MOUNTFORD from Jan 1773 til
the time of his the said SAMUEL decease and was during his the
said SAMUEL's lifetime fully paid for. And whereas said SAMUEL
MOUNTFORD devised all his estate to his wife FRANCES. And not-
withstanding that the land was fully paid for to said WILLIAM
FENWICK, yet the conveyance according to the tenor of said bond
has as yet been neglected. Wit: BENJAMIN ROBINSON, RICHARD
HOWARD. Ackn 5 Feb 1789.

536. 5 Feb 1789. Deed. STAPHEN COSTON, of Broadkiln Hund,
farmer, from NEHEMIAH REED of Broadkiln Hund, farmer, and ISABEL
his wife, for 145 pounds parcel of land in Broadkiln Hund,
beginning at Long Bridge Branch on the w side of Co Road ...
along fence of STEPHEN PARRAMORE's ... to line of the land of
the heirs of WILLIAM CLARK, decd, 81 1/2 ac Wit: N. WAPLES,
STEPHEN PARRAMORE, ANDREW WILLEY. Ackn 5 Feb 1789.

537. Petition of THOS. LAWS adminr of WM. BAGWELL for leave of
court. That WILLIAM BAGWELL by his bond dated 11 Sep 1777
became bound to JOSHUA SPENCER of Suss, afsd under the condition
that WM. BAGWELL, when required make over to JOSHUA SPENCER a
parcel of land in Cedar Creek Hund of 176 ac. WILLIAM BAGWELL
died intestate without making any deed to JOSHUA SPENCER. Now
that SPENCER has paid the remaining portion owed, THOS. LAWS
requests authorization to execute the deed of conveyance.

537. Deed. JOSHUA SPENCER from THOMAS LAWS, Sussex Co, yeoman.
Whereas a parcel of land and marsh in Cedar Creek Hund, 176 ac,
53 perches, pt/o a larger tr whereof HENRY SPENCER late of Suss,
died seized of, leaving issue one son named WILLIAM and one
daughter named ELIZABETH to whom the lands descended, pt/o which
said larger tr of land, namely the above described 176 ac and 53
perches was laid off and alloted to said ELIZABETH who after-

100

wards married JOHN BAGWELL. ELIZABETH and JOHN BAGWELL on 10
Jul 1749 conveyed same to WILLIAM BAGWELL, late of the co, decd,
and WILLIAM BAGWELL by his bond dated 11 Sep 1777 became bound
to JOSHUA SPENCER in the sum of 700 pounds with the condition
that said WILLIAM BAGWELL should, when thereunto required, convey to JOSHUA SPENCER above described 176 ac and 53 perches.
After WILLIAM BAGWELL died intestate without conveying a deed to
JOSHUA SPENCER. The Court of Common Pleas impowered THOMAS LAWS
to execute the conveyance - for 202 pounds, 14 shillings, 10
pence and for the further sum of 194 pounds. Wit: PHILIIPS
KOLLOCK, W. HARRISON. Ackn 5 Feb 1789.

538. 4 Mar 1789. Permanent Power of Attorney THOMAS STOCKELY
from FRANCES MOUNTFORD. Whereas SAMUEL MOUNTFORD late of Suss,
decd, by his last will dated 10 Aug 1784 executed about 17 Jul
1786 devised his estate to FRANCES MOUNTFORD widow of decd,
excepting a legacy of 5 shillings to his three daughters: MARY,
MARGARET and ELIZABETH; as also 5 shillings to his son-in-law
JOHN KING. FRANCES MOUNTFORD now appoints THOMAS STOCKELY,
Esqr., of the town of Washington, PA, her attorney. Wit: ROBT.
JONES, NATHAN CLIFTON. Proved 3 Mar 1789.

539. 4 Mar 1789. Deed. NATHAN CLIFTON, Suss, yeoman, from
THOMAS EVANS, Sheriff. Whereas a parcel of land of 118 ac
originally taken up by a patent from the proprietory of MD,
dated 10 Aug 1753 by THOMAS CLIFTON lately of Suss which tr was
called Good Luck and on 29 Oct 1783 was devised by THOMAS
CLIFTON to FREDRICK CLIFTON his son. And whereas the said
NATHAN CLIFTON and THOMAS CLIFTON lately recovered judgment
agnst said FREDRICK CLIFTON for the sum of 24 pounds and 15
shillings. And 50 ac seized and sold to NATHAN CLIFTON for 25
pounds. Wit: CLEMENT JACKSON, JOS. MILLER. Ackn 9 Mar 1789.

540. 18 Feb 1784. Bond for the conveyance of land RICHARD
BLOXOM, Suss, from THOMAS WHARTON, Sussex Co, yeoman, for 200
pounds. That THOMAS WHARTON convey that pt/o a tr whereon
THOMAS WHARTON now dwells, 54 ac, 122 perches, called Whartons
Chance, in Cedar Creek Hund. Wit: WILLIAM VEACH, WM. POLK.
Proved 12 Feb 1789. THOMAS WHARTON adminr of THOMAS WHARTON
petitions for the authority to convey same to RICHARD BLOXOM on
4 Feb 1789. Approved.

541. 23 Jun 1789. THOMAS STOKELY, Esqr. of Washington Town,
county of Washington, PA, relinquishes power of attorney vested
in him by FRANCES MOUNTFORD.

541. Agreement between JOHN CLOWES Junr, BENJAMIN MIFFLIN and
JOHN JONES being jointly concerned in purchasing sundry trs of
land, swamp and savanah called the Drain, and having made a
division of the same in three parts. That they will bear costs
proportionally to the quantity of the lands that each holds;
that the swamp and drains shall be ditched or canals cut of
sufficient lengths and bigness to draw and keep the water off
the said lands; that as BENJAMIN MIFFLIN's division contains
about 200 ac claimed by JACOB KOLLOCK, if his heirs or assigns
should recover the same the said MIFFLIN shall be reimbursed 2/3
by CLOWES and JONES.

James 47
John 34, 46, 52
William 23, 24
CALE Margaret 20
Calf Paster 80
CALLAWAY Betty 16
  Clement 67
  Isaac 28
  Isaiah 67
  James 67, 82
  John 49
  Jonathan 16
  Lowder 28
  Moses 82
Callaways Intention 58
Callaways Neglect 12, 75
CALWELL John 33
CAMPBELL John 36
CANNON Charles 87
  Clarkson 33, 65, 72
  Easter 87
  Ebenezer 66
  Elijah 2, 52, 66, 67, 75
  George 87
  Hayward 67
  Hudson 12
  Hughit 36
  Jacob 67
  James 12, 67, 74, 99
  Jeremiah 10, 17, 47, 66
  John 12, 93
  Joseph 12, 16, 46, 66, 67, 74
  Levin 61
  Luerecy 12
  Newton 93
  Thomas 47
  William 61
  Wittington 12
Cannons Conclusion 61
Cannons Meadows 67
Cannons Regulation 47
Cannons Swamp 8
Cannons Cypress Swamp 10
CAREY Collins 28
  Ebenezar 1
  John 4
  Thomas 21, 84
CARLETON Joseph 32
CARLILE Mary 89
  Thomas 18, 89
CARPENTER Jacob 11
  William 30
CARRELL Joseph 63
CARTER Joseph 35
CARTY Isaac 97

CARY Ann 35
  Elizabeth 35
  Nancy 42
  Nehemiah 48
  Samuel 32, 35
  Solomon 42
  Thomas 35, 83
  William 35, 83
CASLETES Joseph 25
CATHELL Joshua 23
CAUSEY William 9, 33
CEASER 53
CHAMBERS Anne 30
  John 95
  William 13, 29, 30
Chance 35, 37, 44, 49, 50
CHANCE Banings 3
  John 54, 79
CHARLES 25
Cherry Garden 35
CHIPMAN Margaret 28, 46
  Paris 28
  Parish 46
CIPP 53
CIRWITHIN Caleb 21, 53, 62, 71, 85, 91, 97
CLARK Easter 86
  Elizabeth 62
  Esther 85, 86
  John 2, 3, 28, 30, 54, 82
  Joshua 2, 30
  Lot 11, 85, 86
  Mary 3, 30
  Meirs 2, 3, 30, 40
  Nehemiah 2, 30
  Rebecca 62
  Sarah 5, 29
  Thomas 78
  William 4, 17, 18, 27, 46, 62, 72, 76, 79, 92, 96,
  William 100
CLARKSON Barbezelai 87
Clarkson Forrest 72
Clarksons Industry 3
CLAYPOOLE George 10
  Jehu 52
  Jeremiah 10
  Joseph 10
  Mary 10
  Norton 10
Clearance 10, 31, 69
CLIFTON Anne 27, 46
  Daniel 54
  Elizabeth 26, 98
  Fredrick 101

  Isaac 59
  Jehu 26, 98, 99
  John 26
  Levin 65
  Lurana 59
  Mary 98
  Nathan 42, 101
  Robert 27, 46
  Thomas 90, 101
  William 26, 98
CLINDANIEL Anna 16
  Avory 16
  John 28
CLOWES --- 35
  Catharine 37, 95, 96
  David 37, 95
  Gerardus 95
  Hannah 37
  John 3, 7, 9, 10, 11, 13, 14, 15, 16, 17, 19, 20, 22, 25, 27, 29, 31, 33, 36, 37, 38, 40, 59, 66, 69, 75, 79, 85, 88, 91, 95, 96, 99, 101
  Lydia 95, 96
  Mary 37, 95, 96
  Sarah 30
  William 95, 96
CLOWS John 30
COATES Thomas Peachey 94
Cockland 20
COCKS Moses 59
CODD Berkley 97
  Mary 97
COLE Coverdale 21, 26, 60
COLEMAN Betty 14, 27
  William 14, 27, 46, 96
Collesons Choice 40
COLLICK Simon 6
Colliers 16
Collin's Industry 53
COLLINGHAM Elisha 85
COLLINGS Aberilla 33
  Andrew 10, 11
  Elijah 33
  Elizabeth 60
  John 10, 28, 33, 35
  Joseph Scrogin 52
  Levi 22
  Mary 52
  Shepherd 33
COLLINS --- 97
  Andrew 3, 8, 30, 66
  Betty 52
  Charles 18
  Eli 13, 31
  Elizabeth 44
  Esther 91

DAY Betsey 19
  George 1, 29
  John 28
  Joseph 63
  Owen 19
  Prettyman 25
  William 28
DAZEY Moses 29
DEAN Jemima 72
  Jesse 72
  John W. 55, 79, 88
  John Wilson 11, 19, 20, 75
DEBUTY Jesse 97
Delight 31
DENNIS John 92
  Robert 92
DENNISS John 92
DENWOOD Arthur 2
  Rebecca 2
DEPUTY Charles 91
  Jesse 91
  Joshua 91
  Newnez 38
  Nunez 66
DERICKSON Levin 3, 5, 18, 24, 29, 30, 32, 33, 40, 68
Desire 64
DICKERSON Edmond 11, 37, 60
  Elisha 24, 25
  Somerset 55
  William 60
DICKINSON Catharine 96
  Peter 96
  Samuel 84
  Somerset 16
DILL Abnor 61
DINGEE Daniel 63, 84
  Esther 63
  Jacob 76, 96
  Obediah 76, 96
DINGLE Edward 2, 5, 44, 63, 65
  Edward 69
  William 11
DINGUS Daniel 21
DIRICKSON -- 81
  George 69, 81
  Job 81
  Joseph 15, 94
  Levin 32
  Rhoda 69
  Rody 81
  Samuel 15, 43
  William 69, 81
DIRRICKSON Levin 32, 92

Dispute 33, 76
Dispute Disputed 33, 76
DOBSON Ann 72
  Elinor 57
  Isabella 72
  Jane 10, 57
  Rachel 10, 57
  Richard 10, 57, 72
  Sarah 72
Dobsons Folly 32
DOD Hebron 30
DODD Hebern 85
  Joseph 75
  Lydia 85
  Magdaline 63
  Samuel 63
  Sarah 75
  Solomon 12
  Thomas 12
DOLBY John 8
DONALY Morp 49
  William 49
DONAVAN Foster 66
DONE William 20, 21, 27, 36, 44, 51, 58
DONOLY Jemima 49
  Keziah 49
  Mary 49
  William 49
DONOVAN Forster 11
DORMAN John Sheldon 40
DORMON John S. 92
  John Sheldon 37
  Mary 37
Double Purchase 33, 56
DOWNING John 51
DOWNS Barnet 50
  Jacob 8
Downses Chance 8
DRAIN --- 101
  Elizabeth 36, 88, 89, 90
DRAPER Alexander 2, 9, 17, 18, 30, 36, 39, 54
  Anne 59
  Avery 39
  Charles 36, 39, 91
  Elizabeth 54
  Henry 18, 38, 39, 85
  Isaac 3, 11, 39, 98
  James 54
  Joseph 9, 36, 38
  Mary 17
  Nehemiah 17, 54
  Phebe 54
  Polly 54
  Samuel 39
  Sarah 17, 54

  William 36, 41, 47, 59
Drapers Pattent 39
DRAPPER John 84
DRISKELL William 8
  Drusile 42
  Dublin 31
DUGLASS James 38
DULAVAN Foster 11
DUNCAN Isaac 84
  Thomas 16
DUTTON John 11, 63
  Thomas 11
DYER William 27, 46, 76

EASOM Benjamin 16
Eastwood 66
ECCLESTON Hugh 69
  John 69
EDGAR Dolley 51
  James 26
EDGER James 23
  Edward Furlongs Patent 38
ELBERT Charles 89
  Elbo Rume 66
ELDRIDGE Joseph 96
  Mary 14, 96
  Obediah 76
ELIOTT John 19
ELLEGOOD William 49
ELLES Edward 12
ELLESS Francis 12
ELLIOT Samuel 57
ELLIS Benjamin 70
  Levin 39
EMMOTT William 7
EMORY Thomas 41
ENLESS Richbell 2
ENNES John 25
  William Brittingham 51
ENNIS John 13, 25, 31
  Levin 31
EVANS --- 34
  Caleb 15
  Catharine 43
  Ebenezer 40
  Edward 62
  Jacob 15
  John 24, 35, 41, 43, 45, 69, 73, 94
  Rebecca 62
  Thomas 38, 53, 69, 82, 101
  Walter 41
  William 35, 41
  William Riley 10, 23, 34, 35
EVENS Ebenezer 40
  John 40

Jonathan 12, 66, 67, 82
Samuel 12, 24, 57, 66,
  67, 73, 82
Thomas 67
Hearns Liberty 67
HEAVALOES Anthony 52
HEAVERLO Andrew 66
  Daniel 66
  Samuel 31
  Sarah 66
HEAVERLOE Samuel 52
HEMMONS John 2
  Jonathan 39
HENRY Elizabeth 89
  Gabriel 39
  Isaac 2, 6, 20, 24, 30,
    47, 58, 70, 73, 85
  Jonathan 89
  Sarah 89
  William 88, 89
HEPBURN John 27, 46
  Joseph 27
HERONS Jane 27
HESSE 48
HESTER 80
HICKMAN Baily 42
  Charles 40
  Elizabeth 40
  Jacob 29, 30
  James 31, 40, 65
  John 14, 36, 58
  Joseph 5, 28, 29, 40
  Joshua 18
  Josiah 40
  Margaret 31, 65
  Mary 40, 42
  Nathaniel 4, 39, 40, 58
  Nicholas 90
  Phebe 40
  Thomas 31, 69
  William 5, 18, 25, 29
HICKMAN & DAVIS 14
Hickmans Conclusion 31
Hickmans Lot 25
HIFFERNAN William 30
HILL Brittingham 54, 55,
  82
  Elenor 93
  Elsey 93
  George 1
  Jehu 77
  John 1, 14, 80, 96
  John Stephen 40, 82
  Jonathan 93
  Joshua 10, 92
  Nehemiah 36
  Stephen 94
  Thomas 48

Hills Content 79
HITCH Joshua 3, 52
  Mary 3
Hitchen's Choice 85
HITCHENS Edmond 35
HITCHINS Edward 85
  Sarah 49
Hobs Choice 73, 97
HODGER Robert 29
HODGESON Gamage Evans
  52
HODGSON Gamage Evans 29
  Jacob 59
  Jesse 59
  Mary 59
  Miriam 59
  Robert 58
  Sarah 59
HODSON Constantine 4
  Robert 5, 29
  Sarah 5, 29
  Vienna 4
HOG Gamage Evans 29
HOG Quarter 28, 82
Hog Range 66
Hogg Island 86
Hogg Island Gutt 14
Hogg Quarter 13, 16, 80
Hogg Range 61
HOLDSON Thomas 32
HOLLAND Benjamin 73
  Elizabeth 21
  Isaac 14, 21, 22
  Israel 22, 35, 40,
    43, 69, 73, 94
  John 92
  Samuel 67
  William 21, 22, 40,
    54, 55, 82, 94
HOLMES Ann Catharine 41
  John 29, 59
Holmes's Place 78
HOLSTON Robert 85
HOLT Ryers 87
  Ryves 4, 19, 24
HOMS John 41
HOOPER Henry 61, 70
Hoopers Chance 27
HOPKIN Samuel 77
HOPKINS Archibald 98
  Caty 35
  Ezekiel 43
  Hampton 40, 94
  John 35, 43, 94
  Josiah 43
  Robert 43, 51, 98
  Sarah 43
  Susannah 2

Hopkins Discovery 43
Horse Pound 2
HORSEY Isaac 2, 49, 81,
  93
  Nathaniel 49, 93
  Sarah 99
  Stephen 52
  William 93
HOSEA Daniel 11, 37
HOSEMAN Daniel 89
HOSEY Daniel 11
HOSMAN Comfort 22
  Daniel 22
  Hannah 70, 81
  Jane 22
  Joseph 22
  Stockley 22, 70, 81
Hounds Ditch 20
HOUSTON James 74
  John 8, 14, 28, 49, 56,
    58, 74
  Joseph 15, 31, 50
  Leonard 8, 74
  Magdalene 37, 48
  Mary 74
  Micajah 98
  Polly 31
  Robert 1, 3, 8, 14, 21,
    23, 26, 28, 31, 47,
    49, 50, 51, 52, 56,
    58, 74, 85
HOWARD Comfort 61
  George 11
  Nehemiah 11
  Richard 7, 26, 61, 100
HUBARTT John 61
HUBBART John 61
HUBBERT John 25
  Solomon 25
HUDSON Benjamin 26, 41
  Constantine 12
  James 91, 92
  Jaquesh 43
  John 26, 42
  Richard 12, 26
  Walter 16, 39, 79
  William 26, 42
HUFFINGTON Luke 23, 58
HUGGEN Phillip 70
HUGGENS Phillip 70
HURT William 28

Inclosed 6
Industry 53
INGLISH Joshua 11
  Thomas 13, 28
INGRAHAM Robert 34

MACALLY Betsy 6
MACELLS John 76
MACINTOSH Hugh 32, 95
MACKLIN Annes 32
  Rachel 32
  Thomas 32, 57
MACKNIEL John 12
MADDOX William 12
  Zachariah 12
MADDUX Hezekiah 15
  Zephaniah 67
Maidenhead Thickett 40
MANLOVE Betty 8
  Boaz 3
  Manuel 8
  Mary 28
  William 28, 46, 47
Manloves Grove 70, 71, 74
Manor Plantation 98
MARGARET 80
Mariner Constantine 31
MARRET Mark 86
MARRINER Bowman 98
  Gilbert 77
  Mary 98
  Robert 94, 98
Marsh 40
MARSH John 64
  Mary 36
  Peter 19, 20, 36, 45,
  85
  Polly 36
  Thomas 85
Marsh Point 35, 40
Marsh Point Enlarged 43
Marsh Point Inlarged 26
MARSHAL Diana 3
MARTIN James 14, 22, 72
  Jane 99
  John 90
  Josiah 10, 16, 17, 99
  William 53, 57
Martins Hundred 21, 27
MARVEL Joseph 6
  Philip 10, 24, 34
  Thomas 11, 34, 41, 50
MASON David 20
  Elias 20, 79
  George 20
  Isaac 20
  Jonathan 20
  Keziah 20
  Mary 20
  Rhoda 20
  Sarah 20, 79
MASSEY Easter 56
  Isaac 41
  Job 56

John 23, 24, 29, 34,
  40, 94
  Joseph 56
  Mary 17
  William 17
Masseys Folly 56
MASTON John 90
Maston's Lott 90
MATHEWS Ann 45
  William 45
Mattapany 44
MATTHEWS Ann(e) 72, 77,
  92, 95
  Elilzabeth 72
  Sally 72
  William 72, 77, 92,
  95
MATTOX Safiah 60
MAUL John 40
MAULL John 40, 83
MAXWELL Elizabeth 88,
  89
  J. 7, 31
  John 89
MAY John 8
McCALL Mark 91, 97
McCALLEY Anthalina 13
  Eli 6, 56, 58
  Robert Watson 6, 13,
  56
McCLISH Thomas 15
McCRACKIN John 22
McCREA Robert 22
McCULLAH John 65
McDEAN John W. 88
McDOWEL Isaac 28
  Naomi 39
McDOWELL --- 39
  Isaac 39
  John 39
McELVAIN Andrew 29, 32
  Benjamin 9, 94
McILVAIN Andrew 30, 33,
  84
  Leonard 29, 32, 33
McINTUSH Hugh 15, 35
McIVAIN Lenard 32
McIVER John M. 32
McKAM Thomas 86
McKEMMY Aaron 10
McKEY Robert 29
McKIMMEY Aaron 10
  Elizabeth 10
  Jane 10
  Walter 10
McKIMMY Elizabeth 57
McKINNY Aaron 57
  Jane 57

McKNIT Deborah 80
McMURRAY James 2
McNAIRYTH James 86
McNEILL James 79
  Jane 79
MEGEE Samuel 84
MEIRS James 6, 84
  Jane 84
  John 6, 7, 61, 67, 84
  Mary 6, 7, 62
  Sarah 6
MELLSON Elijah 3
MELSON Betty 31
  John 43
  Joseph 9, 28, 42, 43
MERRELL Mark 19
MERRICK Sarah 8
MESSEX Comfort 80
  Litticy 80
MESSICK Anness 32
  Comfort 66
  Isaac 32, 66
  Jacob 28
  Levi 28
  Minis 2
  Minors 2
  Nehemiah 6
  Obediah 28, 66
  Rachel 66
  Sallie 32
  Sarah 32
MESSICKS Chance 56
MESSIX Comfort 66
METCALF John 8, 17, 38,
  39, 93, 94
MIDCALF John 93
Middleborough,
  Middlebourg, etc. 76,
  78, 87, 88, 89
MIFFLIN Benjamin 11, 94,
  101
  Deborah 56
  Joseph 56
  Sarah 94, 95
MILBEY Ann 51
  Levin 31, 35, 36, 51,
  88
Mill Chance 9
Mill Land 52
Mill Landing Enlarged 56
Mill Lott 49, 51, 52, 53
MILLER Betty 18, 19
  David 55, 56
  James 40
  John 18
  Joseph 26, 29, 31, 34,
  39, 40, 42, 43, 55,
  58, 60, 79, 90, 98,
  101

113

115

POTTER Abraham 45, 77, 95
  John 21
  Zabdiel 19
POWELL William 52
  Zadoc 42
POWER Mary 49
  Naomi 49
  Nehemiah 49
POYNTER Ratliff 48
Presbyterian Glebes 65
PRETTYMAN Benjamin 18
  Comfort 7, 87, 88, 89
  Elizabeth 24, 37, 48
  John 14, 22, 29, 63, 98
  Magdalin 37
  Mary 37, 48
  Perry 7
  Robert 18, 27, 37, 46,
    48, 55, 58
  Sarah 88, 89
  Thomas 13, 37, 48
  William 7, 17, 18, 22,
    24, 29, 32, 35, 37,
    45, 48, 87, 88, 89
PRICE John 70, 81
  Nehemiah 19, 23
Primehook 97
PRITCHARD David 20
PRITCHETT John 61
  Rhoda 61
Proprietary's Dispute 99
Providence 70, 81
PUCKHAM Richard 78
PUCKLE Nathaniel 97
PULLET John 20
Purchase 90
PURNALL Benjamin 73
Pusle 44, 46

Quarter 80

RALPH William 87
Ramble 82
RANKIN David 25
REA Peter 53
READ George 91, 96, 97
  Gertrude 91, 96, 97
  Jesse 93, 94
  John 41, 94
  Mathew 41
Recard's Hundred 97
RECORDS Alexander 3
  John 19, 91
Red Oak Ridge 13, 15, 32,
  95
Red Oak Ridgeway 64
REDDEN Stephen 10, 11,
  17, 28, 59

William 10
REED Alexander 63, 65
  Elizabeth 65
  Isabel 100
  James 11, 12, 30
  Matthew 12, 14
  Nehemiah 12, 13, 34,
    100
  William 4
REGUA John 1, 28, 29
Regulation 31
REID Alexander 63
RELPH William 3
Resurvey 69
REVEL Stephen 33
REVELL John 59
REYNOLDS James 34
  William 56
Rich Bottom 65, 99
Rich Land 87
Rich Ridge 31
RICHARD David 70
RICHARDS Comfort 81
  David 31, 32, 33, 66,
    81, 83, 99
  Esther 32
  Henry 32
  Isaac 70, 81
  Jacob 81
  James 32, 33
  John 31, 32, 33, 97
  Tamsey 32
  Temperance 81
  William 32
RICHARDSON James 11
  William 19
RICKARD James 78
Rickard's Choner 41
RICKARDS Elijah 22, 37
  George 71
  John 94
  Jones 10, 40, 41, 94
  Mary 94
  William 17, 40, 94
RICKETS John 91, 97
RICORDS William 17
RIDGELY John 84
  Nicholas 98
RIGGEN Elizabeth 73
  Isaac 66, 73
  Isabella 46
RIGGIN Anne 44
  Charles 44
  Joshua 44, 46
  Tegue 44
RIGGON Ann 46
  Charles 46
  Joshua 46

RIGHT Peter Fretwell 81
RILEY --- 30
  Benjamin 68
  George 68
  Thomas 36, 68
  William 68
Riley's Forton 68
ROACH Levi 22
  Martha 22
ROBERTS Joseph 9
ROBINS Charles 73
  Elizabeth 39
  John 3
  Levi 39, 40
  Phebe 40
  Thomas 73
  William 10, 57
ROBINSON --- 27
  Arcada 89
  Benjamin 100
  Burton 90
  Cada 84
  Elizabeth 84
  George 60
  John 84, 91, 96
  Joseph 32, 84
  Joshua 49, 50, 73, 94
  Levi 92
  Michael 41
  Parker 4, 12, 39, 77,
    95
  Peter 17, 21, 24, 29,
    30, 37, 39, 45, 60, 88
  Ruth 45, 77, 95
  Thomas 17, 29, 30, 32,
    33, 89
  W. 91
  William 13, 41
Rock Hole 17, 35
RODGERS Custis 58
  Jacob 92
RODNEY -- 52, 66
  Caleb 66
  Daniel 21, 68, 78, 83,
    84, 88
  Elizabeth 6
  John 2, 3, 8, 9, 10,
    11, 15, 16, 17, 19,
    20, 22, 23, 31, 32,
    47, 49, 57, 66, 68,
    71, 73, 74, 77, 78,
    83, 84, 88, 90, 91,
    94, 99, 100
  P. 84
  Ruth 52
  Thomas 6
ROE Mary Ann 71
  William 71

116

117

118

119

WALLER --- 46
  Eunice 60
  Henry 33, 76
  James 35, 49
  John 35
  Nathaniel 12, 16, 35,
    37, 58, 70
  Thomas 12, 35, 39, 46,
    49, 58, 70
  William 49
WALLIS Samuel 84
WALLS --uel 81
  Joshua 81
  William 81
  Walters Land 44
WALTON David 22
  Elizabeth 71
  George 22, 24, 28, 60
  John 32, 47
  Joseph 46
  Mary 24
  William 71
WANGER John Hassel 58
WAPLE John 65
WAPLES Burton 13, 17, 28
  Joseph 18
  N. 29, 35, 50, 66, 100
  Nathaniel 32, 35, 63
  Paul 11, 26, 65
  Peter 11, 18, 65
  Thomas 11, 18
  William 18, 26, 50, 65
WARD George 13, 14, 15,
    21
  Joseph 75
WARDER Jeremiah 79
WARREN Absolam 30
  Alexander 30, 42
  Ally 61
  Bennet 42
  David 41, 42
  Ebenezer 17
WARRING Ebenezer 79
  Thomas 4
WARRINGTON Comfort 4
  Elijah 13
  Jacob 4
  John 4, 28
  John Abbott 4, 40
  Stephen 4
  Thomas 4
WARWICK Jeremiah 20
WATER Million 82
WATKINS Thomas 18
WATSON David 30, 93
  James 50
  Uriah 50
  Watson's Marsh 91, 97

Watsons Folly 67
Watsons's Marsh 97
WATTSON Bethuel 93, 94
  Coston 71
  David 29, 30, 93
  Elizabeth 71
  Hezekiah 71
  James 15, 71
  Jesse 30, 93, 99
  John 71
  Luke 5, 19, 40, 71
  Thomas 71
WEBB John 19, 42, 49
  Webley 4
WELCH Daniel 8
  John 72
  Rachel 50
  William 50
  Welches Delight 72
  Wellbrook 2
WELLS Thomas 15
WEST Ezekiel 1
  George 26, 72
  Isaac 43, 45, 94
  John 26, 34, 35
  Mary 28
  Robert 26
  Thomas 26, 50
  William 19, 20
WESTLEY W. John 15
  Westleys Old Field 14
WESTLY John 22
  Mary 22
  Westons Folly 16
WHARTON Baker 63, 68
  Charles 50
  George 50
  Harvey 43
  Hinman 50, 68
  Jonathan 34
  Thomas 11, 101
  Watson 34, 43
  Whartons Chance 101
WHAYLEY William 75
WHEELER John 28, 46
  Jonathan 28, 46, 47
  Keriah 46
  Keziah 28
  Manlove 28
  Margaret 28
  Mary 47
WHEELOR John 47
  Keziah 28
  Mary 47
WHITE Abraham 44
  Ambros 94
  Edward 23, 66
  Elizabeth 58

George 38, 98
Isaac 58
Isbal 29
Jacob 24, 45, 58, 77,
    95
James 3, 5, 29, 30
Jane Wilkins 58
John 38, 97
Margaret 29, 30
Mary 3, 45, 77, 95
Peter 20, 36, 50, 52,
    74, 75, 81, 87, 94, 95
Robert 58
Sophia 29
Thomas 19, 23
Wrixam 7, 58, 94
Levil 73
Oak Tract 36
White's Island 58
Whitefield 49, 74
WHITEHEAD R. 5, 6
WHORTON David 29
  Hinman 15
WICKOFF Isaac 46
  Widows Contrivance 30
WILDGOOSE Joseph 84
  Thomas 52
WILEY James 92, 95, 96
WILKINS William 10
WILLEY Andrew 100
  John 57
  John Alexander 57
  Levin 71, 72
  Solomon 50
WILLIAMS Aaron 5
  Ann 54
  Arthur 44
  Barbary 86
  Charles 32
  David 8, 13
  Edward 15
  Esther 21
  Isaac 16, 21
  John 17, 64, 71, 84, 86
  Jonathan 17
  Joshua 21
  Lemuel 9
  Mary 15
  Moses 12
  Nicholas 62
  Reynear 39, 54
  Richard 6, 7
  Robert 81
  Samuel 27
  Spencer 21
  William 48
  Williams Beginning 84
  Williams Choice 16

Williams Purchase 69
WILLICE John 38
WILLIN Thomas 58
WILLIS John 38, 67, 97
WILLSON Matthew 95
  Sarah 30, 31
WILSON Hester 36
  Matthew 36
  Moses 78
  Polly 36
  Sarah 30, 31
  Thomas 93, 94
  William 25, 57, 91
Wilsons Swamp 80, 82
WILTBANK -- 81, 89
  Abraham 21, 22, 68
  Catharine 68
  Cornelius 4, 32, 52,
    83, 100
  Hannah 27
  Hermanus 22, 86
  Isaac 22, 86
  Jane 32
  John 1, 2, 3, 4, 5, 7,
    8, 10, 14, 16, 17, 18,
    21, 22, 25, 27, 30,
    31, 33, 34, 35, 36,
    40, 61, 65, 66, 68,
    70, 71, 72, 96, 99
  Neomy 22
  Rachel 83
  Sarah 37
WILTON George 78
WINDSOR James 14
  John 58
  Lydia 14
  Rachel 43
WINEFRED 47
WINGATE John 5, 8, 24,
    49, 50, 57, 76, 99
  Planner 86
  Smith 35
  Suckey, Suky 35
  Traney 86
  Unice 35
WINGGATE John 8
Winter Meadow 74
Witches Savannah 13
WITH James 2
WITHERS Isaac 8
WITTINGTON Suthey 49, 50
WOLF John 64
  Pitt Gutt 92
WOOD Stephen 76
WOODCRAFT William 44
Woodcrafts Venture 52
Wooden Mine 4, 12

WOODS Esther 11
  John 84
WOODWARD Anthoney 95
  Sarah 95
WOOLF Francis 76
  John 7, 78, 88, 96
  Jonathan 27, 74, 75
  Polley Wolley 50
  Reece 27, 57, 58, 78,
    88, 89
  Ruth 27
  Sarah 88, 89
  William 50
WOOTTEN Lovey 23
WOOTTON Benjamin 23
  Elijah 20
Wootton's Orchard 20
Worlds End 35
WORTON Thomas 68
WRIGHT Ann 9
  Comfort 52
  Edward 9, 87
  Francis 3, 33, 65, 94
  John 36
  Joshua 10, 17
  Naomi 55
  Peter 28, 59, 67, 69,
    87
  Peter F. 11, 38, 40,
    56, 57, 60, 77, 78,
    83, 85, 88, 89, 96,
    98
  Peter Fretwell 27,
    28, 33, 38, 39, 41,
    46, 47, 51, 52, 54,
    55, 56, 58, 60, 62,
    74, 78, 87, 91, 98,
    99
  Sarah 10, 17
  Stephen 74
  Thomas 55
Wrights Meadow 9
WROE Mary Ann 70
  William 70, 74
WYATT Eleanor 64
  Jehu 32, 95
  John 59, 64
  Joseph 64, 95
  Mary 64
  Sackar 99
  William 59, 64
WYNCOPE Abraham 79
WYNKOOP --- 63
  Abraham 8, 21, 22,
    62, 84
  Benjamin 8, 21, 62,
    84
  Mary 21, 84
  Phebe 84
  Thomas 21, 62, 84

Wynkoops Island 36

YEATES William 98
YOUNG Benjamin 13
  Catharine 37
  George 32
  Mary 80
  Nathaniel 29, 51, 53,
    90
  Robert 51, 53, 90

Other Heritage Books by F. Edward Wright:

Abstracts of Bucks County, Pennsylvania Wills, 1685–1785

Abstracts of Cumberland County, Pennsylvania Wills, 1750–1785

Abstracts of Cumberland County, Pennsylvania Wills, 1785–1825

Abstracts of Philadelphia County Wills, 1726–1747

Abstracts of Philadelphia County Wills, 1748–1763

Abstracts of Philadelphia County Wills, 1763–1784

Abstracts of Philadelphia County Wills, 1777–1790

Abstracts of Philadelphia County Wills, 1790–1802

Abstracts of Philadelphia County Wills, 1802–1809

Abstracts of Philadelphia County Wills, 1810–1815

Abstracts of Philadelphia County Wills, 1815–1819

Abstracts of Philadelphia County Wills, 1820–1825

Abstracts of Philadelphia County, Pennsylvania Wills, 1682–1726

Abstracts of South Central Pennsylvania Newspapers, Volume 1, 1785–1790

Abstracts of South Central Pennsylvania Newspapers, Volume 3, 1796–1800

Abstracts of the Newspapers of Georgetown and the Federal City, 1789–99

Abstracts of York County, Pennsylvania Wills, 1749–1819

*Bucks County, Pennsylvania Church Records of the 17th and 18th Centuries
Volume 2: Quaker Records: Falls and Middletown Monthly Meetings*
Anna Miller Watring and F. Edward Wright

Caroline County, Maryland Marriages, Births and Deaths, 1850–1880

Citizens of the Eastern Shore of Maryland, 1659–1750

Cumberland County, Pennsylvania Church Records of the 18th Century

Delaware Newspaper Abstracts, Volume 1: 1786–1795

Early Charles County, Maryland Settlers, 1658–1745
Marlene Strawser Bates and F. Edward Wright

Early Church Records of Alexandria City and Fairfax County, Virginia
F. Edward Wright and Wesley E. Pippenger

Early Church Records of New Castle County, Delaware, Volume 1, 1701–1800

Frederick County Militia in the War of 1812
Sallie A. Mallick and F. Edward Wright

Inhabitants of Baltimore County, 1692–1763

Land Records of Sussex County, Delaware, 1769–1782

Land Records of Sussex County, Delaware, 1782–1789
Elaine Hastings Mason and F. Edward Wright

Marriage Licenses of Washington, District of Columbia, 1811–1830

*Marriages and Deaths from the Newspapers of Allegany and
Washington Counties, Maryland, 1820–1830*

Marriages and Deaths from The York Recorder, 1821–1830

*Marriages and Deaths in the Newspapers of Frederick and
Montgomery Counties, Maryland, 1820–1830*

Marriages and Deaths in the Newspapers of Lancaster County, Pennsylvania, 1821–1830

Marriages and Deaths in the Newspapers of Lancaster County, Pennsylvania, 1831–1840

Marriages and Deaths of Cumberland County, [Pennsylvania], 1821–1830

Maryland Calendar of Wills Volume 9: 1744–1749

Maryland Calendar of Wills Volume 10: 1748–1753

Maryland Calendar of Wills Volume 11: 1753–1760

Maryland Calendar of Wills Volume 12: 1759–1764

Maryland Calendar of Wills Volume 13: 1764–1767

Maryland Calendar of Wills Volume 14: 1767–1772

Maryland Calendar of Wills Volume 15: 1772–1774

Maryland Calendar of Wills Volume 16: 1774–1777

Maryland Eastern Shore Newspaper Abstracts, Volume 1: 1790–1805

Maryland Eastern Shore Newspaper Abstracts, Volume 2: 1806–1812

Maryland Eastern Shore Newspaper Abstracts, Volume 3: 1813–1818

Maryland Eastern Shore Newspaper Abstracts, Volume 4: 1819–1824

Maryland Eastern Shore Newspaper Abstracts, Volume 5: Northern Counties, 1825–1829
F. Edward Wright and Irma Harper

Maryland Eastern Shore Newspaper Abstracts, Volume 6: Southern Counties, 1825–1829

Maryland Eastern Shore Newspaper Abstracts, Volume 7: Northern Counties, 1830–1834
Irma Harper and F. Edward Wright

Maryland Eastern Shore Newspaper Abstracts, Volume 8: Southern Counties, 1830–1834

Maryland Militia in the Revolutionary War
S. Eugene Clements and F. Edward Wright

Newspaper Abstracts of Allegany and Washington Counties, Maryland, 1811–1815

Newspaper Abstracts of Cecil and Harford Counties, Maryland, 1822–1830

Newspaper Abstracts of Frederick County, Maryland, 1816–1819

Newspaper Abstracts of Frederick County, Maryland, 1811–1815

Sketches of Maryland Eastern Shoremen

Tax List of Chester County, Pennsylvania 1768

Tax List of York County, Pennsylvania 1779

Washington County Church Records of the 18th Century, 1768–1800

Western Maryland Newspaper Abstracts, Volume 1: 1786–1798

Western Maryland Newspaper Abstracts, Volume 2: 1799–1805

Western Maryland Newspaper Abstracts, Volume 3: 1806–1810

Wills of Chester County, Pennsylvania, 1766–1778